Paul Kane

Reproduced from an oil painting loaned by A. H. O'Brien, M.A., barrister-at-law, Toronto, Canada. The original is unsigned, but it is believed to have been painted by Verner.

WANDERINGS OF AN ARTIST AMONG THE INDIANS OF NORTH AMERICA

Paul Kane

DOVER PUBLICATIONS, INC.
Mineola, New York

TO
GEORGE WILLIAM ALLAN, ESQ.
OF MOSS PARK, TORONTO, CANADA WEST

THIS WORK

DESIGNED TO ILLUSTRATE THE MANNERS AND CUSTOMS OF THE
INDIAN TRIBES OF BRITISH AMERICA

IS RESPECTFULLY DEDICATED

AS A TOKEN OF GRATITUDE FOR THE KIND AND GENEROUS INTEREST
HE HAS ALWAYS TAKEN IN THE AUTHOR'S LABOURS,
AS WELL AS A SINCERE EXPRESSION OF ADMIRATION OF THE
LIBERALITY WITH WHICH, AS A NATIVE CANADIAN,
HE IS EVER READY TO FOSTER CANADIAN TALENT AND ENTERPRISE.

TORONTO: *July 9, 1858.*

Published in Canada by General Publishing Company, Ltd., 30 Lesmill Road, Don Mills, Toronto, Ontario.

Published in the United Kingdom by Constable and Company, Ltd., 3 The Lanchesters, 162–164 Fulham Palace Road, London W6 9ER.

This Dover edition, first published in 1996, is a corrected, slightly amplified, but otherwise unabridged republication of the work published by The Radisson Society of Canada Limited, Toronto, 1925, under the title *Wanderings of an Artist among the Indians of North America from Canada to Vancouver's Island and Oregon through the Hudson's Bay Company's Territory and Back Again.* The 1925 edition was a revised edition of the original publication by Longman, Brown, Green, Longmans and Roberts, 1859 [Toronto?].

The Dover edition replaces the original illustrations (line engravings or feeble halftones) with new reproductions of the corresponding subjects as painted by Kane; corrects the titles of the illustrations, p. ix, and their corresponding captions throughout the book; relocates the painting now on p. x; and adds an eight-page insert of color plates of Kane's paintings. A few typographical errors have been corrected.

The publisher is indebted to the Royal Ontario Museum, Toronto, Ontario, Canada, for supplying copies for reproduction of the art works in this book, along with permission to reproduce them. We are especially grateful for the kind cooperation of the Museum's Ethnology Department in helping to facilitate this publication.

Library of Congress Cataloging-in-Publication Data

Kane, Paul, 1810–1871.
  Wanderings of an artist among the Indians of North America : from Canada to Vancouver's Island and Oregon through the Hudson's Bay Company's territory and back again, 1845, 1846–48 / Paul Kane.
    p.   cm.
  Originally published: The Radisson Society of Canada Limited, Toronto, 1925.
  Includes bibliographical references.
  ISBN 0-486-29031-X (pbk.)
  1. Indians of North America—Northwest, Canadian.   2. Northwest, Canadian—Description and travel.   I. Title.
E88.K3   1996
971.2′00497—dc20
                                                                96-4691
                                                                CIP

Manufactured in the United States of America
Dover Publications, Inc., 31 East 2nd Street, Mineola, N.Y. 11501

EDITOR'S FOREWORD

Before I read Mr Burpee's Introduction, and visited Mr J. Addison Reid in person, I was convinced that Paul Kane was a native of Toronto, Canada. But the proof is conclusive that he was born and baptized and spent his early years in the village of Mallow, Cork County, Ireland.

Mr Marshall Spring Bancroft, a son of the artist's sister, showed Mr Reid a prayer-book, presented to his mother in the Parish Church of Mallow, July 27th, 1816, and permitted him to photograph the presentation plate.

The family name was spelled 'Keane' in Ireland. This is shown by the 'presentation plate,' and by the Parish Register at Mallow. Why and when it was changed to 'Kane' is not known.

Wanderings of an Artist is a valuable book historically and ethnologically, and as basic native literature. With the keen eye and alert mind of a trained observer, everything of interest and value was noted, and simply and vividly recorded; and this while he was busy sketching hundreds of pictures and often suffering prolonged and intense hardships. Indeed, his drawings and diary and subsequent paintings were a great achievement, for which increasing honour and distinction should be accorded him.

The volume was published in 1859 by Longman, Brown, Green, Longmans and Roberts. It is not known who was responsible for the proof-reading, but it was carelessly done. A number of names have two spellings each: 'Sascatchawan, Saskatchawan'; 'Winnipeg, Wennipeg'; 'Ki-use, Kye-use'; 'La Row's Prairie, La Rouge's Prairie'; 'Grand Batteur, Grand Batture'; 'the Pau, the Paw'; 'Saulteaux, Salteaux'; and pimmi-kon, pemmi-kon.' Mackinaw is spelled 'Mackenaw' and Kaministiquia, 'Kaministaqueah''... In a few instances present-day official spellings have been substituted... (See Mr Burpee's 'Notes')... Numerous words that we now spell with 'z', such as 'civilize', 'organize', authorize' &c., were invariably spelled by Kane with 's'. It is thought advisable to substitute the more recent spelling.

Apart from the two signatures reproduced, no specimen of Kane's handwriting has been discovered.

The Appendix of the original volume is not reprinted. It gives the names and the numbers of the several tribes of Indians inhabiting the Pacific slope and islands in 1846, and enumerates their possessions. The total population was 56,262; of this number, 1955 were slaves. The information was given apparently for the benefit of British Traders.

Longmans, Green & Co., in reply to an enquiry, wrote me in February, 1923, "that the copper plate made for this book" (the original volume) "was destroyed in February, 1878; and the blocks were destroyed in 1907."

JOHN W. GARVIN

Note—Since the above was typed, Mr Bancroft has been located in Guelph, Ontario. In a letter to the Editor he says, " Am an old Toronto boy, that being my birth-place nearly 88 years ago." In a second letter he states that the proof in his possession of Paul Kane's birth in Mallow, County Cork, Ireland, was accepted by the 'Historical Society of Toronto,' when Hon. Mortimer Clark was President and Mrs. Fitzgibbon was Secretary.

CONTENTS

ILLUSTRATIONS

[Illustration captions in the original edition have been corrected to conform to those given in the "Catalogue of Paintings" (see p. xxxviii) or, in their absence there, to the captions in *Paul Kane's Frontier* (Amon Carter Museum of Western Art, Fort Worth, 1971). Proper names in the main text may be spelled differently.]

COLOR PLATES
(between pages 10 and 11)

a—Medicine Mask Dance [at Esquimalt, British Columbia]

b—Spokane River Landscape

c—Ojibbeway [Ojibwa] Camp on Spider Islands [Georgian Bay, Lake Huron]

d—Half Breeds Travelling [near Fort Garry, Manitoba]

e—Sioux Scalp Dance [Fort Snelling, Minnesota]

f—Camp Scene with Bark Wigwams and a Canvas Tent

g—River Landscape

h—The Man that Always Rides [seen at Fort Carlton?]

Paul Kane.

Reproduced from an oil painting loaned by A. H. O'Brien, M.A.,
barrister-at-law, Toronto, Canada. The original is unsigned, but it is
believed to have been painted by the artist himself, in his young
manhood.

INTRODUCTION

by

Lawrence J. Burpee

It has been one of our cherished ideas as Canadians that Paul Kane, pioneer in Canadian art, was one of our native born. That idea has been supported by everyone who has hitherto attempted to sketch his life. It has been repeated time and again that he was born in York, now Toronto, in 1810, his father having come out to Canada with Simcoe in 1791.

Unfortunately the only fact that can be relied upon in this statement is that Paul Kane was born in 1810. For the true particulars of his birth we are indebted to Mr J. Addison Reid, of Toronto, who has been as indefatigable in running down meagre clues as he has been generous in putting the results of his researches at the disposal of others interested in the same subject.

Michael Kane, Paul's father, according to the records of the British War Office, was born at Preston, Lancashire, in 1775; enlisted in the Royal Artillery on February 2nd, 1793; served in the Royal Horse Artillery in Ireland during 1798; and was discharged on September 30th, 1801, with the rank of Corporal. He was married, before his discharge, and settled at Mallow, County Cork, where he engaged in business.

He came to Canada in 1818 or 1819, made his home in York, and had his place of business as a wine and spirit merchant on the west side of Yonge Street, between King and Adelaide. Dr Scadding says that Michael Kane's spirit vaults were near Newgate Street, opposite the Sheldon and Dutcher foundry. He died

July 18th, 1851, aged 78 years, according to the inscription on the stone over his grave in St James Cemetery, Toronto. This statement as to his age does not quite agree with the facts recorded in the War Office.

Michael Kane had five children, James, Fred, Oliver, Paul and Mary, the last three being born at Mallow, in 1807, 1808 and 1810 respectively. James died in Bellevue Hospital, New York, in 1829; Fred was fatally burnt in a fire at Warren, N.Y., about 1847; Oliver died in Ireland before the family came out to Canada. Mary married Daniel Bancroft in 1831; and their son, Marshall Spring Bancroft, was living in Toronto in 1916, when he called on Mr J. Addison Reid and gave him certain facts of family history with proofs.

The inscription on Paul Kane's gravestone in St James Cemetery gives the date of his birth as September 3rd, 1810. The Baptismal Register of Mallow Rectory shows that he was baptized September 16th, 1810. The artist was therefore a native of Mallow, Cork County, Ireland, and was about eight or nine years of age when his father settled in York. Apart from the mere fact of birth, however, Paul Kane was a Canadian. His years of boyhood were spent in York, those impression-able years upon which the man's character and person-ality are so largely based, and, looking back upon them in after years, one is not surprised to find Paul Kane referring to York as "my native village".

Particulars as to the early life of Paul Kane are extremely meagre. He himself gives us just a glimpse, in the Preface to his *Wanderings of an Artist*. Referring to the one outstanding achievement of his life, he says that the subject of the North American Indian "was one in which I felt a deep interest in my boyhood. I had been accustomed to see hundreds of Indians about my native village, then Little York, muddy and dirty, just struggling into existence. To me the wild woods were not altogether unknown, and the Indians but recalled old friends with whom I had associated in my childhood."

One finds confirmation of this in Scadding's account of the early years of the District Grammar School at York, where Paul Kane got such training of the mind and character as was obtainable at that time in the little capital of Upper Canada. "During the time of the early settlements in this country" says Scadding, "the sons of even the most respectable families were brought in contact with semi-barbarous characters. A sporting ramble through the woods, a fishing excursion on the waters, could not be undertaken without communication with Indians and half-breeds and bad specimens of the French voyageurs. It was from such sources that a certain idea was derived which, as we remember, was in great vogue among the more fractious of the lads at York. The proposition circulated about, when anything ever went counter to their notions, always was to run away to the Nor'-West! What that process really involved, or what the Nor'-West precisely was, were things vaguely realized. A sort of savage land of Cocagne, a region of perfect freedom, among the Indians, was imagined, and to reach it Lakes Huron and Superior were to be traversed."

The Indians whom Paul Kane fraternized with in his boyhood at York were the Mississaugas, who had occupied the country along the north shore of Lake Ontario. Dr Scadding mentions that in August, 1805, the Mississaugas had sold to the Government 250,880 acres of land, including the site of the future capital of the Province, and extending eastward to Scarborough Heights—for ten shillings.   This was known as the "Toronto Purchase", and is worth bearing in mind when we Canadians are inclined to remind our American cousins how outrageously they exploited the poor Indians.

There is no reason to suppose that Paul Kane was one of the fractious lads of the District Grammar School, but it is clear that his young imagination was fired with what he saw of the Indians and what he understood, or thought he understood, of their wild life. With the soul of an artist, his mind seized upon all that was picturesque in that life, and no doubt contrasted it with all that was prosaic and uninteresting in muddy and dirty little York.   Then and there, one may conjecture, was born the dream, not to be realized for a quarter of a century, of a glorious adventure into the Indian country, into that measureless region of the west, the home of the buffalo, a land of lakes and rivers and forests, of immense plains and towering, snow-capped mountains, a land inhabited by men of another race, tribe upon tribe of them, untamed, untrammelled, self-reliant, wise in the ways of nature, intensely interesting.

Paul Kane, it appears, was not a brilliant pupil, nor one that, in the eyes of its masters, did credit to the Grammar School.   Like many another destined to leave his mark upon the pages of history, he revealed a strong distaste for the dreary round of instruction. One may picture him in the school room, his eyes drawn like a magnet to the window and its glimpses of that out-of-doors life that he loved, his mind drifting far away from the rules of grammar and the laws of mathematics to lands of pure romance.   One only in the Grammar School had any attraction for the embryo artist, an eccentric drawing master named Drury, from whom he obtained the rudiments of his craft.

The times and the place were not propitious to a young artist. York was nothing more than the unkempt capital of a pioneer settlement, where the struggle for mere existence, the strenuous and never-ceasing battle with the wilderness, left little opportunity or desire for higher things. Francis Hall, an English officer who visited York in 1816, has left us an unflattering picture of the town. "Being the seat of government" he says "it is a place of considerable importance in the eyes of its inhabitants; to a stranger, however, it presents little more than about 100 wooden houses, several of them conveniently, and even elegantly built, and I think one, or perhaps two, of brick." The public buildings, such as they were, had been destroyed by the Americans in 1813. It will be remembered that at this time, and for some years later, Kingston was the only town of any importance in Upper Canada. York had perhaps a couple of thousand inhabitants in 1820, Hamilton was a mere village, Ottawa was not yet born.

In York, at any rate, Paul Kane grew from boyhood into early manhood, sheltering as well as he could the seed of genius that lay within him. Schooldays ended early in pioneer Ontario, and Paul was put to work with a Mr Conger, a manufacturer of household furniture, and afterwards sheriff of Peterborough. Some little outlet for artistic feeling was found in ornamenting the more ambitious pieces of furniture, but what Paul was now striving for was money to take him abroad to study art, and money was a rare commodity in York.

Information is lacking as to Paul's relations with his family, as to his father's circumstances and his ability to help his son realize his artistic ambitions, or indeed how he reacted to those ambitions. We are told, however, that he promised to help him, but that financial or other difficulties subsequently made this impossible. Paul at any rate left York, or Toronto as it was now called, for Cobourg, where he painted the portraits of Sheriff and Mrs Conger, her sister Mrs Percy, Sheriff Ruttan, and other local notabilities, and managed to scrape together enough money to take him to the United States. Here he wandered from city to city, from Detroit to New Orleans, doing such odd jobs in art as came to his hand. Dr Morgan, in the biographical sketch in his *Celebrated Canadians,* says that while in the United States the young artist had to endure many hardships, and "fell into many scrapes consequent upon his pecuniary distress. On one occasion on board a steamboat, he had to take the skipper's portrait to pay his fare."

He was in his twenty-sixth year when he left Canada, and he spent the next five years in the United States. One can readily imagine that this was a period of trial to the young artist. Conscious of a capacity to do something worth while; conscious also, no doubt, of his own shortcomings, his lack of training, lack of artistic experience and background and atmosphere, lack of knowledge of the miracles of drawing and colour produced by the great masters of his art; he longed to be where all things were possible to the man who had the spark of genius and the capacity for hard work that would blow the spark into flame. No one who has read Dickens' *American Notes* and *Martin Chuzzlewit,* making all reasonable allowance for exaggeration, can help sympathizing with Paul Kane. The United States, in the Thirties or Forties of the last century, was no place for an artist who respected his art. By hook or by crook, however, by using his pencil and brush in such ways as were possible, he gradually saved enough to pay his way to Europe and keep him there for a few years.

In June, 1841, he sailed from New Orleans for Marseilles. It may be noted here that practically our only authority on this early period in the life of Paul Kane is the biographical sketch in the *Canadian Journal,* 2nd Series, Vol. 13, (1871) by Dr (afterward Sir) Daniel Wilson. Dr Wilson came to Canada in 1853 as Professor of history and English literature in the University of Toronto, of which he afterwards became President. He was a personal friend of the artist, and undoubtedly obtained at first hand the biographical particulars, meagre enough it is true, which he incorporated in his sketch. All subsequent attempts at biographies of Paul Kane, such as those in Nicholas Flood Davin's *Irishman in Canada,* Castell Hopkins' *Canada: An Encyclopaedia,* and Henry J. Morgan's *Celebrated Canadians,* are based almost entirely on Daniel Wilson's article. Much the best of many recent attempts to describe the life and achievements of Paul Kane is J. Addison Reid's series of articles in the Toronto *Sunday World,* November-December, 1916.

From this article, and a note or two from Morgan, we learn that Paul Kane kept a journal during the years he spent in Europe, but unfortunately it was lost, and with it the details of his experiences. It appears, however, that he spent more or less time at Paris, Genoa, Milan, Verona, Venice, Bologna, Florence, Rome and Naples, "living in humble lodgings and content with humble fare." As Morgan says, he "travelled over a great part of the continent of Europe, without one friend to help him, his only resource being in his own talents." One can imagine how the young Canadian artist, whose life hitherto had been spent in towns and villages where art was almost unknown, and where even educated men and women were too preoccupied with other matters to give much serious thought to anything so unpractical, must have revelled in the great galleries of France and Italy, with their almost bewildering wealth of masterpieces, the finest works of all the great masters of painting that the world had known.

While in Naples, he took advantage of the offer of a passage in a Levantine cruiser, to see a corner of Asia and get a glimpse of Africa. Joining a party of Syrian explorers, he was on his way to Jerusalem when they were deserted by their Arab guides and were compelled to hurry back to the coast. It was on the return from this voyage that he landed somewhere on the African coast.

As the result of his European tour, Kane brought back with him not only a more secure grasp of the technique of his art and a broader and more enlightened vision, but also a number of copies of famous paintings in the galleries of Venice, Florence and Rome. These included Raphael's Madonna in the Pitti Palace, and his portraits of the Popes, Paul II and Julius II; Leonardo da Vinci's and Rembrandt's portraits of themselves, in the Florentine gallery; Murillo's Madonna, in the Corsini Palace at Rome; and Busato's portrait of Pope Gregory XVI.

Kane seems to have spent some time in London, after his return from Italy. Stewart Watson, a well known Scottish artist, who had been one of his companions in Italy, returned with him to London, where they shared for a time the same lodgings and studio, at Mr Martin's, Russell Street. Another of his artist friends, Hope James Stewart, writes him from Edinburgh, "After London, this place looks like a dead city, and reminds me much of the way you and I felt the quietness of Rome after our trip to that noisy and favourite place Naples."

After nearly four years in Europe, Paul Kane returned to Canada, determined, as he says, to "devote whatever talents and proficiency I possessed to the painting of a series of pictures illustrative of the North American Indians and scenery." With the same fine courage and determination that had carried him to Europe, he now set forth to spend the better part of three years in travelling through that vast region that we know as Western Canada. To-day the journey from Toronto to Vancouver is made, in a luxurious sleeping car, in eighty-seven hours. In 1845 it meant as many days' strenuous travel in a canoe, accompanied by dangers and hardships, but also by dramatic adventures that are alien to this more prosaic age.

As Paul Kane says, at the commencement of his travels he possessed neither influence nor means for such an undertaking. Yet he set forth with a resolute spirit and a light heart, equipped with a portfolio and box of paints, to sketch the native life and scenery of the great west. Fortunately before he had gone farther than Sault Ste Marie he made the acquaintance of a man thoroughly familiar with the difficulties of travel in the Indian country, and was persuaded to seek the assistance of Sir George Simpson, Governor of the Hudson's Bay Company, who could in many ways smooth the way for him.

He returned to Toronto, and in the spring of 1846 saw Sir George Simpson at Lachine, showed him his sketches, explained his plans, and obtained from him an order for a passage in the Company's spring brigade of canoes.   Incidentally the Governor commissioned him to paint, it is not clear for himself or the Company, a series of twelve paintings of Indian life.

It might be supposed that the artist's course was now comparatively clear, but after all Paul Kane was merely an unknown painter, and Sir George Simpson, though interested and sympathetic, was the head of a great business organization.   He was willing to help Kane, but only so far as it did not interfere in any way with his own plans or those of the Company.   Had it not been for Kane's indomitable pluck and perseverance he would not have got farther west than Mackinaw.   Nothing could throw a clearer light upon the character of this pioneer artist and adventurer than his account of how he forced his way from Mackinaw to Sault Ste Marie, despite all predictions of failure.

He overtook the Governor at Sault Ste Marie, much to the astonishment of the latter, who by this time had, one is inclined to think, grown rather tired of the pertinacity of the young artist.   That same pertinacity, it is abundantly clear, alone carried him forward.   The spring brigade had gone ahead, the Governor's own canoes were too heavily laden to afford Kane a passage, and the only alternative was to wait for the Company's schooner and trust to her intercepting the brigade at Fort William.   Altogether it does not seem necessary to stress too much the generosity of Sir George Simpson in helping the father of Canadian Art to carry out his most notable achievement.

It would serve no useful purpose to follow the narrative of Paul Kane's travels and adventures—surely one of the most fascinating accounts of Western Canada as it was in the days of the fur trade—farther than to describe his route, and touch upon any points that seem to call for comment. This comment as a matter of convenience, has been added in the form of notes at the end of the text.

The story really covers two distinct journeys, that of 1845 and the much longer and more ambitious expedition of 1846-48. In the former, Kane left Toronto on the 17th of June, 1845, travelling by way of Orillia to Sturgeon Bay on Lake Huron, by canoe to Penetanguishene, thence by steam packet to Owen Sound, on foot to Saugeen where he remained ten days making sketches of the Ojibways, then back to Owen Sound where he purchased a canoe and with a companion set out for Manitoulin Island. Here he spent a fortnight among the Indians, making sketches and studying their customs, and then left for Sault Ste Marie by steamer. The same form of conveyance took him to Mackinaw, where he remained three weeks. He then visited Green Bay, and by canoe to Fox river and the Monomanee tribe. From there he returned by way of Fond du Lac and Sheboygan to Buffalo and Toronto.

On the second journey, he left Toronto on the 9th of May, 1846, for Mackinaw and Sault Ste Marie, thence by schooner to Fort William. The spring brigade had gone forward, but by means of a light canoe Kane managed to overtake it at one of the portages. They followed what is known as the Kaministikwia route, first discovered by the French, subsequently abandoned in favour of the Grand Portage route, and re-discovered and re-established by the North-West Company when Grand Portage became territory of the United States.

Their way lay up the Kaministikwia river, thence by a series of small lakes and streams over the height of land and down to Rainy Lake. After a brief rest at Fort Frances, they descended Rainy river to the Lake of the Woods, and Winnipeg river to Fort Alexander near its mouth. All along the route Kane took advantage of every opportunity to make sketches of the Indians and their camps, the portages, and bits of characteristic scenery.

At Fort Alexander he left the brigade with which he had travelled and engaged a party of Indians to take him up Red River to Fort Garry, now Winnipeg. Here he availed himself of the opportunity to accompany a number of half-breeds on a Buffalo hunt, of which he gives a spirited account in his narrative, and of which he secured a number of sketches. Learning that a small sloop was about to sail from Lower Fort Garry to the north end of Lake Winnipeg, he rode down and embarked on her for Norway House, where he remained until the middle of August waiting for the brigade on its way inland from York Factory.

Leaving Norway House, they crossed the foot of Lake Winnipeg, portaged round Grand Rapids, and ascended the Saskatchewan to Carlton House, where they left the boats and proceeded on horseback to Fort Edmonton, witnessing by the way the ancient Indian method of trapping buffalo by means of a pound, and sketching some of the chiefs of the Cree Indians.

From Fort Edmonton, they started on horseback for the Athabaska and entered what is to-day known as Jasper Park. It was now the beginning of

November, they had to travel up to Athabaska Pass through heavy snow, and the horses were abandoned in favour of snowshoes. A difficult journey carried them over the summit and down the Pacific slope to Boat Encampment on the Columbia. Here they again took boats and descended the river to Fort Vancouver, where they arrived December 8th.

Kane remained at Vancouver for about a month, studying the manners and customs of the Chinook and other neighbouring tribes, and making numerous sketches. He then ascended the Willamette to Oregon City, and returning to Vancouver, remained there until the 25th of March, when he started for Vancouver Island in a wooden canoe with a couple of Indians. He travelled by way of the Cowlitz river and Puget Sound, reaching Fort Victoria, April 9th.

From Fort Victoria, Kane made excursions up the east side of Vancouver Island and over to the main shore, visited Indian villages and made sketches of their inhabitants. June 10th he started back to Fort Vancouver, taking with him the despatches that had just arrived on the Company's vessel from London.

On the first of the following month he started on his long journey home, travelling with the east-bound brigade up the Columbia, and by way of Athabasca Pass to Fort Edmonton, where he arrived December 5th. Here he spent Christmas and the New Year, moving down to Fort Pitt on January 7th, 1848, with a wedding party. At Fort Pitt he lingered for a month, studying the habits and manners of the Crees, and making sketches of ceremonial pipes and medicine dresses.

Returning to Edmonton, he remained there until the 12th of April, when he left for Rocky Mountain

House, 180 miles farther up the Saskatchewan, to study
the Blackfeet, a large party of whom were expected on
a trading expedition.   Once more returning to Edmonton, Kane started down the river May 25th with the
York Factory brigade, passing the Mackenzie River
brigade at Grand Rapids and reaching Norway House
on June 18th.   It may be noted in passing that at Fort
Carlton he met Sir John Richardson and Dr Rae on
their way to the Arctic in search of Sir John Franklin
and his ill-fated expedition.   Here he also got word of
the flight of Louis Philippe from Paris, and other
momentous news from far-off Europe.   He was
detained at Norway House for more than a month, waiting for the annual meeting of chief factors, and then
continued his journey by way of Lake Winnipeg and
the Lake of the Woods route to Fort William and
Toronto, where he arrived early in October.

It has been mentioned that Sir George Simpson
commissioned a dozen paintings of Indian life.   The
request was for "buffalo hunts, Indian camps, councils,
feasts, conjuring matches, dances, warlike exhibitions,
or any other pieces of savage life you may consider to
be most attractive or interesting."   No doubt Paul
Kane carried out the commission, but these paintings
like most of his earlier work seem to have dropped out
of sight.   In a letter from F. A. Verner, the Canadian
artist who painted Kane's portrait, to J. Addison Reid,
it is said that twelve of Kane's pictures were in Buckingham Palace in 1858, for inspection by the Royal Family.
It is just possible these were the twelve painted for Sir
George Simpson.

The artist had, however, a much more liberal patron
in George William Allan, of Toronto, to whom he
dedicated his book.   Indeed it would not be too much

to say that it was largely because of Mr. Allan's generous and large-minded support that the artist found
it possible to carry out his memorable expedition to the
Pacific coast. Mr. Allan commissioned a hundred oil
paintings of Indian life and character and western
scenes, and also asked Kane to make a collection for him
of Indian head-dresses and clothing, pipes and other
Indian material. Some of this Indian material is still
in the possession of the Allan family, but much of it
disappeared, having been loaned from time to time for
exhibition purposes and not returned.

The artist had one other patron, the Legislature of
Canada. An examination of the Journals of the Legislative Assembly reveals the following interesting facts:
On July 26th, 1850, a petition was read from Paul
Kane, representing that he had spent several years in
Western America and had obtained more than five
hundred sketches of the country, inhabitants, Indian
chiefs, costumes, curiosities, etc; that he had made notes
of his travels, and praying for aid to enable him to
complete and publish in suitable style his notes and the
accompanying pictures.

In June, 1851, the same or a similar petition was
brought before the Assembly, and referred to the
Standing Committee on Contingencies. In August of
that year, the Committee presented its report to the
Assembly, recommending that "the sum of five hundred
pounds be expended for the purchase of twelve of such
of Mr Kane's best finished oil paintings as shall be
selected by the Library Committee, for the purpose of
being preserved in the Library of the Legislature, and
that one half of the amount (two hundred and fifty
pounds) be paid to him as soon as the selection shall have

been made, specifications furnished of the several pieces selected, and pledges given by Mr Kane that at a time certain to be agreed upon they will be delivered by him to their intended destination; and the remaining two hundred and fifty pounds upon his return from England, (whither it is his intention to proceed, in order to cause his sketches to be engraved or lithographed for sale), and delivery of the paintings that shall have been so selected, to the Clerk of your Honorable House, to be deposited in the Library, pursuant to the present recommendation."

"Your Committee", continues the report, "think it proper to observe that Mr Kane is a native of the City of Toronto, of whom his native city may be proud, as an artist of the first merit. They deemed it their duty to visit his studio, and were highly gratified by the inspection of the splendid paintings and collection of curiosities shown them by that gentleman, illustrative of the remote and interesting parts of our Continent, which he visited during his peregrinations." It is not much to be wondered at that the impression that Kane was a native of York or Toronto became so widespread, when one finds it in a public document and in his own narrative.

The Assembly accepted the recommendation of the Standing Committee on Contingencies, with the amendment that the amount of five hundred pounds was to be paid in one sum when the pictures were selected.

In the Journals of the Assembly for May 12th, 1856, the Standing Committee on Contingencies is asked to enquire and report to the House whether the conditions under which the grant of five hundred pounds to Paul Kane was made had been complied with.

The Committee reported that it had examined the receipt of Paul Kane for the five hundred pounds, in which he engaged to deliver, when called upon, twelve pictures mentioned in a list signed by Lord Mark Kerr, S. Derbyshire and A. T. Hamilton, Esquires, and offered as his guarantee for so doing the Honorable M. Cameron, and recommended that Kane be called upon to execute his agreement.

In reply to a communication from the Clerk of the Assembly, Kane replied:

"Mr Paul Kane begs leave to bring under the notice of the Contingent Committee the following circumstances connected with his agreement to furnish the House of Assembly with twelve Paintings, in consideration of receiving £500, which was paid to him in 1851:—

"In the first place, Mr Kane begs to state that the understanding arrived at between Mr Hincks, Mr Malcolm Cameron, and the other Gentlemen with whom he was in communication when the grant referred to was made, was that the Paintings should only be supplied to the House after Mr Kane had finished his complete series, which he has now been exclusively engaged at for eleven years and has not yet accomplished. The object of his application to the House was for a gratuity to enable him to devote himself entirely to that work with a view to the publication of his Pictures, in illustration of a narrative of his travels and adventures in the North-West, which he intended, and still intends giving to the Press. It will be obvious to the Committee, and this view was at once admitted to be reasonable by the Committee in 1851, that out of a series of Paintings intended for publication under copyright, to make twelve choice selections and expose them in an apartment, public as the Library of the Legislature, would effectually destroy his right, and in fact the necessity of securing such copyright, as nothing could prevent the public from obtaining access to them for any purpose they might desire. The arrangement, therefore, was that these Paintings should be presented to the House as soon as it could be done without any such danger.

"In explanation of the period elapsed since the arrangement was effected, Mr Kane begs the Members of the Committee to consider that he has been many years engaged at the work in question in his own interest, and that no delay that was not absolutely indispensable in so voluminous a work can reasonably be supposed to have been voluntarily incurred.

"These remarks Mr Kane offers in justification of himself and of the time transpired since he undertook that engagement; he has now, however, to inform the Committee that, anticipating that the return of the Government to *Toronto* would be immediately followed by a demand of the nature now made upon him, he waived the consideration above set forth, and has now been for some months occupied in preparing the series intended for the House, which he hopes to complete by the close of the Summer. He, therefore, requests that the Committee will be good enough to withdraw their Report, which was prepared and presented without his being called upon to offer any explanations, and suspend action in the matter until the opening of the next Session, when Mr Kane will be prepared to place the twelve Paintings in the hands of the proper Officer of the House, on the understanding that such precautions as he may suggest will be adopted to prevent his prospective copyright being infringed, in furtherance of the understanding on which was based as well Mr Kane's original application, as the liberal action of the Committee upon it. *Toronto,* 21st May, 1856."

As a result of this communication, the Assembly, on the recommendation of the Standing Committee on Contingencies, suspended any further action until the following session. In the interval the pictures were completed and handed over to the Legislative Library.

A list of these twelve paintings was published in the first printed Catalogue of the Library, and it appears that they hung for a time in the hall of the Legislative Council. It has been said that some of them were destroyed by fire during the time Parliament sat in Quebec, but this, if true at all, could only apply to one picture, as eleven out of the original twelve are in Ottawa at the present time. Five hang in the National Gallery, and the remainder in the Speaker's Chambers in the House of Commons. The Allan collection was purchased some years ago by Sir Edmund Osler, of Toronto, and presented to the University of Toronto. The pictures are preserved in the Royal Ontario Museum of Archaeology for the benefit of those interested in Canadian art and ethnology.

All these finished paintings, it may be noted, were done after Paul Kane returned from his long journey through the west, and were based on his field sketches, of which he is said to have brought nearly four hundred back with him. Many of these sketches were in oils or water colour, and were themselves works of art. They were, it is said, turned over to Mr. Allan with the finished paintings, but subsequently got into other hands. Some two hundred of the original sketches were exhibited at the Art Gallery in Winnipeg in 1922.

In 1853, Paul Kane married Miss Harriet Clench, of Cobourg, a lady who, among other attractions, had, according to Dr Wilson, a skill with her pencil and brush akin to his own. Having completed the manuscript of his book, Kane revisited London in 1858, to make arrangements for its publication and to superintend the execution of the chromolithographic reproduction of such of his paintings as were used to illustrate it.

One little side-light on this visit to London is afforded by the records of Hudson Bay House. Under date of February 25th, 1858, Sir George Simpson sends Paul Kane a letter of introduction to the officials of the Hudson's Bay Company in London. "Introduces Mr Paul Kane an Artist of Toronto who a few years ago travelled through the Company's territories for the purpose of delineating the life and customs of the Aborigines. He is about to publish an account of his travels and has already done the Company good service."

In the covering letter, Sir George Simpson says, "It occurs to me that the mode in which I can best promote the object of your visit to England, is to make you known to the Board of the Hudson's Bay Company, so that you may be in a position to refer to them when necessary (as a well known and influential organization) in your negotiations with publishers and others.—The enclosed letter to Mr Smith, the Secretary, will serve as a general introduction to the individual members of the Board.—I shall also write to Mr Smith privately, requesting him to introduce you personally to the Governor, Deputy Governor & Committee.

"Wishing you every success in your undertaking."

Under date of March, 1858, the minutes of the Board of the Hudson's Bay Company read, "That Mr. Paul Kane of Toronto be cordially received and encouraged."

In the letter, already referred to, from F. A. Verner to J. Addison Reid, the following additional particulars are given in connection with this visit to London:

"When Kane came to England" he says "he took his manuscript, with a list of a number of Canadian subscribers for his book when published, to Longmans and Company, who received the manuscript to look over it.

Kane called frequently to know what they intended doing, but could not get a definite answer. After remaining in London over six months, he called (as he thought) for the last time. Longman on this occasion opened the door of a large room with shelves filled with manuscripts, and said 'How is it that you expect me to look over yours when none in this collection is looked at yet?' Kane's reply was, 'I am independent of the world. Give me my manuscript. I am returning to Canada.' "

It appears, however, that Longman had heard in the meantime of the fact that twelve of Kane's pictures had been sent to Buckingham Palace, and was favourably impressed. He told Kane that if he would call again to-morrow he would arrange with him to have the book published.

In reviewing *Wanderings of an Artist* in the *Canadian Journal,* 1859, Dr. Wilson draws particular attention to the frontispiece, representing a Cree half-breed. "The original painting" he says "presents an exceedingly interesting illustration of the blending of the white and Indian features in the female half-breed. But the London chromo-lithographer has sacrificed every trace of Indian features in his desire to produce his own ideal of a pretty face, such as might equally well have been copied from an ordinary wax doll." Anyone who will compare the original, now in the Royal Ontario Museum at Toronto, with the frontispiece in the original edition, will appreciate the justness of Dr Wilson's criticism.

On his return to Toronto Kane had hoped to carry out the idea forecasted in the Preface to his book, that he might be enabled to publish a much more extensive series of illustrations of the characteristics, habits, and scenery of the country and its occupants, but unfortunately his eyesight began to fail, and before long he was compelled to abandon entirely work with either brush or pencil, a situation which must have been extremely trying to one so enthusiastically devoted to his art.

He had, says Dr Wilson, at least in his later years, "somewhat of the quiet, unimpressible manner of the Indians, among whom he had spent some of the most eventful years of his life. His memory was singularly retentive; and, in spite of his reserved manner, his descriptive powers were great, when he could be induced to give them free scope. In the company of those who did not sympathize with his favourite pursuits, his words were few and abrupt; but he was a man of acute observation, and, when questioned by an intelligent enquirer, abounded with curious information in reference to the native tribes among whom he had sojourned."

"When I was a boy of about fourteen or fifteen" says F. A. Verner, "I called at Paul Kane's studio, which was on King Street near Toronto Street. Rapping at his door, which he opened about two inches, saying 'What do you want?', I replied that I wished to know if he would give me instruction in painting. The door was quickly closed and no answer from him.

"I did not see anything more of him for some years until I returned from Europe. He had given up painting owing to failing eyesight. He told me that his eyes were affected by the glare of the sun on the snow during his long tramps from station to station in the northwest territories."

It has been said elsewhere that the injury to Kane's eyesight dated back to his student days in Europe, when he had done a good deal of sketching in the Alps with the aid of a mirror.

Paul Kane died in Toronto, February 20th, 1871, leaving his widow with two sons and two daughters.

I think one can agree unhesitatingly with Dr Wilson's conclusion that Paul Kane's narrative "is a modest, but interesting and vivid description of novel scenes and incidents of travel; and his career is a creditable instance of the pursuit of a favourite art, by a self-taught artist, in spite of the most discouraging impediments to success."

As to the value of his paintings as art, one prefers to rely upon the opinion of such an acknowledged authority as the well-known Canadian artist, Charles W. Jefferys of Toronto, who in the course of a lecture on Canadian art said that Kane's pictures "possess considerable artistic merit, and are extremely valuable as records of the vanished life of the North-West. It is inevitable" he continues "that a country with such strongly marked physical characteristics as Canada possesses, should impress itself forcefully upon our artists. One can see in the works of our earliest painters, whether native born or adopted sons of the country, the fascination of Canadian landscape. The artist got his technical training abroad but, satiated with the endless repetitions of European landscape motifs, he found in the new land new and interesting features, a wealth of raw material that presented new problems and new subjects. But though the subjects chosen were Canadian, they were, quite naturally, at first seen through European eyes, and executed in European style and with European technique.

"Paul Kane is a good example. Trained abroad, he naturally adopted the European art traditions of his time. Consequently we see in his pictures of the North-West not the brilliant sunlight of the high prairie country and the foot-hills, nor the pure, intense colour of the north; we see instead the dull, brown tone of the studio and gallery picture of the Middle Europe of his day. The topography may be North American, but the atmosphere both physical and mental, which bathes the scene is essentially European. His Indians, though authentic and convincing in details of physiognomy and costume, are incongruously conventional in their action and gestures, and in this respect resemble the poses of the models and the antique classical statues of the academic studios in which he had learned his craft.

"His buffalo is the lineal descendant of the woolly quadruped imagined and depicted by the earliest discoverers on the reports of the shore-dwelling Indians whom they first met. His western horses in build and action are the ideal Arab steeds of the painters of the Romantic School, and recall those of Delacroix and Gericault.

"But with all these conventions and limitations, he possesses an original and personal quality, he has much genuine poetry, he reveals an accurate observation of facial type, of details of costume, of geological structure and natural growth; and the technical excellence of his pictures elevates these authentic records to the rank of works of art. Compared with his paintings, those of Catlin are merely diagrams and inventories, equally valuable perhaps for their ethnographic and historical data, but greatly inferior in artistic quality."

As long ago as 1877, Nicholas Flood Davin, in his *Irishman in Canada,* noticed the same characteristics in the art of Paul Kane, and particularly the influence of the conventions of the Romantic School, picked up in European studios, and too deeply planted to be got rid of. "Though he studied our scenery and Indian customs at first hand," says Davin, "he did not wholly give himself up to nature. The Indian horses are Greek horses; the hills have much of the colour and form of those of Ruysdael and the early European landscape painters; the foregrounds have more of the characteristics of old pictures than of our out-of-doors. All this is more particularly true of his later work, when, instead of going to nature, he remained in his studio, and painted and repainted his early sketches." For that reason, those early sketches, hurriedly drawn or painted, under conditions that must sometimes have been exceedingly trying, have nevertheless in some respects a higher value as art, are indeed truer interpretations of the wild western life they represented, than the finished paintings of the studio.

No complete list exists of the paintings and sketches of Paul Kane. Of the largest collection of finished paintings, those done for George W. Allan, and now in the Royal Ontario Museum of Archaeology at Toronto, a catalogue was printed, and is now reproduced at the end of this Introduction, together with the list of twelve painted for the Legislative Council. The series commissioned by Sir George Simpson, if it still exists, has been lost sight of. No trace of the pictures can be found in Hudson Bay House, nor is there any record of what became of them. A number of the original sketches are, it is understood, now in the possession of members of the artist's family. In addition to Indian pictures, his daughter, Mrs. Frances S. Donaldson, possesses one of Verner's two portraits of Paul Kane, the other being in the Royal Ontario Museum; also another of the artist in early life, said to have been painted by himself, and an Italian scene, "Three Musicians at a Shrine."

Mr. Arthur V. White, of Toronto, has several of the artist's paintings in his collection,—a portrait of Chief Mauza-pau-Kan, or the "Brave Soldier," the Winnebago chief, referred to on page 40 of *Wanderings of an Artist;* a portrait of Peter Jacobs, the Wesleyan Indian missionary, who, as Paul Kane says, on page 72 of his book, accompanied him on horseback to the Upper Fort on Red River; also a painting of Us-koos-koosish, or "Young Grass," a Cree brave of whom the artist says, page 115, that "he was very proud of showing his many wounds, and expressed himself rather disappointed with my picture, as I had not delineated all the scars, no matter what was their locality." Two or three of the paintings in the Royal Ontario Museum were reproduced in 1909 in the "Guide to the Anthropological Collection in the Provincial Museum" of British Columbia, which, incidentally, is a tribute to the scientific value of Paul Kane's work.

The *Wanderings of an Artist* was published by Longmans in 1859. This first and only English edition was followed by a French translation, published at Paris by Amyot in 1861. Two years later appeared a Danish edition, published at Copenhagen. The English edition, though now rare, is found in most of the larger libraries. The French edition is also in most of the great collections. The Copenhagen edition is, apparently, extremely rare. It is not in the British Museum or the Library of Congress or the Library of Parliament at Ottawa, neither is it in that great collection of Aemricana, the New York Public Library. The only copy I have seen is in the possession of Judge F. W. Howay, of New Westminster, B.C. The title-page reads as follows: "En Kunftners Vandringer/blandt/ Indianerne i Nordamerika/fra Canada til Vancouvers

O og/Oregon, gjennem Hudsons-Bai-/Kompagniets Territorium og tilbage/igjen,/Af/Paul Kane;/Overfat fra Engelst/ ved/I. K./Kjobenhavn/F. H. Eibes Forlag-Louis Kleins Bogtrykferi/1863."

Before the publication of the first edition of *Wanderings of an Artist,* Kane had contributed certain portions of the work to the *Canadian Journal,* Toronto. Two of these articles appeared in Vol. I of the New Series, 1856. "Notes of Sojourn among the Half-Breeds, Hudson's Bay Company's Territory, Red River," and "Notes of Travel among the Walla Walla Indians"; and in Vol. 2 of the same Series, 1857, "The Chinook Indians." The latter had also been published in Vol. III of the Old Series, 1855.

The following bibliographical particulars may also be of interest. *Wanderings of an Artist* was reviewed, among other places, in the *Canadian Journal,* 1859, by Daniel Wilson, and in the *Athenaeum,* July 2, 1859. Biographical sketches and comments on the book are also found in the *Canadian Journal,* 1871; *History of Toronto and York,* Vol. 2; Henry Scadding, *Toronto of Old;* Henry J. Morgan, *Celebrated Canadians,* 1862; N. F. Davin, *The Irishman in Canada,* 1877; J. W. L. Forster, A.R.C.A., "Arts and Artists in Ontario," in *Canada: An Encyclopaedia,* Vol. 4; Howay and Scholefield, *British Columbia,* Vol. I; H. H. Bancroft, *History of British Columbia,* pp. 131-2; Marshall, *Acquisition of Oregon,* Vol. 2, pp. 250-53; W. H. Pearson, *Records and Recollections of Old,* Briggs; Kane (P.)—Wanderungen eines Künstlers unter den Indianern Nordamerikas von Canada nach der Vancouvers Insel und nach Oregon. Deutsch von L. Hauthal. Mit 4 color. Tafeln und 62 Holzschnitten. Leipzig 1862. (Catalogue No. 46—Otto Lange, Florence, Italy).

CATALOGUE OF PAINTINGS

BY

PAUL KANE

IN THE ROYAL ONTARIO MUSEUM OF ARCHÆOLOGY, IN TORONTO

(Kane's method of spelling proper names is followed. This Catalogue is reprinted here by permission of the Director of the Royal Ontario Museum of Archæology.)

LAKE HURON

1—*Wah-pus*

2′ 1″ x 1′ 8″

'The Rabbit,' residing at Owen Sound, a celebrated warrior, all of whose hair had been pulled out except the scalp lock.

2—*French River Rapids*

1′ 6″ x 2′ 5″

3—*Ojibbeway Camp on Spider Islands*

1′ 7″ x 1′ 0¼″

Near Bay of Manetouawning, La Cloche Mts. in the background.

4—*Ojibbeway Chief*

2′ 3″ x 1′ 8½″

With frontlet and nose ring.

5—*Aw-bon-waish-cum*

Second Chief of Ojibbeways at Manetouawning.

6—*Shaw-wan-osso-way*

2′ 1″ x 1′ 8″

'One with his Face to the West,' formerly a great war chief but afterwards a great Medicine Man at Manetouawning in Manitoulin Island.

7—*The Daughter of Asabonish*

2′ 1″ x 1′ 10″   Oval 2′ x 1′ 8″

'The Racoon,' Chief of Ahtawwah Indians at Wequimecong near Manetouwaning.

8—*Encampment Among the Islands of Lake Huron*
1' 6" x 2' 5"
Wigwams of birch bark and poles.

MICHIGAN

9—*Sault Ste. Marie*
1' 7" x 2' 6"
From American side.

WISCONSIN

10—*Spearing Salmon by Torchlight*
1' 6" x 2' 5"
Manomanee Indians at Fox River.

11— *Kitchie-ogi-maw*
2' 6" x 2' 1"
The Great Chief of the Manomanee Indians at Fox River.

12—*Muckata*
2' 1" x 1' 8"
A Manomanee Indian, one of the most ill-favoured of any who had been a subject of Kane's pencil.

13—*Wah-bannim*
2' 1" x 1' 8"
'The White Dog,' a Manomanee Indian at Fox River in mourning for his wife.

14—*Coe-coosh*
2' 1" x 1' 8"
'The Hog,' a Pottowattomie blackleg who gambled with the Manomanee Indians at Fox River.

MINNESOTA

15—*Sioux Scalp Dance*
4' x 2' 5"
Great gathering of Sioux at Fort Snelling in Hennepin County.

LAKE SUPERIOR

16—*Maydoc-gan-kinungee*
2′ 6″ x 2′ 1″

'I hear the noise of the Deer,' Head Chief of the Ojibbe-ways at Michipicoton, with his red coat and medals.

17—*The Kakkabakka Falls*
1′ 9½″ x 2′ 5½″

18—*The Mountain Portage*
2′ 1¼″ x 1′ 8″

MANITOBA

19—*Encampment on River Winnipeg*
1′ 7″ x 2′ 6″

A couple of miles below the 'Terre Blanche' Rapid.

20—*The Slave Falls*
1′ 6 x 2′ 5″

The highest of all the Falls of the Winnipeg River.

21—*White Mud Portage*
1′ 6″ x 2′ 5″

On Winnipeg River.

22—*Hunting Ducks*
1′ 6″ x 2′ 5″

At Lake of the Thousand Islands—Ducks attracted by motions of a dog running forwards and backwards along the shore under orders of an ambushed Indian.

23—*Red River Settlement*
1′ 6″ x 2′ 5″

Fort Garry at Junction of Red and Assiniboine Rivers.

24—*Half-Breeds Travelling*
1′ 6″ x 2′ 5″

An expedition to hunt Buffalo near Fort Garry.

25—*Half-Breed Encampment*
1′ 6″ x 2′ 5″

While on such expedition.

26—*Half-Breeds Running Buffalo*
                    1′ 6″ x 2′ 5″

27—*Wounded Buffalo Bulls*
                    1′ 6″ x 2′ 5″

28—*Buffalo Bulls Fighting*
                    1′ 6″ x 2′ 5″

29—*A Sioux Indian*
              2′ 1″ x 1′ 8″   Oval 2′ x 1′ 7″
     In full war paint.

30—*Caw-kee-kee-keesh-e-ko*
                    2′ 1″ x 2′ 6″
     'The Constant Sky.' A Saulteaux woman and scenery
     near the mouth of Behring's River, Lake Winnipeg.

NORTH-WEST TERRITORIES

31—*Brigade of Boats*
                    1′ 6″ x 2′ 5″
     On the Saskatchewan with a fair breeze, crowding on
     all sail to escape a thunder storm rolling fast after them.

32—*Oge-maw-waw-chack*
                    2′ 6″ x 2′ 1″
     'The Spirit Chief,' an Esquimaux from Hudson's Bay,
     supposed to be 110 years old, living at Norway House.

33—*A Buffalo Pound*
                    1′ 6″ x 2′ 5″
     Near Fort Carlton.

34—*A Valley in the Plains*
                    1′ 6″ x 2′ 5″
     On the way from Fort Carlton to Edmonton—showing
     the cabree or prairie antelopes in a valley with sloping
     banks 200 feet high.

35—*The War Cap of Otiskun*
                    2′ 6″ x 2′ 1″
     Or The Horn, a Cree Chief living between Fort Carlton
     and Pitt.

36—*Cree Pipe-stem Bearer*
2' 6" x 2' 1"
At Fort Pitt.

37—*Indian Summer*
1' 6" x 2' 5"
Evening scene on the Saskatchewan, buffalos grazing.

38—*Fort Edmonton*
1' 6" x 2' 5"

39—*A Prairie on Fire*
1' 6" x 2' 5"
Near Fort Edmonton.

40—*Francois Lucie*
2' 6" x 2' 1¼"
A half-breed Cree from Edmonton and celebrated guide, of whose bravery a story is told.

41—*Cun-ne-wa-bum*
2' 1" x 1' 8"   Oval 2' x 1' 7"
'One that looks at the Stars.'   A half-breed Cree beauty at Fort Edmonton.

42—*Kee-a-kee-ka-sa-coo-way*
2' 6" x 2' 1"
'The man that gives the War Whoop.'   Head Chief of the Crees with his pipe-stem.

43—*Cree Indian Chief from Edmonton*
2' 6" x 2' 1"

44—*The Man that Always Rides*
2' x 1' 6¼"
Dexterous Indian rider.   'A Perfect Centaur.'

45—*Catching Wild Horses*
1' 6" x 2' 5"
At Edmonton.

46—*Two Assiniboine Indians Running a Buffalo*
One armed with a spear, the other with a bow.

47—*Group of Buffaloes*
1' 7½" x 2' 5"   Oval 1' 5¼" x 2' 3¼"
At Sturgeon Creek, 16 miles from Edmonton.

48—*Winter Travelling in Dog Sleds*
1' 7" x 2' 5"

The wedding journey to Fort Pitt from Edmonton.

49—*Cree Indians Travelling*
1' 6" x 2' 5"

50—*Six Indian Chiefs*
2' 1" x 2' 6"

Group showing in full war costume the celebrated Blackfoot Chief Big Snake called 'Little Horn;' Wahnistow the 'White Buffalo,' principal chief of the Sarcee tribe; Mis-ke-me-kin 'The Iron Collar,' a Blood Indian and two inferior chiefs.

51—*Indian Horse Race*
1' 6" x 2' 5"

Blackfoot Indians, Blood Indians, Sarcees, Gros-ventres and Paygans.

52—*Big Snake*
2' 1" x 1' 8"

Omoxesisixany, a very celebrated Blackfoot Chief.

53—*The Death of Big Snake*
1' 8" x 2' 1¼"

Omoxesisixany, the great Blackfoot Chief, killed by one of the Cree War Chiefs in single combat.

54—*Big Snake's Brother*
2' 6" x 2' 1"

Blackfoot Indian.

55—*Blackfoot Pipe-stem Carrier*
1' 8" x 1' 2"

56—*Medicine Pipe-stem Dance*
4' 7" x 2' 5"

Blackfoot Indians, Blood Indians, Sarcees, Gros-ventres and Paygans.

57—*Rocky Mountain Fort*
1' 6" x 2' 5"

And Camp of Assiniboine Lodges.

58—*Mah-Min*

2' 6" x 2' 1"

'The Feather,' Head Chief of the Assiniboines at Rocky Mountain Fort.

59—*Wah-he-jo-tass-e-neen*

2' 6" x 2' 1"

'The Half White Man,' Second Chief of the Assiniboines at Rocky Mountain Fort.

INTERIOR OF BRITISH COLUMBIA

60—*Boat Encampment*

1' 6" x 2' 5¼"

At Northern bend of Columbia River, foot of Rockies.

61—*Dalle des Morts*

1' 6" x 2' 5"

On Columbia River about 70 miles below Boat Encampment.

COLUMBIA RIVER AND TRIBUTARIES IN STATES OF WASHINGTON AND OREGON

62—*Indian Camp Colville*

1' 7" x 2' 5¼"

Lodges of Chualpays near Fort Colville, formed of mats on poles with space in which to hang salmon to dry.

63—*See-Pays*

2' 6" x 2' 1"

'The Salmon Chief' or 'Chief of the Waters,' at the Indian Village of Colville.

64—*Falls at Colville*

1' 7" x 2' 5"

The Sometknu, Chaudiere, or Kettle Falls below the old Hudson's Bay Company's Fort at Colville. Modes of Catching Salmon.

65—*Game of Al-kol-lock*

1' 6" x 2' 5"

Played by the Chualpay Indians, Fort Colville.

66—*Scalp Dance*

1′ 7″ x 2′ 5″

Of Chualpay Indians at Fort Colville.

67—*Chimney Rocks*

1′ 6″ x 2′ 5¼″

The extraordinary 'Rocks of the Kye-use Girls,' where the Walla-Walla debouches into the Columbia River.

68—*Scene near Walla-Walla*

2′ 5″ x 1′ 6″

The Rock of the Nezperee Girl.

69—*Peo-peo-mox-mox*

2′ 1″ x 1′ 8″

'The Yellow Serpent,' Chief of the Walla-Walla Indians.

70—*Pelouse Fall*

1′ 6″ x 2′ 5¼″

One sheet 600 feet high from between rocks 400 feet above summit of the fall.

71—*A Sketch on the Pelouse*

1′ 7¼″ x 2′ 6″

72—*Nezperee Indian*

2′ 1″ x 1′ 8″

With bone through nostrils, on the Columbia River near the Nezperees River.

73—*To-ma-kus*   1′ 2″ x 1′ 8″   Oval 2′ x 1′ 7″

Murderer of Dr Whitman—Kye-use Indian from banks of Walla-Walla.

74—*Til-au-kite*

2′ 1″ x 1′ 8″

Who assisted in the murder of Dr Whitman—Kye-use Indian from banks of the Walla-Walla.

75—*Man-ce-muckt*

2′ 1″ x 1′ 8″   Oval 2′ 0¼″ x 1′ 7½″

Chief of the Indians of the Dalles of the Columbia River.

76—*Ca-sa-nov*

2' 6" x 2' 1"

The Great Chief of the Chinooks and Klickataats at Fort Vancouver on the Columbia River.

77—*Coffin Rock*

1' 6" x 2' 5"

Place where Indians deposit their dead on the Columbia River,

78—*Mount St. Helen's*

I' 6" x 2' 5"

Volcano distant about 30 or 40 miles from Fort Vancouver, taken from mouth of Kattlepoutal River, a tributary of the Columbia.

79—*Indian Burying-place on the Cowlitz River*

1' 6" x 2' 5"

80—*Caw-wacham*

2' 6" x 2' 1"

Flathead woman and child of the Indians residing on the Cowlitz, a tributary of the Columbia River.

81—*The Walhamette River from a Mountain*

82—*Oregon City*

1' 6" x 2' 5"

Near Falls of Walhamette, "contains about ninety-four houses and two or three hundred inhabitants."

83—*Prairie de Butte*

1' 6" x 2' 5"

About 22 miles long. Remarkable for having innumerable round elevations touching each other like so many hemispheres of 10 or 12 yards in circumference and 4 or 5 feet in height, near the Nasqually River.

PACIFIC COAST FROM
COLUMBIA RIVER NORTHWARD

84—*A Battle*

1' 6" x 2' 5"

Between Clal-lums and Macaws at I-eh-nus, a Clal-lum fort situated on the Straits of San Juan de Fuca.

85—*A Flathead Woman*
2′ 1″ x 1′ 8″

Wife of the Second Chief at the Village of Toanichum in Whitby's Island.

86—*Chaw-u-wit*
2′ 1″ x 1′ 8″

A Clal-lum Girl, daughter of Chief at Indian Village of Suck.

87—*Babine Chief*
2′ 6″ x 2′ 1″

Chief of the Chimpseyan or Babine Indians. Given as Frontispiece in Sir Daniel Wilson's 'Prehistoric Man.'

88—*A Babine or Big-lip Woman*
2′ 6″ x 2′ 1″

The size of the underlip constitutes the standard of female beauty, and it is enlarged by a flat piece of wood three inches long and an inch and a half wide.

89—*Chea-clach*
2′ 6″ x 2′ 1¼″

Head Chief of the Clal-lums at Esquimalt (Fort Victoria).

90—*The Esquimalt*
1′ 6″ x 2′ 5″

Fort Victoria on Vancouver's Island, showing the Village of the Chal-lums.

91—*Return of a War Party*
1′ 6″ x 2′ 5″

With scalps, in the war canoes. Fort Victoria appears on the right; part of Indian Village on the left.

92—*Medicine Mask Dance*
1′ 6″ x 2′ 5″

Clal-lum Indians at Esquimalt.

93—*Clal-lum Women Weaving a Blanket*
1′ 6″ x 2′ 5″

At Esquimalt. Another woman spinning, etc.

94—*Saw-se-a*

2' 1" x 1' 8"

Head Chief of the Cowitchins from the Gulf of Georgia
on Vancouver's Island.

95—*Culchillum*

2' 6" x 2' 1"

Son of Saw-se-a with medicine cap made of human hair
and ornamented with feathers.

96—*Lodges on Vancouver's Island*

1' 6" x 2' 5"

97—*Interior of a Lodge*

1' 7" x 2' 6"

Of Clallums at Esquimalt, the largest buildings of any
description among Indians, divided in the interior into
compartments to accommodate 8 or 10 families.

98—*A New-a-tee*

2' 1" x 1' 8"

An Indian with conical shaped head, Chief of New-a-tee
Indians at north end of Vancouver's Island. 'Prehistoric
Man,' ii. p. 317.

99—*Chinook Lodge*

1' 6" x 2' 5"

Near Vancouver, Mount Hood in the distance, Indians
weaving net, etc.

100—*Brant*

2' 6" x 2' 1"

Thayendanegea.

101—*Portrait of Paul Kane*
By F. A. VERNER.

LIST OF PICTURES PURCHASED FOR THE LEGISLATIVE COUNCIL

Twelve Oil Paintings, by Paul Kane, from Sketches made by himself in the North-West Territories.

*1—*Big Snake*

A Blackfoot Chief recounting his war exploits to five of his subordinate chiefs.

2—*Boat Encampment*

Situate at the head of the North Branch of the navigable waters of the Columbia River.

3—*Mount Hood*

A mountain about 7000 ft. high, situate near the south bank of the Columbia River. The figures in the foreground are Chinooks a branch of the Flathead tribes of the northwest coast.

4—*Buffaloes at Sunset*

Taken near Edmonton at a small lake near the Saskatchewan River.

*5—*Scalp Dance*

By a party of Spokan Indians; taken on the Upper Columbia.

6—*Assiniboines*

Hunting or Running Buffaloes on Horseback.
Taken on the plains in the vicinity of the Rocky Mountains.

7—*Fishing Lodges of the Clallums*

Vancouver Island. These Lodges are constructed of a coarse description of matting, which is taken down and carried in canoes when travelling.

*8—*Interior of a Winter Lodge of Clallums*

These Lodges are constructed of split cedar, and are consequently not portable and are frequently large enough to accommodate 100 individuals.

*9—*Part of Red River Settlement*

With a view of Fort Garry on the right and the Roman Catholic Church on the left of the River.

*10—*The White Mud Portage*

Situate on Winnipeg River. The picture represents Saulteaux Indians carrying their canoes and baggage, otherwise called Making the Portage.

11—*A Horse Race*

Among the Blackfeet Indians on the Prairies; an amusement of very frequent occurrence and consisting generally of a four-mile race, viz: two miles to and from a given point. The riders were invariably in a state of nudity.

*12—*Two Indians Playing at Alcoloh*

This sketch was taken among the Shualpees near the Falls of the Columbia. The game consists in rolling a ring of iron, three inches in diameter, with six beads of different colours bound by strings to the inner edge of the circle. The ring is rolled along the ground until it strikes against a stick intercepting it. The two competitors who follow it throw each a dart under it at the moment of its rebound the object being that the ring should, in falling, rest upon the darts, when the beads in closest proximity to the latter count towards the game according to their colour. This game is played by all the Indians on the Columbia River.

*Those starred are now in the National Gallery at Ottawa. The remainder, with the exception of No. 2, which is missing, are in the Speaker's Chambers, House of Commons, Ottawa.

WANDERINGS OF AN ARTIST
AMONG THE
INDIANS OF NORTH AMERICA

PREFACE

ON my return to Canada from the continent of Europe, where I had passed nearly four years in studying my profession as a painter, I determined to devote whatever talents and proficiency I possessed to the painting of a series of pictures illustrative of the North American Indians and scenery. The subject was one in which I felt a deep interest in my boyhood. I had been accustomed to see hundreds of Indians about my native village, then Little York, muddy and dirty, just struggling into existence, now the City of Toronto, bursting forth in all its energy and commercial strength. But the face of the red man is now no longer seen. All traces of his footsteps are fast being obliterated from his once favourite haunts, and those who would see the aborigines of this country in their original state, or seek to study their native manners and customs, must travel far through the pathless forest to find them. To me the wild woods were not altogether unknown, and the Indians but recalled old friends with whom I had associated in my childhood, and though at the commencement of my travels I possessed neither influence nor means for such an undertaking, yet it was with a determined spirit and a light heart that I had made the few preparations which were in my power for my future proceedings.

The principal object in my undertaking was to sketch pictures of the principal chiefs, and their original costumes, to illustrate their manners and cus-

toms, and to represent the scenery of an almost unknown country. These paintings, however, would
necessarily require explanations and notes, and I
accordingly kept a diary of my journey, as being the
most easy and familiar form in which I could put
such information as I might collect. The following
pages are the notes of my daily journey, with little
alteration from the original wording, as I jotted them
down in pencil at the time; and although without any
claim to public approbation as a literary production,
still I trust they will possess not only an interest for
the curious, but also an intrinsic value to the historian, as they relate not only to that vast tract of country bordering on the great chain of American lakes,
the Red River Settlement, the valley of Saskatchewan,
and its boundless prairies, through which it is proposed to lay the great railway connecting the Atlantic
and Pacific Oceans, through the British possessions;
but also across the Rocky Mountains down the Columbia River to Oregon, Puget's Sound, and Vancouver's Island, where the recent gold discoveries in
the vicinity have drawn thousands of hardy adventurers to those wild scenes amongst which I strayed
almost alone, and scarcely meeting a white man or
hearing the sound of my own language.

The illustrations—executed from my sketches, or
finished paintings, for the purpose of illustrating the
present work—constitute only a few specimens of
the different classes of subjects which engaged my
pencil during a sojourn of nearly four years among the
Indians of the North-West. In that period I executed
numerous portraits of chiefs, warriors, and medicine-
men of the different tribes among whom I sojourned,

and also of their wives and daughters. The Indian fishing and hunting scenes, games, dances, and other characteristic customs, also occupied my pencil; while I was not forgetful of the interest which justly attaches to the scenery of a new and unexplored country, and especially to such parts of it as were either intimately associated with native legends and traditions, or otherwise specially connected with the native tribes—as their favourite fishing or hunting grounds, the locations of their villages, or the bury-ing-places of the tribes. The whole of these sketches are now in my possession, and I have already been honoured by a commission to execute a series of paintings from them for the Legislature of the Prov-ince of Canada, which now have a place in the Library of the Provincial Parliament. A much more extensive series of oil paintings had been executed by me, from my sketches, for George W. Allan, Esq., of Moss Park, the liberal patron of Canadian art; and I would gladly indulge the hope that the present work will not prove the sole published fruits of my travels among the Indian tribes of North America, but that it will rather be a mere illustration of the novelty and interest which attach to those rarely explored regions, and enable me to publish a much more extensive series of illustrations of the characteristics, habits, and scenery of the country and its occupants.

PAUL KANE

CHAPTER I

Departure from Toronto—An Indian Village—The "Big Pike's" Likeness—
The Chiefs of Saugeen—An Island Labyrinth—The Encampment—An
Indian Kettle of Fish—The Household Drudge—Manetouawning—
Anecdote of the Chief Sigennok—The Egyptian Sphynx on Indian
Pipes—A Serenade—The Conjuror—The Power of Love—The Escape
—Heraldic Devices—Departure for the Sault Ste. Marie.

I left Toronto on the 17th of June 1845, with no
companions but my portfolio and box of paints, my gun,
and a stock of ammunition, taking the most direct route
to Lake Simcoe. Thence I took the steamboat for
Orillia; and crossed over to Sturgeon Bay on Lake
Huron, where I had to hire an Indian with a canoe, the
packet having left for Penetanguishene a few hours
before I reached "Cold Water." After paddling all
night, we overtook her the next morning at Penetanguishene, or the "Rolling Sand Bank," which is seated in
a deep bay, forming a secure harbour for vessels of any
amount of tonnage: it has been so named by the Indians
from a high bank of rolling sand at the entrance of the
bay. There is a small naval depôt here, and a steamer
is employed in making trips of inspection round the
lake and its shores. A larger one has been for some
years laid up in ordinary, and is no doubt now unfit for
use. Besides this depôt, there is a village inhabited by a
few whites and half-breeds.

We left Penetanguishene on the 20th, and arrived
at Owen's Sound the same evening. I here met with
three men bound for Saugeen, about thirty-five or forty
miles west of this place, where a council of chiefs was
to meet for the purpose of negotiating the sale of a
tract of land to the Provincial Government. After
engaging an Indian to carry my pack and act as guide,

1

I started in company with them on foot. Our journey
was a disagreeable one, through woods and swamps,
the rain all the time coming down in torrents. We had
to encamp at night supperless, and without shelter of
any kind, in our wet clothes, as we had omitted to bring
blankets or provisions under the expectation of reaching Saugeen the same evening. We made an early
start the next morning, and arrived there about noon,
where we found a large assemblage of Indians holding
a camp meeting, with its usual accompaniments of
boisterous singing and praying, under the superintendence of six or seven Methodist preachers.

The Indian village of Saugeen, meaning "the Mouth
of a River," contains about 200 inhabitants (Ojibbeways). It is the site of a former battleground between
the Ojibbeways, as usually pronounced, or Chippawas,
and the Mohawks. Of this, the mounds erected over
the slain afford abundant evidence in the protrusion of
the bones through the surface of the ground. The land
hereabouts is excellent, but only a small part is cultivated, as the inhabitants subsist principally on fish,
which are taken in great abundance at the entrance of
the river. They also kill hundreds of deer by erecting
a fence of brushwood many miles in extent, behind
which the Indians conceal themselves; and as the deer,
in their annual migrations, are seeking an opening
through this fence, they fall a prey to the unerring aim
of the red man. I sketched the principal chief, named
Maticwaub, or "the Bow." The band of which he is
the head chief forms a part of the great nation of the
Ojibbeways, which still inhabits the shores of Lakes
Huron, Michigan, and Superior. There is also another
large band of them on the upper Mississippi, 90 or 100
miles above the falls of Saint Anthony; they speak the

same language; their medicine dances, called Matayway, and their feasts are in every respect the same, identifying them as one and the same people, although scattered so widely apart. Another branch of them, called the Pilleurs, is found some 200 or 300 miles farther north. They derive their name from their thievish propensities, and richly deserve it, as I unfortunately experienced some few years afterwards on visiting their country.

I also took a sketch of a chief named Maskuhnoonjee, or the "Big Pike." This man was very proud of having his likeness taken, and put on his chief's medal presented by the Government to those they acknowledge as chiefs. I have never known a chief to barter away one of these marks of distinction, which they seldom wear on unimportant occasions. An interesting girl, the daughter of a chief from Lake St. Clair, gave me much trouble in prevailing on her to sit for her likeness, although her father insisted upon it; her repugnance proceeded from a superstitious belief that by so doing she would place herself in the power of the possessor of what is regarded by an Indian as a second self. Wah-pus, "the Rabbit," also permitted me to take his portrait. He resides at Owen's Sound, and was formerly as much renowned for his unconquerable fierceness and intemperance as he is now for his temperance and wisdom. This change in his character is attributable to the influence of the Methodist missionaries, whose church he has joined. He was the first Indian I had seen whose hair had been pulled out, all except the scalp-lock; this custom is common among many tribes of Indians, though not universal amongst any.

I remained at Saugeen about ten days, residing in the family of an Indian who had been educated as a

Wesleyan missionary. I then returned to Owen's Sound, accompanied by a young man named Dillon, who was extremely desirous of joining in my excursion. On arriving at the Sound I bought a canoe and a stock of provisions, and embarked with my new companion for Penetanguishene in our route for the Manitoulin Islands. On the fourth day we passed Christian Island, on which are still standing the ruins of a fort, said to have been built by two Jesuit priests who took refuge on the island with a large band of Hurons, after they had been defeated by the Iroquoisin. They defended the fort until they were nearly all destroyed by hunger and disease, when the missionaries led the survivors to Quebec. The day after passing this island we again reached Penetanguishene, where we obtained a fresh supply of provisions, after which we threaded a labyrinth of islands of every size and form, amounting, as is said, to upwards of 30,000; and both being strangers to the navigation, we continually lost ourselves in its picturesque mazes, enchanted with the beauty of the ever-varying scenery, as we glided along in our light canoe. We fished and hunted for fourteen days, almost unconscious of the lapse of time so agreeably spent. We saw only two or three Indians, the greater part of them having preceded us to Manetouawning to receive their presents.

Sketch No. 1 represents an Indian encampment amongst the islands of Lake Huron; the wigwams are made of birch-bark, stripped from the trees in large pieces and sewed together with long fibrous roots; when the birch tree cannot be conveniently had, they weave rushes into mats, called Apuckway, for covering, which are stretched round in the same manner as the bark, upon eight or ten poles tied together at the top, and stuck in the ground at the required circle of the tent, a hole being left at the top to permit the smoke to go out. The fire is made in the centre of the lodge, and the inmates sleep all round with their feet towards

1. Encampment Among the Islands of Lake Huron
Courtesy of Royal Ontario Museum

it. These lodges are much more comfortable than one would at first suppose from their loose appearance— that is, as far as warmth is considered. The filth, stench, and vermin make them almost intolerable to a white man; but Indians are invariably dirty, and it must be something very terrible indeed which will induce them to take half an hour's trouble in moving their lodge. As to removing the filth, that is never done. Their canoes are also made of birch-bark stretched over a very light frame of split cedar laths; the greatest attention being paid to symmetry and form. They travel a great deal and are often exposed to rough weather in these boats, which, being extremely light, are carried across "portages" with ease. They make their mohcocks, or kettles, of birch-bark, in which they cook fish and game. This is done by putting red hot stones into the water, and it is astonishing how quickly an Indian woman will boil a fish in this way. The Indians round Lake Huron raise a good deal of corn, which is dried and then pounded in a sort of mortar, made out of a hollow log, as represented in the sketch.

The Indians in this neighbourhood having a direct communication with the whites, use guns and other weapons of civilized manufacture, bows and arrows being seldom seen except with the children. As amongst all other tribes of North American Indians, the women do all the household work, carrying wood, putting up lodges, and cooking. I here noticed a custom amongst the women bearing a curious resemblance to the ancient usages of the Jews. At certain stated periods they are not allowed the slightest intercourse with the rest of the tribe, but are obliged to build a little hut for themselves a short distance from the camp, where they live entirely secluded until their return to health.

Previous to entering the bay of Manetouawning, we put ashore on one of the Spider Islands, to escape from a heavy shower, where we found a single lodge. A woman and her two children were there, but the men were off in the distance fishing, which is the principal occupation of the Indians hereabouts in summer, there being very little game, except occasionally a bear or deer, and, at particular seasons, ducks. The afternoon being clear, I had a fine view of the La Cloche Mountains, and spent the remainder of the evening in sketching.

Manetouawning is situated at the extremity of a bay six miles long, in the great Manitoulin Island, and is

200 miles distant from Penetanguishene by the route we took.

The word Manetouawning signifies "the Spirit Hole." The village consists of forty or fifty log-houses built by the Provincial Government for the Indians. There is a mission, with a church and pastor, an Indian agent, a doctor, and a blacksmith, all paid by the Government. I found nearly 2000 Indians here, waiting the arrival of the vessel that was freighted with their annual presents, comprising guns, ammunition, axes, kettles, and other implements useful to the Indian.

The principal chief here is Sigennok; he is an acute and intelligent Indian; he is appointed to distribute to his tribe their due share of the presents annually consigned to them. He receives a salary from the British Government as interpreter. This is paid him from policy, for although useless as an interpreter, from not speaking the English language, his natural eloquence is such that he possesses great influence over his tribe; indeed, it is to the untiring volubility of his tongue that he owes his name, which signifies "the Blackbird." The following anecdote, illustrative of character, was related to me by Captain Anderson, now superintendent of Indian affairs:—Sigennok was, in his younger days, in the continual habit of drinking to excess, and when under the influence of his potations was a perfect maniac, and only to be controlled by main force; but as the attempt to place him under due restraint was attended with no small personal danger, on account of his Herculean strength, it was the custom of his attendants to increase the amount of stimulus, and ply him with it until he became insensible, rather than expose themselves to danger from his ungovernable violence. One day, when in this state of drunken stupor, Captain

Anderson—who at that time filled the post of Indian agent,—saw him lying in front of his lodge in one of these fits of oblivion, and bound him hand and foot with strong cords, placing a sickly decrepit boy to watch over him, with instructions to hasten to him (Captain Anderson) the moment the sleeper should awake, and by no means to let him know who it was that bound him. After some hours he revived, and angrily demanded of the boy, who had dared to treat him with such indignity. The little fellow, without replying to the inquiry, hobbled away to the captain: he at once hastened to his prisoner, who put the same interrogatory to him as he had before done to the boy, and furiously demanded his instant liberation. The captain replied that the boy had bound him by his own orders, and that he had lain for hours exposed to the derision of the whole camp. He took the opportunity also of commenting forcibly on the disgrace to which so great a warrior had thus subjected himself, merely to gratify a vile and disgusting propensity, which reduced him manifestly beneath the level of the brute beast, which never sacrificed its reason, or the power to protect itself from annoyance or insult from its fellows.

Sigennok, his pride humbled, and greatly mortified at the degraded position in which he had placed himself—in the power, as it were, of the most helpless of his tribe—formed the prompt resolution of at once and for ever abandoning his favourite habit, and promised Captain Anderson that if he would release him from his bonds, he would never again taste ardent spirits. The captain took him at his word, and unbound him. Twenty-three years had elapsed since the occurrence, during which Sigennok had never been known to violate the promise then made.

Sketch No. 2 represents Awbonwaishkum. This head possesses the characteristics of the Indian to a striking degree: the small piercing eyes, high cheek-bones, large mouth, protuberant and hanging lips, are

2. Aw-bon-waish-cum [Second Chief of Ojibbeways]
Courtesy of Royal Ontario Museum

strongly indicative of the race. This chief is a man of great ingenuity and judgment. The sketch No. 3 is that of a pipe carved by Awbonwaishkum out of a dark-coloured stone, his only tools being an old knife and broken file. I leave it to antiquaries to explain how the bowl of this pipe happens to bear so striking a resemblance to the head of the Egyptian sphynx. I questioned Ambonwaishkum as to whether he knew of any tradition connected with the design, but the only explanation he could offer was, that his forefathers had made similar pipes with the same shaped head for the bowl, and that he therefore supposed the model had always existed among the Indians.

Strolling one evening in the vicinity of the camp, I heard the sound of some musical instrument, and upon approaching the performer, who was lying under a

3. Stone Pipe Carved by Aw-bon-waish-cum
Courtesy of Royal Ontario Museum

tree, I found that he was playing on an instrument resembling a flageolet in construction, but much softer in tone. This instrument is principally used by lovers, who play for hours in the vicinity of their mistress's lodge. I have often listened with pleasure to this music, as its simple and plaintive notes stole through the stillness of the forest. The lover made no secret of his object, but conversed with me freely upon the subject of his love.

The Indians assemble annually at Manetouawning from all parts of the shores of Lakes Huron, Nipissing, and Superior, as well as from all the neighbouring islands. On the arrival of the presents, the Indians, male and female, accompanied by their children, immediately seated themselves in rows on the grass, each chief heading his own little band, and giving in their number and names to Sigennok, who here appears in his proper element, dividing the goods among them with great impartiality. He is really a very useful man. His voice

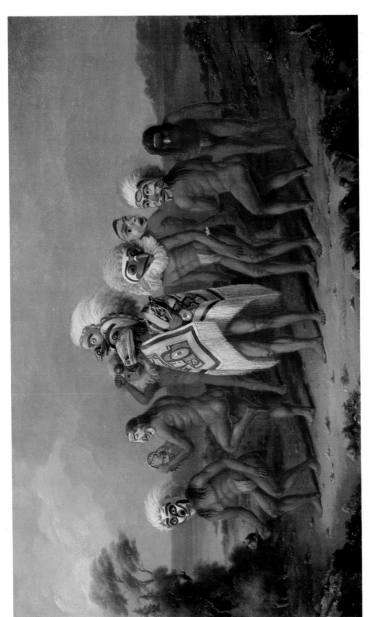

a. Medicine Mask Dance [at Esquimalt, British Columbia] • *Courtesy of Royal Ontario Museum*

b. Spokane River Landscape • *Courtesy of Royal Ontario Museum*

c. Ojibbeway [Ojibwa] Camp on Spider Islands [Georgian Bay, Lake Huron] • *Courtesy of Royal Ontario Museum*

d. Half Breeds Travelling [near Fort Garry, Manitoba] • *Courtesy of Royal Ontario Museum*

e. Sioux Scalp Dance [Fort Snelling, Minnesota] • *Courtesy of Royal Ontario Museum*

f. Camp Scene with Bark Wigwams and a Canvas Tent • *Courtesy of Royal Ontario Museum*

g. River Landscape • *Courtesy of Royal Ontario Museum*

h. The Man that Always Rides [seen at Fort Carlton?] • *Courtesy of Royal Ontario Museum*

is heard everywhere above the universal din of tongues, his native eloquence is unceasing, and seems to have the effect of allaying every envious and unpleasant feeling, and keeping all in good humour and proper order.

Among the numerous Indians assembled here, was one that particularly attracted my attention from his venerable and dignified appearance. In reply to my inquiry, as to who he was, I learned that he was called Shawwanossoway, or "One with his Face towards the West," and that he was a great medicine-man, skilled in the past, present and future. As I happened to lose, some days previously, some articles from my tent, I resolved for the sake of an introduction, and the gratification of my curiosity, to apply to the seer. On laying my case before him, he told me that his power was of no avail wherever the pale faces were concerned, and, notwithstanding my offer of a very liberal remuneration, I could not prevail upon him to put his incantations into practice. He had been, I was told, a celebrated warrior in his youth, but that owing to a romantic incident, he had abandoned the tomahawk and scalping-knife for the peaceable profession of the medicine-man, or, in common parlance, the necromancer or conjuror, in which he has obtained great repute among his people.

There dwelt many years before, on the shores of one of the great lakes, a band of Ojibbeways. Among them was a family consisting of a father and mother, with a grown-up son and daughter, the latter named Awh-mid-way, or, "There is music in her footsteps:" she exceeded in beauty the rest of the tribe, and was eagerly sought in marriage by all the young warriors of her nation. It was not long before Muck-e-tick-enow, or "Black Eagle," renowned for his prowess in battle and the chase, had, by his assiduities, won her undivided affections; nor did she conceal from him this favourable state of her feelings, but, in accordance with the customs of her people, she had unhesitatingly extinguished the blazing bark which he had sent floating down the stream that glided past her lodge, and thus acknowledged him as her accepted lover. Confident of possessing her heart, he directed all his endeavours to the propitiation of her parents, and eagerly sought how to compensate them for the loss they would undergo in relinquishing a daughter so dearly loved. For this purpose he departed on a long and distant hunt, and while straining every faculty of his mind and body in collecting trophies and presents wherewith to conciliate them, and show his entire devotion to the object of his adoration, their evil destiny brought Shawwanossoway, then a great war chief, in all the pride of manly strength and vigour, to their camp, on his return from a war excursion, in which he had greatly distinguished himself, and spread his fame far and wide, as the terror of his enemies and the boast of his friends.

Having heard of the transcendent charms of Awhmid-way, he presented himself before her, girded with the scalps of his enemies, and loaded with other trophies of victory. No sooner did he behold her, than, overcome by her charms, he devoted himself to her service and endeavoured by every art that the most passionate love could dictate, to win her regard. He recounted the numerous battles he had won, the enemies he had slain: he displayed the reeking scalps he had torn from the defeated enemy,—warriors who had been the terror of his nation: he named the many chiefs who had sued to him for peace, and at the same time plied every artifice to win the good-will of her parents, who, proud of what

they considered their daughter's superb conquest, listened to him with delight, and urged her, by every
persuasive argument, to accept so distinguished a chief
as her husband, expatiating on the honour such an
alliance would confer on their family. Constant, however, to her first love, she turned a deaf ear to all the
protestations of his rival, whose tales of conquest and
bloody trophies only excited her abhorrence.

But, nothing daunted, and determined to win her,
either by fair means or by foul, Shawwanossoway perse-
vered in his suit, trusting to time and accident to attain
his object. The poor girl, now made truly wretched by
his undeviating persecution, accompanied by the men-
aces of her parents, who were determined to conquer
what they regarded as the rebellious obstinacy of their
child, at length came to the resolution of appealing to
the generosity and honour of her persecutor, and, in the
hope of propitiating his forbearance, in an evil hour she
confessed her long-cherished affection for Muck-e-tick-
enow. He no sooner discovered the cause of her rejection of his suit, than rage and jealousy took full
possession of his heart, and plans of vengeance rapidly
succeeded each other, until he decided on the assassination of his rival. Having learned from his unsuspecting charmer the route her lover had taken, he tracked
him, and came up with his camp, and, concealing himself from observation, crawled towards the fire, where
his victim sat alone preparing his evening repast, and
shot him from behind a tree. Hiding the body among
some brushwood, he took possession of the game of his
murdered rival as a means of accounting for his own
absence, and hastened back to the village, where he
renewed his suit more ardently than before, to the utter
disappointment and distress of Awh-mid-way who still

rejected all his overtures with indignation, until, urged by the positive commands and threats of her parents, she at last, hoping by some artifice still to put off the evil day, consented to name a time when she would receive him as her husband, trusting that her lover would in the meantime return and rescue her from the impending sacrifice, and concealing, as well as she could, her increasing aversion to her persecutor.

The dreaded day at last, however, arrived, but no lover of course returned. Little did she think that his mangled remains had fallen a prey to the ravenous beasts of the forest—for still hope fondly directed her gaze in the direction she had seen him take at his departure, when all was sunshine and prospective happiness. With aching eyes and a bursting heart she saw the evening approach that was to bind her irrevocably to one she abhorred.

The bridal canoe which, according to the Indian custom, had been prepared with all the necessary stores to convey the betrothed pair on a month's excursion together, which is, in fact, the only marriage ceremony, was already lying upon the beach. Night had come—the nuptial feast was prepared—the last she was to partake of in her father's lodge—when lo! the bride was missing, and consternation usurped the place of gaiety in the bridal throng. Eagerly did they seek her with torches and shouts through the neighbouring forests, but no answering sound met their ears, although the search was continued with untiring eagerness till daylight. Then, for the first time, it was discovered that the bridal canoe was gone, and, concluding that the bride had availed herself of it to aid her escape, Shaw-wanossoway, accompanied by her brother, started in pursuit on foot, following the direction of the shore.

After proceeding for several hours, they caught sight of the canoe and its fair occupant in the distance. Increasing their speed, they reached a point which the canoe must necessarily pass round. Here the lover swam out, hoping to intercept it. In vain did he endeavour, by every means he could devise, to induce her to stop and take him on board. Defeated by her resolute refusal and the vigour and skill with which she plied her paddle, he was obliged to reliquish the pursuit and return to the shore. He had scarcely landed, when a violent storm, accompanied with thunder, lightning, and heavy rain, compelled the pair to encamp for the night. Notwithstanding the tempest, she continued her efforts until the shades of night hid her from their view. The clouds dispersed with the dawning day, and they continued their pursuit until they at length espied the canoe lying on the shore. Thinking they had at last attained their object, they quickened their steps; but, on coming up to it, they encountered a troop of wolves, and their horror may well be conceived on discovering the remains of the being they loved almost wholly devoured, and only to be recognized by her torn and scattered garments. With aching hearts, they carefully gathered the cherished remains, and, placing them in the canoe, returned to the camp, where she was wept and mourned over for many weeks by her disconsolate relatives and friends, and buried with all the ceremonies of her tribe.

It was evident that the heavy storm had driven the canoe ashore, and it is probable that her materials for kindling a fire having become soaked with water, she had been debarred the only means of protecting herself from these ravenous animals.

Shawwanossoway was so much grieved at the misery

which his ungovernable passions had brought upon the
object of his warmest love, that he formed the resolution of abandoning his warlike pursuits; and, throwing
up the tomahawk to the Great Spirit, that it might be
employed only as an instrument of justice, he took
in its stead the rattle of the medicine-man; nor did he
ever after act inconsistently with his altered character.

Six miles from Manetouawning is another village
called Wequimecong, comprising fifty or sixty houses,
and a Catholic mission with a church. I made a sketch
of the principal chief, named Asabonish, "the Racoon,"
and his daughter. He belongs to the tribe of Ahtawwah
Indians. This tribe is now scarcely distinct from the
Ojibbeways, with whom they have numerously inter-
married, and speak the same language. The Indians
of this village subsist chiefly on salmon and white fish,
which they take in such quantities as to be able to barter
away a surplus beyond their own wants for other necessaries. The inhabitants also make abundance of maple
sugar, which they sell to the traders; nor are they so
very deficient in agricultural skill and industry, having,
under the able and kind guidance of the missionary,
cultivated many patches of wheat, corn, and potatoes, as
well as erected a neat little church.

While I was at Manetouawning, the successor of
Mr. Anderson, Captain Ironsides, arrived there; and
as he was a half-breed and chief of the Wyandots, I
have introduced him among my Indian sketches. His
name signifies, "walk in the water:" he is a descendant
of Tecumseh, and uses the same *to-tem,* a turtle, each
Indian family having a sort of heraldic device, which
they use as a signature on important occasions. Sometimes a family passing through the woods will cut a
chip out of a tree, and mark their to-tem on the fresh

surface, so that the next may know who passed; or should a chief wish to send to a post for any articles, he draws the articles on a piece of birch-bark, and puts his to-tem, a fox, a dog, a bear, or whatever it may be, at the bottom; these are perfectly well understood, and answer every purpose of a written order.

I remained at the Manitoulin Island for a fortnight, parting with Mr. Dillon, who returned in the schooner that brought the presents.   I left for the Sault Ste. Marie on board the steamer "Experiment," a Government vessel; Captain Harper, who commanded, kindly taking my canoe on board, and giving me a passage. At the Sault Ste. Marie I made the acquaintance of Mr. Ballantyne, the gentleman in charge of the Hudson's Bay Company's Post, who was exceedingly kind. He strongly advised me against attempting to penetrate into the interior, except under the auspices of the Company, representing it as almost impossible and certainly very dangerous; but urged me to apply to Sir George Simpson, the Governor of the Company at Lachine, who, he thought, when aware of the object I had in view, would send me forward with the spring brigade of canoes next year. Hoping that, by following this advice, I should be able to travel further, and see more of the wilder tribes, I determined upon confining my travels for the present to a mere summer campaign.

As it is my intention to speak of the Sault Ste. Marie
in my next trip, I will pass over any mention of it here.
After remaining a few days, I embarked on board a
steamer for Mackinaw, a distance of ninety miles,
There I found a large band of Indians to the number
of 2600, who had come from all quarters to receive their
pay of $25,000 for land ceded to the United States;
these Indians were also Ojibbeways and Ottawas. On
arriving among them, I at once pitched my tent in their
midst, and commenced to sketch their most remarkable
personages. I soon had to remove my tent, from the
circumstance that their famishing dogs, which they
kept for the purpose of hunting and drawing their sleds
in winter, contrived to carry off all my provisions, and
seemed likely to serve me in the same way. This will
appear by no means improbable, when I state that,
while I was one evening finishing a sketch, sitting on
the ground alone in my tent, with my candle stuck in
the earth at my side, one of these audacious brutes un-
ceremoniously dashed in through the entrance, seized the
burning candle in his jaws and bolted off with it, leaving me in total darkness.

The next day, as I approached my tent, I saw a dog
running away from it, and thinking it probably the
same rascal that had stolen my candle, I thought to
inflict summary justice upon the marauder, and fired
the contents of my pistol into his carcase. Beyond my

expectations, which had only been to wound, I saw that
I had killed him, and was immediately assailed with a
demand, from the owner of the dog and his wife, for
payment for the loss of his services, which I agreed to
liquidate on their paying me for the losses I had sus-
tained in hams and other provisions which their dog
had stolen from me. Hereupon they balanced accounts,
and considered that we were about even, giving me an
invitation to join them at supper, and partake with them
of the slaughtered animal, in which operation I afterwards saw them happily engaged.

The Indian name of the island is Mitchi-mac-inum,
or "the Big Turtle," to which animal it bears a strong
resemblance in form when seen from a certain point.

It is situated in the straits between Lakes Huron
and Michigan; it contains some picturesque spots, one
in particular, a natural bridge, which all strangers visit.
There is a garrison on the island, consisting of a company of soldiers. The inhabitants support themselves
chiefly by fishing, the straits here yielding an immense
supply of large salmon and white fish. Many traders
assemble at Mackinaw, at the periods of payment,
bringing with them large quantities of spirituous liquors,
which they sell clandestinely to these poor creatures, it
being prohibited by Government; and many an Indian
who travels thither from a long distance returns to his
wigwam poorer than he left it, his sole satisfaction being
that he and his family have enjoyed a glorious bout of
intoxication.

I took the likeness of a chief named Mani-tow-wah-
bay, or "He-Devil." He anxiously inquired what I
wanted the likeness for. In order to induce him to sit,
I told him that they were going home to his great
mother, the Queen. He said that he had often heard of

her, and was very desirous of seeing her, and that had
he the time and means, he would pay her a visit. It
pleased him much that his second self would have an
opportunity of seeing her. He told me, with much pride
that he had been a successful warrior, and had taken
nine scalps in his warfare. He was very fond of liquor,
and, when under its influence, was one of the most
violent and unmanageable among them.

Having remained at Mackinaw for three weeks, I
left for Green Bay, which is well situated for a commercial port, and must eventually become a place of importance, from the rich farming country in its vicinity; but
owing to over speculation in every way in the years
1836 and 1837, it has been paralysed, and houses might
now be obtained for the keeping them in repair. Here
I amused myself with shooting snipe, which are met
with in abundance. In about a week I left in company
with three gentlemen going to Fox River to see the
Manomanee Indians, who were now assembling to
receive their payment for lands sold to the United States
Government in the vicinity of Lake Winebago. We
embarked in my little canoe, and proceeded up stream,
arriving on the second night about 11 o'clock at an
Indian log-house on the shore of Lake Winebago, or,
"Muddy Lake." Two Indian girls, sisters, reside here
alone. I remained with them the next day, and took
their likenesses; the elder was named Iwa-toke, or,
"the Serpent," the younger was called Ke-wah-ten,
"the North Wind." We then proceeded up the lake to
Fox River, entering which we found an Indian trading-
house, round about which a number of idlers were
pledging everything they possessed for liquor, under
the influence of which dozens were lying about in a state
of beastly intoxication.

An Indian called Wah-bannim, or, "the White Dog," sat to me for his likeness. He was in mourning for his wife, who had died some three months before; the mourning suit consisting of a coat of black paint with which he had smeared his face. He apologized for not appearing in full mourning costume to have his likeness taken, lamenting that a part of the paint had worn off; he was eagerly seeking to obtain whisky to console him for his loss. We gladly quitted this disgusting scene of dissipation, and continued our course

4. Spearing Salmon by Torchlight [Fox River]
Courtesy of Royal Ontario Museum

up the monotonous stream. After paddling for two days, we reached the Monomanee camp.

The evening previous to our arrival, we saw some Indians spearing salmon; by night, this has always a very picturesque appearance, the strong red glare of the blazing pine knots and roots in the iron frame, or light-jack, at the bow of the canoe throwing the naked

figures of the Indians into wild relief upon the dark
water and sombre woods. Great numbers of fish are
killed in this manner. As the light is intense, and being
above the head of the spearsman, it enables him to see
the fish distinctly at a great depth, and at the same time
it apparently either dazzles or attracts the fish. In my
boyish days I have seen as many as a hundred light-
jacks gliding about the Bay of Toronto, and have often
joined in the sport. This, I suppose, gave me additional
interest in the scene; and although very tired with my
long day's paddling, I sat down by the fire, and while
my companion was cooking some fish in a moh-cock,
Indian fashion (for we had lost our kettle), I made the
sketch No. 4.

Here we found about 3000 Indians assembled anxiously awaiting the arrival of the agent with their money;
there was also a large number of traders collected, all
busily occupied in the erection of booths for the display
of their finery. In about a week the bank of the river
wore the aspect of a little town; the booths, placed in
rows, presented a scene of bustle and animation: the
finery was, of course, all displayed to the best advantage
on the outsides of the booths. On the arrival of the
Indian agent a council was immediately called in a place
erected for the occasion, in which thirty chiefs assembled.
I attended in compliance with an invitation I had received from the head chief, Oscosh, or, "the Bravest of
the Brave."

He opened the council by lighting a pipe, and hand-
ing it to all present, each person taking a whiff or two,
and passing it to the next. The mingling clouds of
smoke raised by each are supposed to ascend to the Great
Spirit, in token of the harmony that pervades the
assembly, and to attest the purity of their intentions.

After this ceremony the main business of the council began: it almost exclusively consisted of complaints to be forwarded to the Government. After several of the minor chiefs had delivered their sentiments, Oscosh himself rose, and spoke for about an hour, and a finer flow of native eloquence—seasoned with good sense— I never heard, than proceeded from the lips of this untutored savage. Although a small man, his appearance, while speaking, possessed dignity; his attitude was graceful, and free from uncouth gesticulation. He complained of numerous acts of injustice which he supposed their great father, the President, could not possibly know, and which he desired might be represented to him, through the agent, accompanied with a pipe-stem of peace richly ornamented.

One of the grievances he specified was, that their money passed through too many hands before it reached them, and that a great part of it was thus lost to them. He wound up his long harangue by descanting upon the narrow limits in which they were pent up, which did not allow them sufficient hunting grounds without encroaching upon the rights of other tribes. He said that, like the deer chased by the dogs, they would have to take to the water.

When Oscosh aspired to the dignity of head chief, his election was opposed in the council by another chief, who insisted on contesting the post of honour with him. Oscosh replied, that as there could be only one head chief, he was quite willing on the instant to settle the dispute with their knives by the destruction of one or the other. This proposal was declined, and his claim has never since been disputed. This tribe is remarkably partial to gaudy decorations, and ornament themselves with great quantities of beads, silver ornaments, and

feathers. This passion for display is confined chiefly
to the men.

They are much addicted to gambling, and I have
seen them commence playing, covered with highly-
prized decorations, which have gradually changed
hands, as the game proceeded, until its close has left the
original possessor without a blanket to cover him. The
principal despoilers of the Manomanees are the Potto-
wattomies, some of whom make it their business to visit
the Manomanee camp on a regular black-leg expedition
at the time the latter receive their Government pay, in
order to fleece them of whatever they can, and they
generally return home laden with booty. Liquor, whenever they can obtain it, is their chief bane, and lays them
more open to the fraudulent schemes of their despoilers.

I made a sketch of Coe-coosh, "the Hog," one of
these Pottowattomie black-legs, whom I saw intently
engaged in gambling. The introduction of spirits
among the Indians is, as before mentioned, prohibited
under severe penalties by the laws of the United States,
and with the greatest propriety, as an Indian, when
under its influence, is one of the most dangerous animals
in existence, and there being so few whites to control
them at the period of payment, we should have been in
no small danger of losing our lives had it been readily
attainable.

I was myself, on this occasion, called up in the dead
of the night by the United States' marshal, who had
been commissioned to prevent its introduction among
them; he required my assistance, in common with all the
other whites on the spot, in order to make a search
throughout the camp to detect the person who was selling liquor, as some of the Indians were already drunk.
Having a suspicion that a half-breed was engaged in the

illicit traffic, we all proceeded to his tent. Although we plainly smelt the liquor in his tin pots, not a single keg was to be found in spite of the most vigilant search, carried even to the extent of digging up the earth in his tent. When I was leaving the neighbourhood, I got him to confess that he had sunk several kegs, with buoys attached to them, in the middle of the river. By keeping watch by turns through the night, it fortunately passed over without mischief.

Among other Indians whose likeness I took, is that of Kitchie-ogi-maw, or, "the Great Chief," a Mano-manee, who was celebrated among his tribe for many acts of daring, one of which was narrated to me by his half brother: it occurred eight or ten years previously.

His maternal uncle, who was then at Mackinaw, chanced to be present in a grocery store, where ardent spirits were sold, when two soldiers entered, one of whom treated him with so much indignity, that, seizing him in his powerful grasp, and being the stronger and more active man, he threw the soldier down with great violence on the ground upon his back, and planting his knee upon his breast, assured him that he would do him no further injury, if he would behave himself properly. This assurance given in his own language, was, un-fortunately, not understood by either of the soldiers; the second of whom, seeing his comrade in the power of a savage, and his life, as he thought, in peril, instantly drew his side-arms and stabbed the ill-fated Indian to the heart. No punishment of any importance followed the commission of this crime; the offender was merely sent away from Mackinaw to escape the vengeance of the relatives of the murdered man.

A year or two subsequently to this unhappy occur-rence, as two white men, a Mr. Clayman and a Mr.

Burnett, were coming down the Fox River in a canoe, they chanced to pass the lodge of Kitchie-ogi-maw's father, the brother-in-law of the deceased Indian, who, with his family, was camped on the banks of the river. They were noticed by the squaw, the dead man's sister, who called to her husband that now had arrived the opportunity of revenging her brother's death, and that it was his duty, as a man, not to let so good a chance escape him; but her husband, unwilling to risk so hazardous an encounter without other aid than that of his son, Kitchie-ogi-maw, then a stripling of only four-teen years, hesitated to comply with her request. On which, in order to show her contempt of what she considered his pusillanimity, she hastily divested herself of the breech cloth usually worn by Indian women, and, throwing it insultingly in his face, told him to wear it, for that he was no man. The husband, stung by the opprobrious imputation, caught up his gun, and commanded his son to follow him. The boy declined having any concern in killing the white men, but consented to accompany him for his protection.

The two Americans had now landed and were pre-paring their camp for the night; one of them was upon his knees engaged in kindling a fire, the other approach-ing at a distance with an armful of wood; the father raised his gun, but dropped it again to his side in evi-dent agitation, the boy thereupon turned to him, say-ing, "Father, you tremble too much; give me the gun, and let me do it," and, taking the weapon from his father's hands, he approached the kneeling man from behind, and shot him dead; the other one, hearing the report and catching sight of the Indians, threw down the wood he had collected and ran for his life; the boy seeing a double-barrelled gun lying on the ground near the man he had killed, seized it and followed the fugitive, telling his father to assist in the pursuit, as if this man escaped they might be punished through his evidence for killing the other.

The father was unable to keep up with the boy, who gained on the white man, and, when within twenty or thirty yards of him, took aim and endeavoured to fire; but being unused to the double trigger, and not having cocked both locks, he pulled the wrong one: determined to make sure of his next aim, he cocked both and pulled the two triggers together; part of the charge entered the victim's shoulder, but the recoil of the two barrels going off at once, knocked the boy backwards on the ground. He was, however, only stunned for the moment, and soon recovered his feet; drawing his scalping knife, the young assassin continued his pursuit of the now almost exhausted man, who, in endeavouring to leap over a log lying on the ground, stumbled and fell.

The bloody young wretch now made sure of his victim, and before the latter could recover his feet, had come up within a few yards of him. The white man seeing that the youngster was alone, and the father not within sight, faced his pursuer, armed likewise with a knife, and resolved to grapple with him. But the boy dexterously kept out of his reach, dodging him round the fallen log, until his father should come up when they could unitedly overpower him. The wounded fugitive having now recovered breath, and noticing the father in the distance, took to flight once more, dogged by his indefatigable tormentor, and continued his speed till the morning dawned, when he fell in with some friendly Indians, who protected him and dressed his wounds, none of which were mortal; they supplied all his wants, until he was strong enough to return to his home. Kitchie-ogi-maw now deemed it the safest plan to keep away from any of the White Settlements, and he continues still to observe the same precaution.

I found some Indians of the Winebago tribe at the camp on a visit. The word Winebago signifies "dirty water;" and they are so called from living on the margin of a lake of that name. They are easily distinguished from other tribes, as they have the custom of pulling out their eyebrows.

I took the likeness of their chief, Mauza-pau-Kan, or the "Brave Soldier." I remained here for three weeks, and received much kindness and attention from the Manomanees. Hearing that I was taking sketches of the most noted Indians in the camp, a fellow named Muck-a-ta paid me a visit. He was one of the most ill favoured of any that had been the subjects of my pencil, and by all accounts his physiognomy did not belie his character.

The Indians had no sooner received their money than a scene ensued that baffles description. Large quantities of liquor immediately found their way into the camp from some unknown quarter, and the sad effect was almost instantaneous. There was scarcely a man, woman, or child, old enough to lift the vessel to its mouth, that was not wallowing in beastly drunkenness; and we gladly availed ourselves of the arrival of a small steamer that plies on Lake Winebago and the Fox River to make our escape from the disgusting and dangerous scene of singing and dancing and fighting going on around us. We disembarked at a place called "Fond du Lac," where we hired a waggon, and crossed over to the Sheboygan on Lake Michigan, and embarked on board another steamer for Buffalo, which I left again on the 30th of November and arrived the day following at Toronto.

Chapter III

In the ensuing March I repaired to Lachine to seek an interview with Sir George Simpson. Having exhibited to him the sketches which I had made, and explained the nature of the objects which I had in view, Sir George entered cordially into my plans; and, in order to facilitate them, ordered a passage in the spring brigade of canoes.

Accordingly on the 9th of May, 1846, I left Toronto in company with Governor Simpson for the Sault Ste. Marie, in order to embark in the brigade of canoes which had left Lachine some time previously, taking the route of the Ottawa and Lake Huron.

On my arrival at Mackinaw in the evening, I was informed by the master of the steamboat that he would not leave until 9 o'clock next morning. Trusting to this assurance, I went on shore for the night; but on coming down to the wharf on the following day, I found that the vessel with Sir George Simpson had departed about twenty minutes previously. This was indeed a damper of no ordinary magnitude, as, should I fail in seeing Sir George before he left the Sault, I should not be able to accompany the canoes. I was aware, likewise, that the governor would not remain longer than a few hours; but how to overtake him was the difficulty, as no boat would leave for four days.

Determined, however, not to be disappointed in my proposed expedition, I used every exertion to procure

29

a mode of conveyance. Walking along the beach, I saw a small skiff lying, and having found the owner, inquired if I could hire it, and whether there was any chance of procuring a crew. The man strongly advised me not to attempt such a perilous voyage, as it was blowing hard, and that it was not in mortal power to reach the Sault by daylight next morning. Resolved, however, to make the attempt, I at length succeeded in chartering the skiff and engaging a crew, consisting of three boys, the eldest being under nineteen years of age. It must be added that they were all well acquainted with boating. The striplings held out no hopes of being able to accomplish the undertaking within the given time, and were only induced to make the attempt by the offer of a high reward. Thus, in a tiny skiff, with a blanket for a sail, and a single loaf of bread along with a little tea and sugar for stores, we launched out in the lake to make a traverse of forty-five miles.

The wind being favourable, the boat shot ahead with tremendous rapidity, but the danger was imminent and continuous from the moment we left the shore until we reached the mouth of the river of Ste. Marie, which we did at sunset.

Here we remained about twenty minutes, and discussed our tea and bread with appetites sharpened to intensity. But now commenced another difficulty, the navigation of forty-five miles of a river with which we were totally unacquainted, in a dark night against the current and through a channel dotted with numerous islands. All this was to be accomplished by daylight, or the toil and anxiety would be of no avail.

We however set forth unflinchingly; and after a night of the most violent exertion, after running into all sorts of wrong places and backing out again, after giving up half a dozen times in despair, and as often renewing the struggle, our exertions were crowned with success. When morning dawned, there lay the eagerly looked-for steamer not two miles from us.

On getting up in the morning, Sir George Simpson was astonished at seeing me; and his amazement was not lessened when he learned the mode of my conveyance The voyage on no former occasion had been performed in so short a time under corresponding circumstances, and to this day the undertaking is still talked of as a rather notable adventure in Mackinaw and the Sault.

The Sault Ste. Marie is situated at the lower extremity of Lake Superior, where it debouches into the river Ste. Marie, in its course to Lake Huron: having in this part of the river a considerable fall, for about a mile and a half in length, it soon becomes a foaming torrent, down which, however, canoes, steered by practised guides, ordinarily descend safely, although with terrific violence. Sometimes, indeed, the venture is fatal to the bark and its occupants. A short time before our arrival on the present occasion, a canoe, in running down the rapid, had struck upon a sunken rock that made a hole through her bottom. She instantly filled, but, owing to the extreme buoyancy of the birch-bark these canoes are made of, the men, by balancing themselves adroitly in her, and squatting up to their necks in the water, thereby lessening their weight materially, were enabled to steer her with safety down the foaming billows, and run her on the shore in an eddy at the foot of the rapids.

I took a sketch of the rapids alluded to, from the American side. There is a small town called the Sault Ste. Marie, on the American side, containing 700 or 800 inhabitants, with a well-built garrison, prettily situated

on the river's bank. On the Canadian side, about half
a mile direct across, the Hudson's Bay Company have
a trading establishment, and the Customs House officer,
Mr. Wilson, a tolerably handsome house. With these
two exceptions, the British side presents to the traveller
a collection of poor miserable hovels, occupied solely
by half-breeds and Indians. In strolling among these
hovels, I made a sketch of a good-looking half-breed
girl, whose sudden appearance, emerging from such a
wretched neighbourhood, took me by surprise.

As the brigade of canoes had passed up two days
before my arrival at the Sault, and Sir George's canoes
were too heavily laden, he was unable to give me a
passage. My only alternative was to wait until the
"White Fish," a small schooner belonging to the Company, and lying at the upper end of the portage, was
unloaded, and trust to the chance of her intercepting
the canoes at Fort William. This was very doubtful,
depending, as it entirely did, upon the wind; but I had
no alternative. Sir George had embarked on the 14th
in his canoe, leaving me to follow in the way above
named. It took four days to unload the schooner, so
that she was not ready to leave before the 20th of May.
We had a fair wind at starting, which continued until
the night of the 23rd, when it came to blow a gale off
"Thunder Point." The night being very dark, we were
apprehensive of driving on the rocks at the base of this
formidable mountain—Thunder Point, as it is called,
being in fact, a perpendicular rock of twelve to fifteen
hundred feet high. Seeing it, as I then did, for the
first time, by the glare of the almost incessant flashes of
lightning, it presented one of the grandest and most
terrific spectacles I had ever witnessed. As our crew
consisted of only two men, I was under the necessity of

assisting to work the vessel, so that all hope of a comfortable sleep in my warm hammock had to be abandoned, and I was obliged to remain the whole night on deck.

At daybreak we succeeded in rounding this dangerous point, and soon passed El Royal, which island is supposed to contain valuable mineral wealth, and cast anchor near the mouth of the Kaministiquia River, which we ascended about two miles to Fort William in a small boat. This fort, during the existence of the North-west Company, was one of considerable importance as a depôt for all the trade carried on in furs, &c. This importance it has lost, in consequence of the goods which formerly passed by the route of Lake Superior now passing by Hudson's Bay since the two rival companies have merged into one; but as it possesses the best land in the vicinity of Lake Superior, it might still be made a place of much consideration in an agricultural point of view.

On delivering my letter of introduction to Mr. Mackenzie, the gentleman in charge of the fort, I learned, to my great disappointment, that the brigade had passed up the river the day before. I was compelled, in this dilemma, to trespass on the kindness of this gentleman for the supply of a light canoe and three men, in order to overtake them if possible before they reached the mountain portage, forty miles in advance. In the course of half an hour, thanks to Mr. Mackenzie's kindness, we were straining at the paddles, and, ten hours afterwards, had the satisfaction of coming up with the brigade about thirty-five miles from our starting point.

I found a gentleman named Lane in charge of the brigade, which consisted of three canoes with eight men in each. We all camped immediately, and at 3 o'clock

next morning were again *en route* in our canoes. These
are constructed of the bark of the birch tree, and are
about twenty-eight feet long and four to five feet beam,
strong, and capable of carrying, besides their crew of
eight men, twenty-five pieces; but at the same time so
light as to be easily carried on the shoulders of two men.
All goods taken into the interior, and all peltries
brought out, are made into packs of 90 lbs. each, for the
purpose of easy handling at the frequent *portages* and
discharges; these packs are called pieces.

After pulling our canoes up a rapid current, we
arrived about 8 o'clock at the mountain portage, whose
falls surpass even those of Niagara in picturesque
beauty; for, although far inferior in volume of water,
their height is nearly equal, and the scenery surrounding
them infinitely more wild and romantic. Whilst the
men were engaged in making the portage, I took advantage of the delay to make a sketch.

I have since been informed that the large flat rock
which divided the torrent in the centre has fallen in.
The interruption thus caused by the falls is about two
miles of very steep ascent, up which the men have to
carry the canoes and baggage, the former on their
shoulders, the latter on their backs, by means of what
is technically named a portage-strap, both ends of which
are attached to the load of two pieces, while the middle
of the strap goes round the forehead, which thus supports the principal part of the burden. The men who
usually work this brigade of canoes are hired at Lachine,
and are called by the uncouth names of *Mangeurs du
Lard,* or pork-eaters, among the old hands in the interior, to whom they are unequal in encountering the difficulties incident to a voyage from Lachine to the mouth
of the Columbia, whither some of them are sent, and

become almost skeletons by the time they reach their destination, through the unavoidable privations and hardships they have to undergo.

Launching our canoes again, we proceeded for about a mile, and made another portage called "The Lost Men's Portage," owing to three men having lost themselves in the woods in crossing it. I very nearly met with the same fate myself; for, having gone up to the rapids to take a sketch, I endeavoured, when I had finished, to find my way back, and spent two hours in an unsuccessful attempt to gain the path. I then fortunately thought of discharging my fowling-piece as a signal, and had the pleasure of immediately hearing an answering shot, which guided my steps to the party who were anxiously awaiting my return to embark.

Proceeding a few miles up the stream, we reached the "Pin Portage," so called from the rocks over which we had to carry the canoes being so sharp as actually to cut the feet of the men, who usually go barefooted or only wearing light mocassins. We made, in all, six portages in one day, viz., "Ecarté," "Rose Décharge," and "De l'Isle," and the three before named, travelling a distance of forty-three miles: the current was so impetuous, even where we could avail ourselves of our canoes, that the men found the greatest difficulty in forcing up against it with poles.

On the 26th of May we journeyed twenty-six miles, making the following portages and discharges, viz.:— "Recousi Portage," "Couteau Portage," "Belanger Décharge," "Mauvais Décharge," "Tremble Décharge," "Penet Décharge," "Maître Portage," "Little Dog Portage," "Dog Portage," and the "Big Dog Portage;" the latter affords a splendid view from its summit of the Kaministaqueah River, meandering in the distance, as far as the eye can reach, through one of the loveliest valleys in nature. This view I wished much to have sketched but time is of so much importance in the movement of these brigades, that I did not consider myself justified in waiting.

The "Big Dog Portage" derives its name from an Indian tradition that a big dog once slept on the summit, and left the impression of his form on the highest point of land, which remains to this present time. The length of this portage is two miles; we camped at the upper end; and while here I made a sketch of the fall, during one of the heaviest showers of rain I ever experienced.

One of our *Mangeurs du Lard* presenting himself at the camp fire in a handsome rabbit-skin blanket, was asked by Mr. Lane where he had obtained it. He replied that he had found it among the bushes. Mr. Lane, knowing that it is customary among the Indians to place offerings of all descriptions upon the graves of their deceased relatives, first rendering them unserviceable to any evil disposed persons in this world, under the idea that the Great Spirit will repair them on the arrival of the deceased in the next, and that they hold in the greatest abhorrence, and never fail to punish, any one who sacrilegiously disturbs them, ordered him immediately to return to the place whence he took it, and replace it exactly as he had found it, unless he wished to have us all murdered. When the man understood what he had done, he replaced the blanket immediately.

On the 27th, Sir George Simpson passed us with his two canoes, accompanied by his secretary Mr. Hopkins. Sir George only stopped a few minutes to congratulate me on my having overcome the difficulties of my starting: he seemed to think that the perseverance and determination I had shown augured well for my future success, and as his canoes were much lighter and better manned than ours, he passed on rapidly in advance. As there were no more currents to overcome, the men this day threw away their poles as useless, and started on a race with their paddles for about fifteen miles through "Dog Lake" and entered "Dog River." We now had to make a long portage of three miles over a high mountain into a small lake. At the upper end of this portage we again overtook Sir George, and were invited to dine with him at the next, some four or five miles further on, but we unluckily could not again come up with him.

On inquiring the cause of some loud shouting that I heard in the woods, I was told that some of our men had surrounded a bear which had given them battle, but that, unarmed as they were, they had deemed discretion the better part of valour, and sounded a retreat. We camped on the banks of a small river. We had hitherto stemmed against the stream of waters that emptied itself into the Atlantic; but we had now reached streams that flowed at a much more rapid rate, and coursed on to Hudson's Bay. At the close of this day we had accomplished a distance of thirty-three miles, having made the following portages, viz.:—"Barrière Portage," "Joudain Portage," and "Prairie Portage."

May 28*th*—To-day we passed over one of the largest and most difficult portages in the whole route; it is called the "Savan Portage;" it passes through about four miles of swamp. It formerly had logs laid lengthwise, for the convenience of the men carrying the loads; but they are now for the most part decayed, so that the poor fellows had sometimes to wade up to the middle in mud and water. In all, we made to-day about thirty miles, including the following portages, viz.:—"Milieu Portage" and "Savan Portage," from whence we went twenty miles down the Savan River, and camped near its mouth, where it empties into "Mille Lacs."

On the 29th, we passed through the Lake of the Thousand Islands, thirty-six miles long, a name it well deserves. The scenery surrounding us was truly beautiful; the innumerable rocky islands varying from several miles in length to the smallest proportions, all covered with trees, chiefly pine. This lake is filled with innumerable ducks, which the Indians entice in the following curious manner:—A young dog is trained by dragging a piece of meat attached to a string up and down the edge of the shore several times, and putting the dog on the scent, who follows it rapidly, wagging his tail. After the dog has followed it for some time, he is given the meat; this is done repeatedly until the dog will do so whenever he is ordered, and his motions attract the ducks swimming in the distance to within

38

reach of the Indian, who lies concealed on the banks. The flock of ducks is so crowded and numerous, that I have known an Indian kill forty ducks by firing at them whilst in the water, and rapidly loading and firing again whilst the same flock was circling above his head. Our first portage after leaving this lovely lake was "Portage de Pente." We camped at the end of the next portage, called "Little Discharge," having made a distance altogether of fifty-six miles.

May 30*th*—We made an early start, reaching the "French Portage" by breakfast-time. Here we lightened the canoes of the principal part of the baggage, and carried it across the portage, a distance of three miles, in order that we might be able to send the canoes round by the river, which had now become very shallow, to meet us at the further end of the portage. We camped this evening at a small lake called Sturgeon Lake, having come a distance of forty-eight miles, passing "French Portage," and "Portage de Morts."

May 31*st*—We passed down the "Rivière Maligne" until we came to what are termed the First, Second, and Third portages, and, making the portage "De l'Isle" and "Du Lac," camped near "Lac la Croix Traverse," accomplishing a distance of only twenty-seven miles.

June 1*st*—We passed down the river "Macau," where there are some beautiful rapids and falls. Here we fell in with the first Indians we had met since leaving the Lake of the Thousand Islands; they are called "Saulteaux," being a branch of the Ojibbeways, whose language they speak with very slight variation. We purchased from an Indian man and woman some dried sturgeon. The female wore a rabbit-skin dress: they were, as I afterwards learned, considered to be cannibals, the Indian term for which is *Weendigo,* or "One

who eats Human Flesh." There is a superstitious belief
among Indians that the Weendigo cannot be killed by
anything short of a silver bullet. I was informed, on
good authority, that a case had occurred here in which
a father and daughter had killed and eaten six of their
own family from absolute want. The story went on to
state, that they then camped at some distance off in
the vicinity of an old Indian woman, who happened to
be alone in her lodge, her relations having gone out hunting. Seeing the father and daughter arrive unaccom-
panied by any other members of the family, all of whom
she knew, she began to suspect that some foul play had
taken place, and to feel apprehensive for her own safety.
By way of precaution, she resolved to make the entrance
to her lodge very slippery, and as it was winter, and the
frost severe, she poured water repeatedly over the
ground as fast as it froze, until it was covered with a
mass of smooth ice; and instead of going to bed, she
remained sittting up in her lodge, watching with an axe
in her hand. When near midnight, she heard steps
advancing cautiously over the crackling snow, and looking through the crevices of the lodge, caught sight of the
girl in the attitude of listening, as if to ascertain whether
the inmate was asleep; this the old woman feigned by
snoring aloud. The welcome sound no sooner reached the
ears of the wretched girl, than she rushed forward, but,
slipping on the ice, fell down at the entrance of the lodge,
whereupon the intended victim sprang upon the mur-
deress and buried the axe in her brains: and not doubt-
ing but that the villainous father was near at hand, she
fled with all her speed to a distance, to escape his
vengeance. In the meantime, the Weendigo father,
who was impatiently watching for the expected signal
to his horrid repast, crept up to the lodge, and called to

his daughter; hearing no reply, he went on, and, in place of the dead body of the old woman, he saw his own daughter, and hunger overcoming every other feeling, he saved his own life by devouring her remains.

The *Weendigoes* are looked upon with superstitious dread and horror by all Indians, and any one known to have eaten human flesh is shunned by the rest; as it is supposed that, having once tasted it, they would do so again had they an opportunity. They are obliged, therefore, to make their lodges at some distance from the rest of the tribe and the children are particularly kept out of their way; however, they are not molested or injured in any way, but seem rather to be pitied for the misery they must have endured before they could be brought to this state. I do not think that any Indian, at least none that I have ever seen, would eat his fellow-creature, except under the influence of starvation; nor do I think that there is any tribe of Indians on the North American continent to whom the word "cannibal" can be properly applied.

We traversed to-day a distance of forty-one miles, passing four portages before entering Lake Meican, which is nine miles long, to "Portage Neuf," entering the "Lac la Pluie," where we camped; its name did not seem inappropriate, for we were detained here two days by the incessant torrents of rain that poured down. It took us until the evening of the 4th to reach Fort Frances, at the lower end of the lake, a distance of fifty miles, where I found a letter from Sir George Simpson, enclosing a circular.

There is a beautiful fall of water here within sight of the fort, at the commencement of the river which runs from Lac la Pluie to the Lake of the Woods. Vast quantities of white fish and sturgeon are taken at the

foot of the rapids, with which our mess-table at the fort
was abundantly supplied; indeed, the chief food here
consists of fish and wild rice, with a little grain grown
in the vicinity of the fort, this being the first land I had
seen fit for agricultural purposes since I left Fort
William.   We continued at the fort until the morning
of the 5th. There was a large camp of Saulteaux Indians
in the immediate vicinity: a considerable party of them
came to the establishment in the morning to see the
"great medicine-man" who made Indians, Mr. Lane
having given them to understand that my object in
travelling through the country was to paint their likenesses.

I applied to the head chief, Waw-gas-kontz, "the
Little Rat," to take his likeness, but was refused, on the
grounds that he feared something bad would result to
him; but after Iacaway, "the Loud Speaker," had sat
for his, Waw-gas-kontz seemed ashamed of his cowardice, and became very anxious to have it done, following
me down to the canoe. I had not time, however, to do
so; but I could not get rid of him until I promised to
take his likeness on my return.

June 5th—We left the fort at 10 this morning; the
rain continued all day, and obliged us to camp at 4 in
the afternoon, the distance we went being about thirty
miles.

June 6th—It was a remarkable fact that the trees
on each side of the river, and part of the Lake of the
Woods, for full 150 miles of our route, were literally
stripped of foliage by myriads of green caterpillars,
which had left nothing but the bare branches; and I was
informed that the scourge extended to more than twice
the distance I have named, the whole country wearing

the dreary aspect of winter at the commencement of summer.

As it was impossible to take our breakfast on land, unless we made up our minds to eat them dropping incessantly as they did from the trees among our food, and the ground everywhere covered with them *en masse,* we were compelled to take it in our canoes. We met some Indians, from whom we purchased seven fine sturgeons, each weighing perhaps forty or fifty pounds. We paid for the whole one cotton shirt. We next entered the Lake of the Woods, and camped on a beautiful rocky island, having made fifty-three miles in one day.

June 7th—We passed through the above lake, sixty-eight miles long. When passing a small island about the middle of it, the steersman of my canoe put ashore on this island, and running to a clump of bushes returned with a small keg of butter, which he told us he had left hidden, or, as they call it, *en cache,* the year before: it proved an acquisition to our larder, although its age had not improved its flavour. We next made the "Rat Portage," at the foot of which is the fort, a small establishment where they were so badly supplied with provisions as to be able to afford us only two white fish. We consequently thought it advisable to leave the place, although late in the evening, and camped a few miles lower down the Winnipeg River; having travelled to-day a distance of seventy-two miles.

June 8th—We continued our course down the river Winnipeg, which is broken by numerous beautiful rapids and falls, being indeed one of the most picturesque rivers we had passed in the whole route. Our bowsman caught a pike, which in appearance had two tails, one at each end; but we found on examination that the tail and part of the body of another fish or sucker, nearly as large as himself, which he had tried to swallow, was protruding from his mouth, evidencing the extreme voracity of this species. We passed to-day a Catholic missionary station called "Wabassemmung" (or White Dog), which, on my return, two years and a half afterwards, I found deserted, from the circumstance that the Indians of this quarter did not prove very willing converts. We camped for the night a few miles below this station, and still found the caterpillars before alluded to extremely annoying, covering as they did completely our blankets and clothing. We had passed the following places, viz.: "the Dalles," "Grand Décharge," "Terre Jaune Portage," "the Charrette Portage," "Terre Blanche Portage," "Cave Portage," and Wabassemmung, a distance of seventy-one miles.

June 9th—We passed the "Chute de Jaques," so called from a man thus named, who, being dared by one of his companions to run his canoe over a fall of fifteen or twenty feet, an exploit never attempted before or since, unhesitatingly essayed the bold feat, and pushing off his frail bark, jumped into it, and on rounding a small island darted down the main sheet, his companions meanwhile anxiously watching for his safety from the shore. As might have been expected, he was dashed to pieces and no more seen. We camped this evening, after completing a distance of sixty miles, and making the following portages, viz.: "Portage de l'Isle," "Chute de Jaques," "Point des Bois" (the Indian name of this fall is Ka-mash-aw-aw-sing, or "the Two Carrying-Places"); "Rochers Boules," "the Slave Falls," which is the highest of all the falls of the Winnipeg River; I never heard the reason of its bearing this name. At "Barrière Portage" we found the black flies and mosquitoes so annoying all night, as to deprive us entirely of sleep.

June 10*th*—We ran three or four beautiful rapids to-day in our canoes, the men showing great expertness in their management, although so much risk attends it that several canoes have been lost in the attempt. We made about sixty miles to-day down the Winnipeg passing the following places, viz.: the "Grand Rapid," six portages, all within sight of each other, and about five miles in length inclusively: they are known collectively by the name of "The Six Portages"—the first and second portage of the "Bonnet," "the Grand Bonnet," "Petits Rochers," and "Terre Blanche." We encamped about a couple of miles below the rapids at 5 o'clock— earlier than usual, as our canoes had received some little injury and required repairs. It is usual to start every morning between 3 and 4 o'clock and proceed till 8 for breakfast, then continue steadily on until an hour before dark, just so as to give the men time to prepare for the night. The only rest allowed being at intervals of about an hour, when all hands stop two or three minutes to fill their pipes. It is quite a common way of expressing the distance of one place to another to say that it is so many pipes; and this, amongst those who have travelled in the interior gives a very good idea of the distance. The evening was very beautiful, and soon after we had pitched our tents and lighted our fires, we were visited by some Saulteaux Indians. As I had plenty of time, I sketched the encampment. Our visitors, the clear stream reflecting the brilliant sky so peculiar to North America, the granite rocks backed by the rich foliage of the woods with Indians and voyageurs moving about, made a most pleasing subject.

CHAPTER V

Fort Alexander—Mr. Lane—A Western Career—Value of Bark to the
Indian—The Medicine Lodge—A Double Shot—Fort Garry—The
Nearest Market Town—Red River Settlement—White Horse Plain—
Hunting the Buffalo.

June 11th—We made an early start with a fine
breeze, filling our sail, and arrived at Fort Alexander
to breakfast, a distance of seventeen or eighteen miles
including three portages: "First Eau Qui Merit,"
"Second Eau Qui Merit," "Third Eau Qui Merit."
Fort Alexander is situated on Winnipeg River, about
three miles above where it disembogues into Lake Winnipeg, and has some good farming land in its vicinity.
I here took my farewell of Mr. Lane with great regret,
and left the brigade of canoes, which proceeded with
him to Norway House, on his route to Mackenzie River.
Mr. Lane had entered the Hudson's Bay Company's
service when very young, and having served for twenty-
six years, he became dissatisfied with the slowness of his
promotion, and determined to resign and return to
Ireland, his native land. However, on his return home,
he found himself lost in civilized life, and quite unable
to occupy himself with any business pursuits there; and
when I met him, he was again in the employment of the
Company, at a lower salary than he had before received,
and was going to Mackenzie River, one of the most
remote and bleak posts in the whole region, accompanied
by his wife, a half-breed. The last that I heard of him
was that he had arrived at his post almost starved to
death, after travelling about 700 miles on snow-shoes
through the depth of winter.

Hearing that a camp of Indians lay within a few

miles, I requested a Mr. Setler, in charge of the establishment, to procure me a guide to them. I found it
indispensably necessary to wear a veil all the way, as
a protection from the mosquitoes, which I had never
before seen so numerous. I found a very large camp
of Saulteaux Indians assembled. They had a medicine
lodge erected in the centre of their encampment, to which
I at once directed my steps. It was rather an oblong
structure, composed of poles bent in the form of an
arch, and both ends forced into the ground, so as to
form, when completed, a long arched chamber, protected
from the weather by a covering of birch bark. This
bark is one of the most valuable materials that nature
supplies to the Red-man, as by its friendly aid he is
enabled to brave the inclemency of the weather on land,
and float lightly and safely over the vast inland seas
that so abound in his wild domain; and when any transi-
ent impediments present themselves to his using it on
water, so light is its weight, that he easily carries it on
his shoulder. Such also is its compactness and closeness
of texture, that he forms his culinary and other utensils
of it, and, as it is quite impervious to water, he is able,
by the aid of heated stones, to boil his fish in them. It
also serves for a material or papyrus on which to trans-
mit his hieroglyphic correspondence.

On my first entrance into the medicine lodge (the
reader is already apprised of the mysterious meaning
the Indian attaches to the term "medicine") I found
four men, who appeared to be chiefs, sitting upon mats
spread upon the ground gesticulating with great violence, and keeping time to the beating of a drum. Something, apparently of a sacred nature was covered up in
the centre of the group, which I was not allowed to see.
They almost instantly ceased their "pow-wow," or

music, and seemed rather displeased at my intrusion, although they approached, and inquiringly felt the legs of my fustian pantaloons, pronouncing me a chief on account of their fineness.

On looking around me, which I now ventured to do, I saw that the interior of their lodge or sanctuary was hung round with mats constructed with rushes, to which were attached various offerings consisting principally of bits of red and blue cloth, calico, &c., strings of beads, scalps of enemies, and sundry other articles beyond my comprehension. Finding they did not proceed with their "pow-wow," I began to think I was intruding, and retired. But no sooner had I emerged from the lodge, than I was surrounded by crowds of women and children, whom nothing would satisfy short of examining me from head to foot, following me in swarms through the camp, not apparently with any hostile intentions, but for the mere gratification of their curiosity. I passed a grave surmounted with a scalp hung on a pole, torn, doubtless, from an enemy by the warrior buried beneath. I now returned to the fort, first engaging six of the Indians to proceed with me to Red River. We left at four o'clock in the afternoon in a small boat, accompanied by Mr. Setler, and camped on the shore of Lake Winnipeg.

June 12th—I wrote this part of my journal by the light of a blazing fire in the above encampment, surrounded by my six painted warriors sleeping in the front of the tent, their hideous faces gleaming in the fire-light: a head wind all day had prevented our making any great progress.

June 13th—We entered the mouth of the Red River about 10 this morning. The banks of this river, which here enters the lake, are for five or six miles low and marshy. After proceeding up stream for about twenty miles, we arrived at the Stone Fort, belonging to the Company, where I found Sir George Simpson and several of the gentlemen of the Company, who assemble here annually for the purpose of holding a council for the transaction of business. I remained here until the 15th, and left for the Upper Fort, about twenty miles higher up. We rode on horseback, accompanied by Mr. Peter Jacobs, Wesleyan Indian missionary, and arrived there in about four hours, after a pleasant ride of eighteen or twenty miles through a considerable part of Red River Settlement. Here there are a judge and a court house. A Salteaux Indian was hung here last year for shooting a Sioux Indian and another of his own tribe at one shot, the ball having passed through the Sioux and entered the Saulteaux's body: his intention was to kill the Sioux only, with whom his tribe then was, and had been from time immemorial, at war, so that the killing of the Saulteaux was accidental. The country here is not very beautiful; a dead level plain with very little timber, the landscape wearing more the appearance of the cultivated farms of the old country with scarcely a stick or stump upon it.

This settlement is the chief provision depôt of the Hudson's Bay Company, and it is also here that large quantities of pemmican are procured from the half-breeds, a race who, keeping themselves distinct from both Indians and whites, form a tribe of themselves; and, although they have adopted some of the customs and manners of the French voyageurs, are much more attached to the wild and savage manners of the Red-man. Fort Garry, one of the most important establishments of the Company, is erected on the forks of the Red River and the Assiniboine, in long. 97° W., and in

lat. 50° 6′ 20″ N., as will be seen in sketch No. 5. On
the opposite side of the river is situated the Roman
Catholic church, and two or three miles further down
there is a Protestant church. The settlement is formed
along the banks of the river for about fifty miles, and
extends back from the water, according to the original
grant from the Indians, as far as a person can distinguish
a man from a horse on a clear day.

5. Red River Settlement
Courtesy of Royal Ontario Museum

Lord Selkirk first attempted to form a settlement
here in 1811, but it was speedily abandoned. A few
years afterwards several Scotch families, including some
from the Orkney Islands, emigrated under the auspices
of the Hudson's Bay Company, and now number about
3000, who live as farmers, in great plenty so far as mere
food and clothing are concerned. As for the luxuries
of life, they are almost unattainable, as they have no
market nearer than St. Paul's, on the Mississippi River,
a distance of nearly 700 miles over a trackless prairie.

The half-breeds are more numerous than the whites, and now amount to 6000. These are the descendants of the white men in the Hudson's Bay Company's employment and the native Indian women. They all speak the Cree language and the Lower Canadian patois; they are governed by a chief named Grant, much after the manner of the Indian tribes. He has presided over them now for a long period, and was implicated in the disturbances which occurred between the Hudson's Bay and North-West Companies. He was brought to Canada charged with the murder of Governor Semple, but no sufficient evidence could be produced against him.

The half-breeds are a very hardy race of men, capable of enduring the greatest hardships and fatigues: but their Indian propensities predominate, and consequently they make poor farmers, neglecting their land for the more exciting pleasures of the chase. Their buffalo hunts are conducted by the whole tribe, and take place twice a year, about the middle of June and October, at which periods notice is sent round to all the families to meet at a certain day on the White Horse Plain, about twenty miles from Fort Garry. Here the tribe is divided into three bands, each taking a separate route for the purpose of falling in with the herds of buffaloes. These bands are each accompanied by about 500 carts, drawn by either an ox or a horse. Their cart is a curious-looking vehicle, made by themselves with their own axes, and fastened together with wooden pins and leather strings, nails not being procurable. The tire of the wheel is made of buffalo hide, and put on wet; when it becomes dry, it shrinks, and is so tight, that it never falls off, and lasts as long as the cart holds together.

Chapter VI

I arrived at Fort Garry about three days after the half-breeds had departed; but as I was very anxious to witness buffalo hunting, I procured a guide, a cart for my tent, &c., and a saddle horse for myself, and started after one of the bands. We travelled that day about thirty miles, and encamped in the evening on a beautiful plain covered with innumerable small roses. The next day was anything but pleasant, as our route lay through a marshy tract of country, in which we were obliged to strain through a piece of cloth all the water we drank, on account of the numerous insects, some of which were accounted highly dangerous, and are said to have the power of eating through the coats of the stomach, and causing death even to horses.

The next day I arrived at the Pambinaw River, and found the band cutting poles, which they are obliged to carry with them to dry the meat on, as, after leaving this, no more timbered land is met with until the three bands meet together again at the Turtle Mountain, where the meat they have taken and dried on the route is made into pemmican. This process is as follows:— The thin slices of dried meat are pounded between two stones until the fibres separate; about 50 lbs. of this are put into a bag of buffalo skin, with about 40 lbs. of melted fat, and mixed together while hot, and sewed up, forming a hard and compact mass; hence its name in the Cree language, *pimmi* signifying meat, and *kon,* fat.

52

Each cart brings home ten of these bags, and all that the half-breeds do not require for themselves is eagerly bought by the Company, for the purpose of sending to the more distant posts, where food is scarce. One pound of this is considered equal to four pounds of ordinary meat, and the pemmican keeps for years perfectly good exposed to any weather.

I was received by the band with the greatest cordiality. They numbered about two hundred hunters, besides women and children. They live, during these hunting excursions, in lodges formed of dressed buffalo skins. They are always accompanied by an immense number of dogs, which follow them from the settlements for the purpose of feeding on the offal and remains of the slain buffaloes. These dogs are very like wolves, both in appearance and disposition, and, no doubt, a cross breed between the wolf and dog. A great many of them acknowledge no particular master, and are sometimes dangerous in times of scarcity. I have myself known them to attack the horses and eat them.

Our camp broke up on the following morning, and proceeded on their route to the open plains. The carts containing the women and children, and each decorated with some flag, or other conspicuous emblem, on a pole, so that the hunters might recognise their own from a distance, wound off in one continuous line, extending for miles, accompanied by the hunters on horseback. During the forenoon, whilst the line of mounted hunters and carts was winding round the margin of a small lake, I took the opportunity of making a sketch of the singular cavalcade.

The following day we passed the Dry Dance Mountain, where the Indians, before going on a war party, have a custom of dancing and fasting for three days and nights. This practice is always observed by young warriors going to battle for the first time, to accustom them to the privations and fatigues which they must expect to undergo, and to prove their strength and endurance. Should any sink under the fatigue and fasting of this ceremony, they are invariably sent back to the camp where the women and children remain.

After leaving this mountain, we proceeded on our route without meeting any buffalo, although we saw plenty of indications of their having been in the neighbourhood a short time previously. On the evening of the second day we were visited by twelve Sioux chiefs, with whom the half-breeds had been at war for several years. They came for the purpose of negotiating a permanent peace, but, whilst smoking the pipe of peace in the council lodge, the dead body of a half-breed, who had gone to a short distance from the camp, was brought in newly scalped, and his death was at once attributed to the Sioux. The half-breeds, not being at war with any other nation, a general feeling of rage at once sprang up in the young men, and they would have taken instant vengeance, for the supposed act of treachery, upon the twelve chiefs in their power, but for the interference of the old and more temperate of the body, who, deprecating so flagrant a breach of the laws of hospitality, escorted them out of danger, but, at the same time, told them that no peace could be concluded until satisfaction was had for the murder of their friend.

Exposed, as the half-breeds thus are, to all the vicissitudes of wild Indian life, their camps, while on the move, are always preceded by scouts, for the purpose of reconnoitring either for enemies or buffaloes. If they see the latter, they give signal of such being the case, by throwing up handfuls of dust, and, if the former, by running their horses to and fro.

Three days after the departure of the Sioux chiefs, our scouts were observed by their companions to make the signal of enemies being in sight. Immediately a hundred of the best mounted hastened to the spot, and, concealing themselves behind the shelter of the bank of a small stream, sent out two as decoys, who exposed themselves to the view of the Sioux. The latter, supposing them to be alone, rushed upon them, whereupon the concealed half-breeds sprang up, and poured in a volley amongst them, which brought down eight. The others escaped, although several must have been wounded, as much blood was afterwards discovered on their track. Though differing in very few respects from the pure Indians, they do not adopt the practice of scalping; and, in this case, being satisfied with their revenge, they abandoned the dead bodies to the malice of a small party of Saulteaux who accompanied them.

The Saulteaux are a band of the great Ojibbeway nation, both words signifying "the Jumpers," and derive the name from their expertness in leaping their canoes over the numerous rapids which occur in the rivers of their vicinity.

I took a sketch of one of them, Peccothis, "the Man with a Lump on his Navel." He appeared delighted with it at first; but the others laughed so much at the likeness, and made so many jokes about it, that he became quite irritated, and insisted that I should destroy it, or, at least, not show it as long as I remained with the tribe.

The Saulteaux, although numerous, are not a warlike tribe, and the Sioux, who are noted for their daring and courage, have long waged a savage war on them, in consequence of which the Saulteaux do not venture to hunt in the plains except in company with the half-breeds. Immediately on their getting possession of the bodies, they commenced a scalp dance, during which they mutilated the bodies in a most horrible manner. One old woman, who had lost several relations by the Sioux, rendered herself particularly conspicuous by digging out their eyes and otherwise dismembering them.

The following afternoon, we arrived at the margin of a small lake, where we encamped rather earlier than usual, for the sake of the water. Next day I was gratified with the sight of a band of about forty buffalo cows in the distance, and our hunters in full chase; they were the first I had seen, but were too far off for me to join in the sport. They succeeded in killing twenty-five, which were distributed through the camp, and proved most welcome to all of us, as our provisions were getting rather short, and I was abundantly tired of pemmican and dried meat. The fires being lighted with the wood we had brought with us in the carts, the whole party commenced feasting with a voracity which appeared perfectly astonishing to me, until I tried myself, and found by experience how much hunting on the plains stimulates the appetite.

The upper part of the hunch of the buffalo, weighing four or five pounds, is called by the Indians the little hunch. This is of a harder and more compact nature than the rest, though very tender, and is usually put aside for keeping. The lower and larger part is streaked with fat and is very juicy and delicious. These, with the tongues, are considered the delicacies of the buffalo. After the party had gorged themselves with as much as they could devour, they passed the evening

in roasting the marrow bones and regaling themselves
with their contents.

For the next two or three days we fell in with only
a single buffalo, or small herds of them; but as we proceeded they became more frequent. At last our scouts
brought in word of an immense herd of buffalo bulls
about two miles in advance of us. They are known in
the distance from the cows, by their feeding singly, and
being scattered wider over the plain, whereas the cows
keep together for the protection of the calves, which are
always kept in the centre of the herd. A half-breed,
of the name of Hallett, who was exceedingly attentive
to me, woke me in the morning, to accompany him in
advance of the party, that I might have the opportunity
of examining the buffalo whilst feeding, before the commencement of the hunt. Six hours' hard riding brought
us within a quarter of a mile of the nearest of the herd.
The main body stretched over the plains as far as the
eye could reach. Fortunately the wind blew in our
faces: had it blown towards the buffaloes, they would
have scented us miles off. I wished to have attacked
them at once, but my companion would not allow me
until the rest of the party came up, as it was contrary
to the law of the tribe. We, therefore, sheltered ourselves from the observation of the herd behind a mound,
relieving our horses of their saddles to cool them. In
about an hour the hunters came up to us, numbering
about one hundred and thirty, and immediate preparations were made for the chase. Every man loaded his
gun, looked to his priming, and examined the efficiency
of his saddle-girths.

The elder men strongly cautioned the less experienced not to shoot each other; a caution by no means
unnecessary, as such accidents frequently occur. Each

hunter then filled his mouth with balls, which he drops
into the gun without wadding; by this means loading
much quicker and being enabled to do so whilst his horse
is at full speed. It is true, that the gun is more liable
to burst, but that they do not seem to mind. Nor does
the gun carry so far, or so true; but that is of less consequence, as they always fire quite close to the animal.

Everything being adjusted, we all walked our horses
towards the herd. By the time we had gone about two
hundred yards, the herd perceived us, and started off in
the opposite direction at the top of their speed. We now
put our horses to the full gallop, and in twenty minutes
were in their midst. There could not have been less than
four or five thousand in our immediate vicinity, all bulls,
not a single cow amongst them.

The scene now became one of intense excitement;
the huge bulls thundering over the plain in headlong
confusion, whilst the fearless hunters rode recklessly in
their midst, keeping up an incessant fire at but a few
yards' distance from their victims. Upon the fall of
each buffalo, the successful hunter merely threw some
article of his apparel—often carried by him solely for
that purpose—to denote his own prey, and then rushed
on to another. These marks are scarcely ever disputed, but should a doubt arise as to the ownership, the
carcase is equally divided among the claimants.

The chase continued only about one hour, and extended over an area of from five to six square miles,
where might be seen the dead and dying buffaloes, to the
number of five hundred. In the meantime my horse,
which had started at a good run, was suddenly con-
fronted by a large bull that made his appearance from
behind a knoll, within a few yards of him, and being thus
taken by surprise, he sprung to one side, and getting

his foot into one of the innumerable badger holes, with which the plains abound, he fell at once, and I was thrown over his head with such violence, that I was completely stunned, but soon recovered my recollection. Some of the men caught my horse, and I was speedily remounted, and soon saw reason to congratulate myself on my good fortune, for I found a man who had been thrown in a similar way, lying a short distance from me quite senseless, in which state he was carried back to the camp.

I again joined in the pursuit; and coming up with a large bull, I had the satisfaction of bringing him down at the first fire. Excited by my success, I threw down my cap and galloping on, soon put a bullet through another enormous animal. He did not, however, fall, but stopped and faced me, pawing the earth, bellowing and glaring savagely at me. The blood was streaming profusely from his mouth, and I thought he would soon drop. The position in which he stood was so fine that I could not resist the desire of making a sketch. I accordingly dismounted, and had just commenced, when he suddenly made a dash at me. I had hardly time to spring on my horse and get away from him, leaving my gun and everything else behind.

When he came up to where I had been standing, he turned over the articles I had dropped, pawing fiercely as he tossed them about, and then retreated towards the herd. I immediately recovered my gun, and having reloaded, again pursued him, and soon planted another shot in him; and this time he remained on his legs long enough for me to make a sketch. This done I returned with it to the camp, carrying the tongues of the animals I had killed, according to custom, as trophies of my success as a hunter.

I have often witnessed an Indian buffalo hunt since, but never one on so large a scale. In returning to the camp, I fell in with one of the hunters coolly driving a wounded buffalo before him. In answer to my inquiry why he did not shoot him, he said he would not do so until he got him close to the lodges, as it would save the trouble of bringing a cart for the meat. He had already driven him seven miles, and afterwards killed him within two hundred yards of the tents. That evening, while the hunters were still absent, a buffalo, bewildered by the hunt, got amongst the tents, and at last got into one, after having terrified all the women and children, who precipitately took to flight. When the men returned they found him there still, and being unable to dislodge him, they shot him down from the opening in the top.

Our camp was now moved to the field of slaughter,
for the greater convenience of collecting the meat. However lightly I wished to think of my fall, I found myself
the next day suffering considerably from the effects of
it, and the fatigue I had undergone. The man whom
I had brought with me as a guide was also suffering
much from an attack of the measles. Next day our
hunters sighted and chased another large band of bulls
with good success. At night we were annoyed by the
incessant howling and fighting of innumerable dogs and
wolves that had followed us to the hunt, seemingly as
well aware of the feast that was preparing for them as
we could be ourselves. The plain now resembled one vast
shambles: the women, whose business it is, being all
busily employed in cutting the flesh into slices, and
hanging them in the sun on racks, made of poles tied
together. In reference to the immense number of
buffaloes killed, I may mention that it is calculated that
the half-breeds alone destroy thirty thousand annually.

Having satisfied myself with buffalo hunting
amongst the half-breeds, I was anxious to return to the
settlement, in order to prosecute my journey. On pro-
posing to set out I found my guide so unwell, that I
feared he would not be able to travel. I tried to procure
one of the hunters to take his place and return with
me, but none of them would consent to travel alone over
so large a tract of country, from fear of the Sioux, in

whose territory we then were; and who, they dreaded
from the late occurrence, would be watching to cut off
any stragglers. Being unable to procure a fresh man,
I was about to start alone, when my guide, who thought
himself better, proposed to accompany me, on condition
that he should ride in the cart, and not be expected to
attend to the horses or cooking. This I readily agreed
to, as his services as guide were of the utmost importance.

We started next morning for the settlement, a distance which I supposed to be somewhat over two hundred miles. A party of twenty of the hunters escorted
us for eight or ten miles, to see that there were no Sioux
in the immediate vicinity. We then parted, after taking
the customary smoke on separating from friends. I
could not avoid a strong feeling of regret at leaving
them, having experienced many acts of kindness at
their hands, hardly to be expected from so wild and
uncultivated a people. We found a great scarcity of
water on our return, most of the swamps that had supplied us on our way out being now dried up by the heat
of the season.

We fell in with a great many stray dogs and wolves,
which appeared to be led on by the scent of the dead
carcasses. After hobbling the horses, putting up my
tent, and cooking the supper, I then turned in for the
night, not without some apprehensions of a hostile visit
from the Sioux, as we were still on their hunting
grounds, and in the territory of the United States,
being still a few miles south of the boundary line. During
the night my guide, who was very ill and feverish, cried
out that the Sioux were upon us. I started up with my
gun in my hand, for I slept with it by my side, and rushing out in the dark, was near shooting my own horse,

which, by stumbling over one of the tent pins, had alarmed my companion.

We travelled on the next day with as great rapidity as the ill health of my guide would permit, and on the evening of the 30th of June, we encamped on the bank of the Pambinaw. I lost considerable time next morning in catching the horses, as they are able from habit to run a considerable distance, and pretty fast, in spite of their hobbles. In the afternoon we arrived at the Swampy Lake, about fourteen miles across. A little before sunset we reached about the middle of it, but my guide complained so much that I could not proceed further.

I succeeded in finding a small dry spot above water large enough for me to sit on, but not affording room for my legs, which had to remain in the water, there being no more room in the small cart than was necessary for the sick man. Having no means for cooking, I was compelled to eat my dried meat raw. I tried to compose myself to sleep, but found it impossible, from the myriads of mosquitoes which appeared determined to extract the last drop of blood from my body. After battling with them until 4 o'clock next morning, my eyes almost blinded by their stings, I went in search of the horses, which had strayed away to some distance into deeper water, tempted by some sort of flags growing there. I had to wade up to my middle in pursuit of them, and it was not until 9 o'clock that we were able to proceed.

After leaving this dismal swamp we were within a day's march of the settlement; and my guide, believing himself to be much better, insisted upon my leaving him to drive the cart, whilst I proceeded at a more rapid rate on horseback. This, however, I would not do until

I had seen him safe across Stinking River, which the horses had almost to swim in crossing. Having got him over safely, I left him, and proceeded onwards in the direction of the fort. But I had not gone far before I encountered one of the numerous swampy lakes that abound in this region, and render travelling extremely difficult. I had no doubt got on a wrong track, for in endeavouring to cross, my horse quickly sank up to his neck in mud and water. Seeing that I could neither advance nor recede, I dismounted, and found myself in the same predicament, scarcely able to keep my head above the surface. I managed, however, to reach the dry land; and, with the lasso, or long line, which every voyageur in these parts invariably has attached to his horse's neck, succeeded in getting the animal out. I remounted, and endeavoured to cross in another direction, but with no better success. I now found myself surrounded on all sides, as far as I could see, with nothing but swamp. My horse refused to be ridden any further. I had therefore, to dismount, and drag him along as best I could, wading up to my very middle in mud and water abounding with reptiles.

That I had lost my way was now certain; and as it was raining hard, I could not see the sun, nor had I a compass. I, however, determined to fix upon one certain course, and keep that at all hazards, in hopes that I might reach the Assiniboine River, by following which I could not fail to reach the settlement. After travelling in uncertainty for ten or twelve miles, I had at length the satisfaction of reaching the river, and in two hours afterwards I arrived safe at Fort Garry. The next morning I learned that my guide had been brought in by two men who were looking for stray horses. The poor fellow had got rapidly worse after my leaving, and had only proceeded a short distance when he was compelled to stop. He only survived two days after his arrival.

Fort Garry is one of the best built forts in the Hudson's Bay territory. It has a stone wall, with bastions mounted with cannon, inclosing large storehouses and handsome residences for the gentlemen of the establishment. Its strength is such that it has nothing to fear from the surrounding half-breeds or Indians. The gentleman in charge was Mr. Christie, whose many acts of kindness and attention I must ever remember with feelings of grateful respect.

The office of Governor of the Red River Settlement is one of great responsibility and trouble, as the happiness and comfort of the whole settlement depend to a great extent upon the manner in which he carries out his instructions. The half-breeds are much inclined to grumbling, and although the Company treat them with great liberality, they still ask almost for impossibilities; indeed, as far as the Company is concerned, I cannot conceive a more just and strict course than that which they pursue in the conduct of the whole of their immense traffic. In times of scarcity they help all around them, in sickness they furnish them with medicines, and even try to act as mediators between hostile bands of Indians. No drunkenness or debauchery is seen around their posts, and so strict is their prohibition of liquor, that even their officers can only procure a small allowance, which is given as part of their annual outfit on voyages.

Without entering into the general question of the policy of giving a monopoly of the fur trade to one company, I cannot but record, as the firm conviction which I formed from a comparison between the Indians in the Hudson's Bay Company territories and those in the

United States, that opening up the trade with the Indians to all who wish indiscriminately to engage in it, must lead to their annihilation. For while it is the interest of such a body as the Hudson's Bay Company to improve the Indians and encourage them to industry, according to their own native habits in hunting and the chase, even with a view to their own profit, it is as obviously the interest of the small companies and private adventurers to draw as much wealth as they possibly can from the country in the shortest possible time, although in doing so the very source from which the wealth springs should be destroyed. The unfortunate craving for intoxicating liquor which characterizes all the tribes of Indians, and the terrible effects thereby produced upon them, render it a deadly instrument in the hands of designing men.

It is well known that, although the laws of the United States strictly prohibit the sale of liquor to the Indians, it is impossible to enforce them, and whilst many traders are making rapid fortunes in their territories, the Indians are fast declining in character, numbers, and wealth, whilst those in contact with the Hudson's Bay Company maintain their numbers, retain native characteristics unimpaired, and in some degree share in the advantages which civilization places within their reach.

Chapter VIII

Hearing that two small sloops belonging to the
Company which ply between the Red River and Norway House would leave the Lower, or Stone Fort,
immediately, I rode down on the 5th of July, in company with Mr. W. Simpson, a brother-in-law of Sir
George's, and reached our destination in about three
hours. This establishment is larger than the Upper
Fort, and built with still greater strength, but not so
neatly arranged in the interior. We rested about an
hour, and then embarked on one of the sloops; two
Catholic missionaries, Mr. Le Fleck and Mr. Taché,
who were bound for Isle La Croix, occupying the other.
We dropped down the river a few miles, and cast
anchor in front of the residence of Mr. Smithers, the
Episcopalian missionary, and his larder and cellar being
well supplied, we passed a most agreeable evening, notwithstanding the mosquitoes, which were very troublesome. Early next morning we went round his very extensive farm, which seemed to be in a high state of
cultivation. He works it principally by Indians, who
receive a share of the produce according to their labour.

After a hearty breakfast, we bid a reluctant farewell
to our kind host, and drifted down the current, there not
being enough wind to fill our sails. When night had set
in, I distinctly heard the noise made by the Red River
sun-fish, which I have only noticed in this river. The
fish resemble our Canadian black bass, weighing from

two to three pounds, and during the night they make
a singular noise, resembling a person groaning; how
they produce these sounds, I was unable to ascertain.
We proceeded only a short distance to-day, the current
running very slow. After casting anchor for the night,
the mosquitoes became so troublesome on board, that
Mr. Simpson and I took our blankets on shore and went
to an Indian lodge within a short distance of the river,
the smoke which pervades these places generally keeping
them free from the nuisance. There were three or four
families of women and children in the lodge, but the
men were all absent hunting. They cleared a corner for
us to sleep in, but one of the most awful thunder storms,
accompanied by heavy rain, that I have ever witnessed,
set in, and effectually prevented our repose. Such tem-
pests are here of frequent occurrence; so vivid was the
lightning, and so near the rattling and crashing of the
thunder, that I fancied several times during the night
that I heard our vessels dashed to pieces by it. The
missionaries on board were much terrified, and spent, I
believe, the whole night in prayer. A short time previously, a lodge containing seven persons was struck by
the electric fluid; four of them were immediately killed,
the other three were much injured, but recovered. These
accidents are of very frequent occurrence about Red
River.

July 7th—We embarked in the morning, and proceeded at a slow rate. On arriving at the mouth of the
river we were obliged to cast anchor, as it still remained
a dead calm.

July 8th—This morning we had a strong head wind,
putting a stop to our further progress for the present.
Mr. Simpson and I took a small boat, and returned up
the river to an Indian camp of Saulteaux which we had

passed the day before. The Indians crowded round the boat on our arrival, inquiring what we wanted. Our interpreter told them that I had come to take their likenesses. One of them, a huge ugly-looking fellow, entirely naked, stepped up telling me to take his, as he was just as the Great Spirit had made him. I declined, however, as I wanted to sketch one of the females, but she refused, as she could not dress herself suitably for such an occasion, being in mourning for some friends she had lost, and therefore only wearing her oldest and dirtiest clothes.

After some difficulty, I succeeded in getting a young girl to sit in the costume of this tribe, although her mother was very much afraid it might shorten her life. But on my assuring her that it was more likely to prolong it, she seemed quite satisfied. After finishing my sketch, which they all looked at with great astonishment, a medicine-man stepped up and told us that he would give us three days' fair wind for a pound of tobacco. As the demand was so enormous for so small a supply of wind, we declined the bargain, whereupon he hesitatingly reduced his price, offering a greater quantity of wind for a smaller amount of tobacco, till at length, having reduced his price to a small plug for six days, we closed the bargain, declining his invitation to stay and partake of a large roasted dog, which we had seen slaughtered on our arrival. We returned to our vessel to pass another uncomfortable night, tormented by the mosquitoes, which all our efforts at smoking failed to drive out of our hot little cabin.

July 9th—Hauled up our anchor and left the mouth of the river with a fair wind, and proceeded up Lake Winnipeg.

July 10th—To-day we were wind-bound under the

lee of a low rocky island, and although the surf ran very high on the beach, we determined to explore it as a relief to the monotony of our voyage. The attempt furnished us with plenty of excitement, as the boat filled before we reached the shore. We, however, arrived safe, and walked across the island about half a mile. It was literally covered with gulls and pelicans, which were hatching, and all rose in one body on our approach in such a dense mass as to give the appearance of the island itself taking wings. The rocks were so covered with eggs and young birds, that it was difficult to tread without crushing them. Wearied with the discordant screeching of the birds over our heads, and the smell from their dung being very offensive, we soon returned to our vessels. Large quantities of eggs are collected on this island by the voyageurs and Indians, gulls' eggs being considered a great delicacy at certain seasons. There did not appear to be any considerable collection of guano here, as probably the island is washed almost clean by the high water and heavy rains in the spring of the year.

July 11*th*—We entered the Straits between Lake Winnipeg and Playgreen Lake. The lake derives its name from a green plain which the Indians frequent to play their great game of ball. We cast anchor here, and having a small net on board, we set it, and caught a great number of jack-fish or pike, which we found excellent eating.

July 12*th*—Sailed on through Playgreen Lake, a distance of twenty-five miles, the channel lying between numerous small rocky islands, some of them so near that we could easily have sprung on shore from the vessel; from Playgreen Lake we entered Jack-fish River, and the current soon carried us to Norway House, a distance of nine miles, where we arrived in the afternoon. Mr. Ross, the gentleman in charge, received us with great kindness and hospitality. Notwithstanding the barrenness of the soil and the severity of the cold in this region, which prevents all hope of deriving any advantage from agricultural pursuits, a Wesleyan Methodist mission is established within a few miles of the fort. It is under the superintendence of the Reverend Mr. Mason, and consists of about thirty small log houses, with a church and dwelling-house for the minister. It is supported by the Company with the hope of improveing the Indians; but, to judge from appearances, with but small success, as they are decidedly the dirtiest Indians I have met with, and the less that is said about their morality the better.

The Indians belong to the Mas-ka-gau tribe, or "Swamp Indians," so called from their inhabiting the low swampy land which extends the whole way from Norway House to Hudson's Bay. This race is rather diminutive in comparison with those who inhabit the plains, probably from their suffering often for want of food; and instances of their being compelled by hunger to eat one another are not uncommon. Their language somewhat resembles the Cree, but is not so agreeable in sound. I made a sketch of one of them, called the I-ac-a-way, "the Man who is gone on a Hunt without raising his Camp."

I remained at Norway House until the 14th of August, waiting for the brigade of boats which had gone down in the Spring to York Factory, in Hudson's Bay, with the furs, and was now expected back on their return with the outfit of goods for the interior trade. Our time passed very monotonously until the 13th, when Mr. Rowand, chief factor, arrived with six boats:

one of the boats under the charge of a clerk, Mr. Lane, was entirely devoted to the carriage of the furs paid annually by the Hudson's Bay Company to the Russian Government, for the privilege of trading in their territory. These consisted of seventy pieces or packs, each containing seventy-five otter skins of the very best description. They are principally collected on the Mackenzie River, from whence they are carried to York Factory, where they are culled and packed with the greatest care; they have then to be carried up the Saskatchewan, across the Rocky Mountains, down the Columbia River, to Vancouver's Island, and then shipped to Sitka. I mention these furs particularly here, as they were the source of much trouble to us in our future progress.

On the morning of the 14th we left Norway House, in the boats, for Playgreen Lake. These boats are about twenty-eight feet long, and strongly built, so as to be able to stand a heavy press of sail and rough weather, which they often encounter in the lakes: they carry about eighty or ninety packs of 90 lbs. each, and have a crew of seven men, a steersman and six rowers. Mr. Lane was accompanied by his wife, a half-breed, who travelled with us all the way to Fort Vancouver, on the Columbia. We had scarcely got into Playgreen Lake when a heavy gale separated the boats and drove ours on to a rock in the lake. Here we were compelled to remain two nights and a day, without a stick to make a fire, and exposed to the incessant rain, as it was not possible to raise our tents. In the distance we could perceive our more fortunate companions, who had succeeded in gaining the mainland, comfortably under canvas, with blazing fires; but so terrific was the gale that we dared not venture to leave the shelter of the rock.

On the 16th, the wind having somewhat abated, we were enabled to join the rest of the party, when the blazing fires and comfortably cooked food soon restored our spirits. Being sufficiently recruited, and the wind being fair, we again embarked, although the lake was still very rough.

This lake is about 300 miles long, but so shallow, that in high winds the mud at the bottom is stirred up, from which it derives the name of Winnipeg, or Muddy Lake. On the present occasion the waves rose so high that some of the men became sick, and we were obliged to put into a lee shore, not being able to find a landing-place. On nearing the shore some of the men jumped into the water and held the boats off, whilst the others unloaded them and carried the goods on their heads through the dashing surf. When the boats were emptied, they were then enabled to drag them up on the beach. Here we were compelled to remain until the 18th, occupying ourselves in shooting ducks and gulls, which we found in great abundance, and which proved capital eating.

The waves having abated on the morning of the 18th, we made an early start, and arrived in the afternoon at the mouth of the Saskatchewan River. The navigation is here interrupted by what is called the Grand Rapid, which is about three miles long, one mile of which runs with great rapidity, and presents a continual foamy appearance, down which boats are able to descend, but in going up are obliged to make a portage.

I was told a story of one of the steersmen of our brigade, named Paulet Paul, who in steering his boat down by an oar passed through a ring in the stern of the boat, fell overboard, from the oar, on which he was leaning with his whole force, suddenly breaking. His great bodily strength enabled him to gain a footing, and to stand against the rapid until the boat following came past, into which he sprang, and urging the men to pull, he eventually succeeded in jumping into his own boat and guiding her safely down, thereby saving the valuable cargo which might have otherwise been lost. He was a half-breed, and certainly one of the finest formed men I ever saw, and when naked, no painter could desire a finer model. We encamped on the shore, and were obliged to remain here till the third day, for the purpose of getting the goods across, as it required the crews of all the boats to haul each over in succession. There are usually Indians to be met at this portage, who assist the men for a small consideration, but on this occasion they were unfortunately absent.

August 21*st*—Embarked in the afternoon, and on the 22nd passed through Cedar Lake, and again entered the Saskatchewan River; the land in the neighbourhood of which is very flat and marshy, innumerable small lakes being scattered over the whole region. We met with nothing worth recording till the 25th, when we arrived at the "Pau," a Church of England missionary station, occupied by the Rev. Mr. Hunter. He resides in a neat house most brilliantly decorated inside with blue and red paint, much to the admiration of his flock, which consists of only a small band of the same tribe of Indians as are met with about Norway House. Mr. Hunter and his amiable lady invited us to their table, where we found some bread made from wheat of their own raising, ground in a hand-mill, and they spared no exertions to make us as comfortable as possible.

Mr. Hunter accompanied me to a medicine-man's lodge, a short distance from his own residence. Seeing a very handsomely worked otter-skin bag, apparently well filled, hanging up in the lodge, I inquired as to its purpose, when the Indian informed me it was his medicine-bag, but would not let me examine its contents until he had seen some of my sketches, and was informed that I was a great medicine-man myself, upon which he opened it for my inspection. The contents consisted of bits of bones, shells, minerals, red earth, and other heterogeneous accumulations, perfectly incomprehensible to my uninitiated capacity.

August 26*th*—We left the hospitable mansion of Mr. Hunter with many kind wishes for our safety and success, and continued our journey along the low and swampy banks of the river. On the 28th, we passed the mouth of the Cumberland River. Here the men had to harness themselves to the boats with their portage straps and drag the boats up the river for several days. We passed a large quantity of the bones of buffaloes which had been drowned in the preceding winter in attempting to cross the ice. The wolves had picked them all clean.

On the 29th I fired both barrels loaded with ball at a large buck moose, which was swimming across the river. He, however, arrived at the other side and trotted up the bank. Thinking I had missed him, I went on, but on my return the following year, two Indians, who had been attracted by the shots, told me that he had dropped 200 yards from the river.

August 30*th*—We this day fell in with a small band of Crees, from whom we procured some buffalo meat, tongues, and beaver tails; the last is considered a great delicacy. It is a fat, gristly substance, but to me by no means palatable; the rest of our party, however, seemed to enjoy it much. The tongues were decidedly delicious; they are cured by drying them in the smoke of the lodges.

The river as we ascended presented a more inviting

appearance, the banks becoming bolder and covered
principally with pine and poplar, the latter trees springing up wherever the former are burned off. The men
suffered severely from the heat, which was very oppres-
sive.

September 6th—We were within about eighteen or
twenty miles of Carlton, when about dark in the evening we heard a tremendous splashing in the water, but
so far off that we could not see the cause. Mr. Rowand
at once conjectured it to be a large party of Blackfeet
swimming their horses across the river, which they do
by driving the horse into the water till he loses his
footing, when the rider slips off and seizes the tail of the
animal, and is thus towed to the opposite shore. We were
somewhat alarmed, and immediately loaded our guns,
the Blackfeet being the most hostile tribe on the continent; but on coming up to the spot, we found it was
the horsekeeper at Fort Carlton, who was swimming his
horses across to an island in the middle of the river to
save them from the wolves, which had killed several of
them, owing to the scarcity of buffaloes. As we had but
a short distance to travel next day we encamped for
the night.

September 7th—When we arrived within a couple
of miles of Carlton, we halted for the purpose of arrang-
ing our toilets previous to presenting ourselves at the
establishment. This consisted chiefly of a thorough
washing; some, indeed, put on clean shirts, but few,
however, could boast of such a luxury. This compliment
to the inhabitants was by no means unnecessary, as we
were in a most ragged and dirty condition.

The country in the vicinity of Carlton, which is
situated between the wooded country and the other
plains, varies much from that through which we had

been travelling. Instead of dense masses of unbroken forest, it presents more the appearance of a park; the gently undulating plains being dotted here and there with clumps of small trees. The banks of the river rise to the height of 150 or 200 feet in smooth rolling hills covered with verdure. The fort, which is situated about a quarter of a mile back from the river, is enclosed with wooden pickets, and is fortified with blunderbusses on swivels mounted in the bastion. This fort is in greater danger from the Blackfeet than any of the Company's establishments, being feebly manned and not capable of offering much resistance to an attack. Their horses have frequently been driven off without the inmates of the fort daring to leave it for their rescue. The buffaloes are here abundant, as is evident from the immense accumulation of their bones which strew the plains in every direction.

The whole of the boats not having yet arrived, we remained here for several days. On the second evening after our arrival we were rather alarmed by the rapid approach of fire, which had originated far off to the west on the prairies. Fortunately, when within about half a mile of the fort, the wind changed, and it turned to the south. We, however, remained up nearly all night for fear of accidents. There were some Cree Indians about the fort, which is one of the trading ports of that nation who extend along the Saskatchewan to the Rocky Mountains, and is one of the largest tribes of Indians in the Hudson's Bay Company's dominions. This tribe has been from time immemorial at war with the Blackfeet, whom they at one time conquered and held in subjection: even now the Crees call the Blackfeet slaves, although they have gained their independence, and are a fierce and warlike tribe. These wars are kept up with unremitting perseverance from year to year; and were they as destructive in proportion to the numbers engaged as the wars of civilized nations, the continent would soon be depopulated of the whole Indian race; but, luckily, Indians are satisfied with small victories, and a few scalps and horses taken from the enemy are quite sufficient to entitle the warriors to return to their friends in triumph and glory.

I made a sketch of Us-koos-koosish, "Young Grass," a Cree brave. He was very proud of showing his many wounds, and expressed himself rather dissatisfied with my picture, as I had not delineated all the scars, no matter what was their locality. He had a younger brother killed by one of his own tribe in a quarrel; this he considered incumbent on him to avenge, and tracked the offender for upwards of six months before he found an opportunity of killing him, which he however effected at last.

This custom of taking life for life is universal amongst all Indians; and the first death often leads to many, until the feud is stayed either by the intervention of powerful friends, or by one party paying the other a satisfaction in horses or other Indian valuables. An Indian, however, in taking revenge for the death of a relative does not in all cases seek the actual offender; as should the party be one of his own tribe any relative will do, however distant. Should he be a white man, the Indian would most probably kill the first white man he could find.

Mr. Rundell, a missionary, whose station was at Edmonton, was at Carlton awaiting our arrival, for the purpose of returning in company with us. He had with him a favourite cat which he had brought with him in the canoes from Edmonton, being afraid to leave her behind him, as there was some danger of her being eaten during his absence. This cat was the object of a good deal of amusement amongst the party, of great curiosity amongst the Indians, and of a good deal of anxiety and trouble to its kind master.

Mr. Rowand, myself, and Mr. Rundell, having determined to proceed to Edmonton on horseback, as being the shortest and most agreeable route, we procured horses and a guide, and, on the morning of the 12th September, we arose early for our start. The Indians had collected in numbers round the fort to see us off, and shake hands with us, a practice which they seem to have taken a particular fancy for. No sooner had we mounted our rather skittish animals than the Indians crowded around, and Mr. Rundell, who was rather a favourite amongst them, came in for a large share of their attentions, which seemed to be rather annoying to his horse. His cat he had tied to the pummel of his saddle by a string, about four feet long, round her neck, and had her safely, as he thought, concealed in the breast of his capote. She, however, did not relish the plunging of the horse, and made a spring out, utterly astonishing the Indians, who could not conceive where she had come from. The string brought her up against the horse's legs, which she immediately attacked. The horse now became furious, kicking violently, and at last threw Mr. Rundell over his head, but fortunately without much injury. All present were convulsed with laughter, to which the Indians added screeching and yelling as an accompaniment, rendering the whole scene indescribably ludicrous. Puss's life was saved by the string breaking; but we left her behind for the men to bring in the boats, evidently to the regret of her master,

notwithstanding the hearty laugh which we had had at
his expense.

We were accompanied by a party of hunters proceeding to a buffalo pound about six miles off. These
pounds can only be made in the vicinity of forests, as
they are composed of logs piled up roughly, five feet
high, and enclose about two acres. At one side an
entrance is left, about ten feet wide, and from each side
of this, to the distance of half a mile, a row of posts of
short stumps, called dead men, are planted, at the
distance of twenty feet each, gradually widening out
into the plain from the entrance. When we arrived at
the pound we found a party there anxiously awaiting
the arrival of the buffaloes, which their companions
were driving in. This is accomplished as follows:—A
man, mounted on a fleet horse, usually rides forward
till he sees a band of buffaloes. This may be sixteen or
eighteen miles distant from the pound, but of course
the nearer to it the better. The hunter immediately
strikes a light with a flint and steel, and places the lighted
spunk in a handful of dried grass, the smoke arising
from which the buffaloes soon smell and start away
from it at the top of their speed. The man now rides
up alongside of the herd, which, from some unaccountable propensity, invariably endeavour to cross in front
of his horse. I have had them follow me for miles in
order to do so. The hunter thus possesses an unfailing
means, wherever the pound may be situated of con-
ducting them to it by the dexterous management of his
horse. Indians are stationed at intervals behind the posts,
or dead men, provided with buffalo robes, who, when the
herd are once in the avenue, rise up and shake the robes,
yelling and urging them on until they get into the enclosure, the spot usually selected for which is one with

a tree in the centre. On this they hang offerings to propitiate the Great Spirit to direct the herd towards it. A man is also placed in the tree with a medicine pipe-stem in his hand, which he waves continually, chaunting a sort of prayer to the Great Spirit, the burden of which is that the buffaloes may be numerous and fat.

As soon as all the herd are within the pound, the entrance is immediately closed with logs, the buffaloes running round and round one after another, and very rarely attempting to break out, which would not be difficult, from the insufficiency of the structure. Should one succeed in doing so the whole herd immediately follow. When once in the enclosure the Indians soon despatch them with their arrows and spears.

Whilst the buffaloes were being driven in, the scene was certainly exciting and picturesque; but the slaughter in the enclosure was more painful than pleasing. This had been the third herd that had been driven into this pound within the last ten or twelve days, and the putrefying carcasses tainted the air all round. The Indians in this manner destroy innumerable buffaloes, apparently for the mere pleasure of the thing. I have myself seen a pound so filled up with their dead carcasses that I could scarcely imagine how the enclosure could have contained them while living. It is not unusual to drive in so many that their aggregate bulk forces down the barriers. There are thousands of them annually killed in this manner; but not one in twenty is used in any way by the Indians, so that thousands are left to rot where they fall. I heard of a pound, too far out of my direct road to visit, formed entirely of the bones of dead buffaloes that had been killed in a former pound on the same spot, piled up in a circle similarly to the logs above described. This improvidence, in not saving the meat, often exposes them to great hardships during the seasons of the year in which the buffalo migrates to the south.

As is frequently the case on buffalo hunts, a large band of wolves hovered round us in expectation of a feast, and a young Indian, for the purpose of showing his dexterity, galloped off towards them mounted on a small Indian horse. He succeeded in separating one from the pack, and notwithstanding all the dodging of the wolf, managed to drive him quite close to us. As he approached he entirely abandoned his bridle, and to look at them, one would imagine, from the rapid turnings of the horse without the apparent direction of the rider, that he was as eager in pursuit as his master. When he had succeeded in getting the wolf close to us, he transfixed him with an arrow at the first shot. We selected a comfortable place on the banks of the river, and, on the boats coming up, we formed our encampment for the night.

September 13*th*—In the morning we passed a small island on which we saw a herd of eighteen deer. Our hunter went round to the other side, the water being shallow enough to wade across, and, getting behind the bushes, fired twice at them before they could escape, and brought down two. The rest crossed over to our side of the river, and, as a noble buck was ascending the bank, we all fired at him. He escaped, notwithstanding, into the woods, and I hobbled my horse and pursued him on foot, tracking him readily by the blood which flowed from his wounds. I soon saw him lying down, apparently so exhausted that I forbore to fire again. This forbearance cost me the deer, for on my coming up, he made a sudden plunge into the thicket and escaped. I followed his track a long distance, but could not come up to him. On my return I found two wolves making a dead set at my poor horse, who was trembling with fear. One of them was in the act of springing at him. It was impossible for him to get away, as his fore feet were tied together. I instantly levelled my double-barrelled gun and killed both, one after the other.

CHAPTER IX

Beautiful Valley—Crossing the Water—The Curious Cabree—A Shouting
Aide-de-Camp—Strange Memento Mori—The Love of Indian Mothers—
No Coat, no Fire—The "Little Slave"—A Voyageur's Trust—Surrounded
by Beef—A Spirited Cow.

On my coming back to the party, I found them
hanging up the two deer for the use of the crews of the
boats, having taken what they wanted for themselves.
This they did by forming a triangle with poles about
twelve feet high in a conspicuous place on the bank, so
that the wolves could not reach the meat, and fastening a
red handkerchief above it to keep off the crows. Towards evening, as we were approaching the place where
we were to cross the river, I saw some buffaloes idly
grazing in a valley, and as I wished to give a general
idea of the beauty of the scenery which lies all along
the banks of the Saskatchewan from this point to
Edmonton, I sat down to make a sketch, the rest of the
party promising to wait for me at the crossing place.
It was the commencement of Indian summer; the evening was very fine, and threw that peculiar soft, warm
haziness over the landscape, which is supposed to proceed from the burning of the immense prairies. The
sleepy buffaloes grazing upon the undulating hills, here
and there relieved by clumps of small trees, the unbroken
stillness, and the approaching evening, rendered it
altogether a scene of most enchanting repose.

On coming up to Mr. Rowand, we prepared to cross
for the purpose of avoiding a strong bend in the river.
Our ammunition, and other things that required to be
kept dry, were put into a sort of basket made of a few
willow twigs, with a buffalo skin drawn by a running

string over them, something in the form of large bowls. This basket was floated in the water, and dragged by a string held in the teeth. The horse was then driven in, and the traveller, holding on by his tail, was safely ferried to the other side with his baggage.

September 14*th*—Saw an immense number of cabrees, or prairie antelopes. These are the smallest of the deer tribe, amazingly fleet, and very shy, but, strange to say, possessed of great curiosity, apparently determined to look at everything they do not understand, so long as they do not scent it. Our hunter set off into the valley, to show me the manner of shooting them, while I made a sketch. A small stream wound its way through this most beautiful and picturesque valley in a course unusually tortuous, and was fringed on each side by a border of small, dense, and intensely green and purple bushes, contrasting beautifully with the rich yellow grass of the gradually sloping banks, about 200 feet in height, and the golden hues of the few poplars which had just begun to assume the autumnal tints.

The hunter stole forward and hid himself behind a small bush, so as to have the wind blowing from them, and gently waved a piece of rag tied to his ramrod; as soon as the cabrees perceived this, they gradually came up to him, until within shot, when he knocked one over; this was of course all he could expect, as the rest were off in an instant.

In the evening we saw smoke in the distance, which we supposed to proceed from a camp of Indians; we waited, therefore, till the boats arrived, with a view to our mutual protection, should they prove to be a hostile tribe. The boats arrived after a short time, and we remained with them all night without molestation.

September 15*th*—About an hour after leaving our

encampment, we crossed the river again in our boat, and found a large camp of Cree Indians. They came down to us in great numbers. Mr. Rowand, being acquainted with their chiefs, they were very friendly with us, and we bought a large quantity of dried meat from them. About a year and a half after this, on my return, I met the head chief, Kee-a-kee-ka-sa-coo-way, or the "Man who gives the War-whoop," and learned something of his history, which will be introduced in the latter part of my journal. When I was in his company for some time at Fort Pitt, in January 1848, the second chief, Muck-e-too, or "Powder," acted as a sort of aide-de-camp to the other, the head chief issuing his commands in a low tone, while the other mounted his horse and delivered them to the rest of the camp in a loud commanding manner. Muck-e-too is a great warrior and horse thief, the two most important qualifications for a chief, skill in stealing horses being regarded with as much respect as taking scalps. We had much difficulty in getting away from them, as they wished to have a long talk, but our time not permitting, we resumed our journey. They, however, adroitly detained a boat that had not yet come up, and the persons in charge had to give them some tobacco before they would allow them to proceed.

September 16th—We rode on till the middle of the day through a most delightful country, covered with luxuriant herbage, the plains being enamelled with flowers of various kinds, presenting more the aspect of a garden than of uncultivated land. While roasting some meat before the fire for our breakfast, and allowing our horses to feed, we espied a party of Indians on the opposite side of the river, who were evidently making signals to another party in our rear whom we did not see. Upon this, eight of their young men came down to reconnoitre, and finding we were friends, kindly conducted us to their camp. We bartered with them for some horses.

I made a sketch of one of their chiefs, Otisskun, or "the Horn," or rather I made a sketch of his back. I did this for the purpose of showing his war-cap, and also to delineate the bag which he carries at his back. These bags are constantly worn, and contain some of the bones or hair of their deceased relatives. These relics they regard with the greatest veneration, and make them their constant companions, whether riding, walking, or sleeping. They are generally worn for a period of three years. Not only amongst this tribe, but also amongst others, the affection for their relatives is very remarkable, though of course sometimes exhibited in a strange manner, as appears to us. As an instance of this, I may mention the universal custom of Indian mothers eagerly seeking another child, although it may be of an enemy, to replace one of her own, whom she may have lost, no matter how many other children she may have. This child is always treated with as great, if not greater, kindness than the rest; but all the mother's care evidently arises from, and has reference to, the love which she bore to the departed.

I had an unexpected trouble to catch my horse, which had got loose, in consequence of the hungry Indian dogs having eaten the lasso of raw hide with which I had fastened him.

September 17th—We were aroused in the night by our hunter, who told us that the horses were stolen, and as he would not leave the fire unless we accompanied him, we all started in pursuit. After a run of about a mile, we came up with the horses pursued by a band of

wolves; the billets of wood attached to their lassoes
having retarded their further escape; the wolves were
loth to leave their expected prey, but after a shot or two
they took to flight. The horses were evidently much
terrified, as they showed by remaining close to the camp-
fires all night afterwards.

In the course of our ride to-day we killed a cabree,
which was fortunate, as Mr. and Mrs. Lane arrived at
our camp fire in the evening in a state of severe exhaustion, having left the boats in the morning and walked the
whole day without tasting food. The boats had reached
the other side of the river, and, for want of a channel,
had been unable to cross over and take them in. It was
unfortunately a very cold night, and very little wood
could be procured; besides which, we were unprovided
with either tents or blankets, having dispensed with
these luxuries since we left Carlton, where we began our
journey on horseback. The greatest sufferer probably
from the cold of the night was a young clerk who had
walked with them, and left his coat and waistcoat in the
boat.

September 19th—The boats this morning found a
channel and crossed over to take in the party, who had
left them the morning before. We reached Fort Pitt
in the evening. It is a neat and compact little fort, and
is, like all the rest of the forts except those at Red River,
constructed of wood. The country here abounds in
buffalo; grain and other produce might be raised plentifully here if cultivated. We remained till the 23rd, and
I took a sketch of Chimaza, "the Little Slave," a Chip-
pewayeen Indian. He was the only one of that tribe
I ever saw, as they live far north of Fort Pitt, on the
Athabasca Lake; his prowess and dexterity in hunting
won him a degree of notoriety amongst the traders. He

had, when I saw him, upwards of a hundred moose skins, besides furs to a considerable amount, which he had brought to the fort to trade with.

September 23rd—I left the fort on horseback, accompanied by Mr. Rowand, Mr. Rundell, an Indian boy, and a fresh hunter; on reaching the river we crossed in a boat, and swam our horses by the bridle. We left this establishment in true voyageur style, unburthened with food of any kind, and, although contemplating a journey of 200 miles, trusting solely to our guns, having not even a grain of salt. After leaving the boat, we saddled our horses, and had not proceeded more than ten miles, when we fell in with immense numbers of buffaloes.

During the whole of the three days that it took us to reach Edmonton House, we saw nothing else but these animals covering the plains as far as the eye could reach, and so numerous were they, that at times they impeded our progress, filling the air with dust almost to suffocation. We killed one whenever we required a supply of food, selecting the fattest of the cows, taking only the tongues and boss, or hump, for our present meal, and not burdening ourselves unnecessarily with more. Mr. Rowand fired and wounded a cow, which made immediately for a clump of bushes; he followed it, when the animal turned upon him, and bore him and his horse to the ground, leaping over them, and escaping among the rest. Fortunately, he received no hurt beyond the mortification of being thrown down and run over by an animal which he felt assured he should see roasting at our evening camp fire.

Chapter X

Long Grass Prairie—An Obstinate Bear—Abandoning a Tired Horse—Dried-up Lakes—Shooting Wild Geese—A Dangerous Swim—Boat-building—The Blazing Prairie—Setting Fire to fight Fire—A Cool Confession—Indian want of Gallantry—An Indian Strongbow.

September 24th—We passed through what is called the Long Grass Prairie. The bones of a whole camp of Indians, who were carried off by that fatal scourge of their race, the small-pox, were here bleaching on the plains, having fallen from the platforms and trees on which it is their custom to suspend their dead, covered with skins,—which latter, as well as the supports, time had destroyed. An immense grisly bear was drinking out of a pond, and our hunter went ahead of the party to try and get a shot at him. The bear quietly awaited his attack, and the Indian, seeing him so cool, rather hesitated to advance, not deeming it prudent or safe to depend on the fleetness of his horse unless he had a good start of the bear. He fired, therefore, at too great a distance for his shot to tell. The bear rose up very composedly on his hind legs, and regarding the hunter for a moment, turned about and walked away. I then determined to try my luck. As I was very well mounted, I rode up to within forty or fifty yards of him, and as he turned to look at me, I discharged both barrels; one wounded him in the shoulder, and, with a savage growl, he turned and pursued me. I set off at full gallop towards Mr. Rowand, who waited till he came within shot, when he put another ball into him,—but still the bear advanced.

In the meantime, the Indian and I had both managed to reload, and, as the bear came forward, the Indian fired, and must have hit, as the bear again rose on his hind legs; when, taking deliberate aim, I lodged a ball in his heart, and the huge monster fell to the ground. The Indian now skinned him and cut off his paws, which we found most delicious picking when roasted in the evening. The claws, which I preserved, measured four and a half inches. There is no animal on the whole continent that the Indians hold in so much dread as the grisly bear, and few will attack one of them alone, unless with a very fleet horse under him.

We had much difficulty that evening in finding a place to encamp away from the immense number of buffaloes that surrounded us, and we found it necessary to fire off our guns during the night to keep them away. We passed through a spot covered with great quantities of shed antlers of the deer. We had ridden so fast as to knock up Mr. Rowand's horse, but, having driven several loose horses with us, to provide against such emergencies, we were not inconvenienced, leaving the poor brute a prey to the wolves, which were constantly hovering about us.

We encamped this evening on the borders of a very beautiful fresh water lake. We had passed in our route daily many *dried-up* lakes, principally small, the basins covered with an incrustation of sub-carbonate of soda. Many of these are bordered with a dense growth of plants resembling in structure the well-known marine production called samphire, but of a rich purple colour. So unbroken is the incrustation of soda, as to give the spots the appearance of being covered with snow.

September 26th—Mr. Rundell remained at the encampment this morning with the Indian boy, being completely knocked up by the hard riding of the preceding days. We were reluctant to leave him, but were under the necessity of going on as fast as possible, as I had still a long journey before me, and the season was drawing to a close. Mr. Rowand and myself, therefore, left the camp at half-past 3 a.m., and pursued our journey almost at a gallop the whole way, having stopped only once for about an hour, for breakfast and to breathe our horses.

About 5 o'clock in the afternoon, when about eight or ten miles from Fort Edmonton, we were met by a party of gentlemen from the fort, who were out shooting wild geese, in which they had been very successful, and on seeing the jaded condition of our horses, they were kind enough to exchange with us, so that we started off for the remaining distance at a round gallop.

On getting to the edge of the river, which it was necessary to cross to reach the fort, Mr. Rowand, having a fine large horse under him, plunged in. Though my horse was very small, I did not hesitate in following him. Mr. Rowand's horse carried him over in fine style, but mine, not being equal to the task, sank under me; still, however, I held firmly on to him, till, drifting into the rapid, he struck a sunken rock in striving to obtain a footing, on which he nearly brought me under him; but, on drifting a little further down, he fortunately found footing in a more shallow part, and was able to ford across, Mr. Rowand appearing greatly to enjoy the scene from his safe position on the shore. We were greeted by the occupants of the fort in their gayest attire, the day being Sunday.

Edmonton is a large establishment: as it has to furnish many other districts with provisions, a large supply is always kept on hand, consisting entirely of dried meat, tongues, and pemmican. There are usually here a chief factor and a clerk, with forty or fifty men with their wives and children, amounting altogether to about 130, who all live within the pickets of the fort. Their employment consists chiefly in building boats for the trade, sawing timber, most of which they raft down the river from ninety miles higher up, cutting up the small poplar which abounds on the margin of the river for fire-wood, 800 cords of which are consumed every winter, to supply the numerous fires in the establishment. The employment of the women, who are all, without a single exception, either squaws or half-breeds, consists in making moccasins and clothing for the men, and converting the dried meat into pemmican.

On the night of our arrival at Edmonton, the wind increased to a perfect hurricane, and we had reason to be thankful to Providence for our timely escape from the awful scene we now witnessed from our present place of safety, for, had we been one day later, we might have been involved in its fiery embrace. The scene on which our attention was now riveted, was the conflagration of the prairie through which we had passed but a few hours before. The scene was terrific in the extreme; the night being intensely dark gave increased effect to the brilliancy of the flames. We were apprehensive at one time of its crossing the river to the side on which the fort is situated, which must in that case have been destroyed. Our fears, too, for Mr. Rundell, whom we had left behind with the boys, were only relieved three days afterwards, when he arrived in safety. It appeared that he had noticed the fire at a long distance off, and immediately started for the nearest bend in the river, which with great exertions he reached in time, and succeeded in crossing. The mode resorted to by the Indians, when in the immediate vicinity of a prairie on fire, is to set fire to a long patch in front of them, which they follow up, and thus depriving the fire in the rear of fuel, escape all but the smoke, which, however, nearly suffocates them.

As we had to remain here until the arrival of the boat with Mr. Lane and the Russian packs of otters, I took a sketch of the fort, and having leisure, I went a good deal amongst the Indians, who are constantly about the fort for the purpose of trading; they were principally Crees and Assiniboines: Potika-poo-tis, "the Little Round Man," an Assiniboine chief, sat for me. He was well known about the fort, and was commonly called the Duke of Wellington, I suppose from his small person and his warlike feats. He was on one occasion set upon by a party of Blackfeet, and, while in the act of discharging his gun, received a wound, which he showed me, of rather a remarkable nature. The ball entering his wrist, passed through the arm, entered the neck, and came out near the upper part of the spine. He had received several wounds, but none that seemed seriously to endanger his life, as at the time I saw him he was in good health.

After relating various stories of his war and hunting exploits, he, to my great astonishment, told me that he had killed his own mother. It appears that, while travelling, she told him that she felt too old and feeble to sustain the hardships of life, and too lame to travel any further, and asked him to take pity on her, and end her misery, on which he unhesitatingly shot her on the spot. I asked him whereabouts he had directed his ball. His reply was, "Do you think I would shoot her in a bad place? I hit her there;" pointing his finger to the region of the heart. "She died instantly, and I cried at first; but after I had buried her, the impression wore off."

It must not be supposed that Indians look on the softer sex with feelings at all resembling those entertained towards them in civilized life; in fact, they regard them more in the light of slaves than as companionable beings. As might be expected, this is most evident in their treatment of aged women, whom they consider as scarcely fit to live.

Some of the Company's servants were going up the Saskatchewan river on the ice in the winter, with a sledge of dogs drawing a load, comprising, amongst other things, an eight-gallon keg of spirits; and in crossing over a piece of bad ice, the dogs went through sledge and all, and were instantly carried under by the force of the current. In the following summer, some Indians, while bathing near the shore, picked up the cask safe and sound; and finding, on examination, that it was full of rum, made up their minds to have a booze. One of them, however, suggested the possibility that the white men had put poison in it, to be revenged on them for having fired on the inland brigade of canoes while going up the river the year before. This deterred them from drinking any until they had tested its quality. For this purpose they selected eight of the oldest women in the camp to try the experiment on. The women fell into the snare; and, becoming intoxicated, commenced singing with great glee. But an old chief soon put a stop to their potations, saying there could be no poison in it, and that it was far too good to be thrown away upon old women. The whole tribe then set to, and were not long in draining the cask.

One day, whilst wandering some distance to the south of the fort, I saw two Assiniboine Indians hunting buffaloes. One was armed with a spear, formed of an ashpole about ten feet long, ornamented with tufts of hair, and having an iron head, which is procured from the trading posts; the other with a bow formed of ash, with the sinews of a buffalo gummed to the back of it. These they use with great dexterity and force; I have known an instance of the arrows passing through the body of the animal, and sticking in the ground at the opposite side.

Chapter XI

Leaving Fort Edmonton—The Last of the Buffaloes—Sir George's Highland Piper—An Indian Delicacy—Freak of an Evil Spirit—Singular Cradle—Jasper's House—The Snow and the Cold—First Steps in Snow-shoes—Nearly Roasted Alive—Going down Hill—Wading an Icy Torrent—Making up for Lost Time—Shooting the Dalle de Mort—A Narrow Escape—A Wet Voyage.

We remained at Edmonton till the morning of the 6th, preparing for the arduous journey which now lay before us. On that morning we started at daybreak. Our party consisted of Mr. Lane and his wife, a young man named Charles, a clerk, who was going to a post on the west side of the Rocky Mountains, a person of the name of M'Gillveray, and sixteen men. We had with us sixty-five horses to carry our baggage and provisions. This seems a large supply of horses for so small a party; but it must be taken into consideration that Edmonton is the last post at which we could get a supply of provisions on this side of the mountains; so that we were necessarily obliged to carry a large quantity with us, owing to the difficulty which always arises in getting the men away from comfortable quarters to commence a long and difficult journey, coupled with the wildness of the horses on the first day's march. We only succeeded in reaching Sturgeon Creek, a distance of about sixteen miles, on the first day. Seeing a group of buffaloes reposing near a small lake, I took a sketch (No. 6). They were the last that I should see for some time; and it was easy for me to keep up with the party at the slow rate at which they proceeded.

October 7th—The prairies were now fast receding behind us, our course lying to the northward. The track became almost impassable, being wet and swampy; and the horses often stuck fast, and threw off their loads in their struggles to extricate themselves from the mire. We were lucky enough to vary our provisions by killing a great many geese of the kind called "wavy." Could

6. Buffaloes at Sunset
Courtesy of Royal Ontario Museum

we have procured a little salt, I should have found them more palatable.

October 8*th*—The tremendous hurricane above alluded to had torn up immense trees by the roots, and scattered them in piles one on another in all directions, detaining us sometimes for hours, while the men cut a path through them for the horses. Our progress through the thick woods, which we had now fairly entered, was necessarily very slow and fatiguing.

October 9*th*—The track still continued bad, and we saw no game; so that our time passed very monotonously, as we had to keep pace with the loaded horses. A Highlander of the name of Colin Frazer had joined our party. He was on his way to a small post, of which he had the charge, at the head of the Athabasca River, in the Rocky Mountains, where he had resided for the last eleven years. He had been brought to the country by Sir George Simpson, in the capacity of his piper, at the time when he explored Frazer's River, and made an extensive voyage through a country hitherto little known, and among Indians who had seen few or no white men. He carried the pipes with him, dressed in his Highland costume; and when stopping at forts, or wherever he found Indians, the bagpipes were put in requisition, much to the astonishment of the natives, who supposed him to be a relation of the Great Spirit, having, of course, never beheld so extraordinary a looking man, or such a musical instrument, which astonished them as much as the sound produced. One of the Indians asked him to intercede with the Great Spirit for him; but Frazer remarked, the petitioner little thought how limited his influence was in that quarter.

October 10*th*—I left the party this morning and proceeded on, and at two o'clock in the afternoon, after a smart ride, I arrived at Fort Assiniboine, on the Athabasca River. This establishment, although honoured with the name of a fort, is a mere post used for taking care of horses, a common man or horsekeeper being in charge of it. The rest of the party arrived late the same evning.

October 11*th*—We found two boats here, which our men immediately overhauled and set to work to repair and pitch. At 2 o'clock P.M., we embarked, and continued travelling slowly on, against a very strong current, for five days. The water was very low, which added greatly to our difficulties. We saw no game nor

Iroquois

Indians to break the monotony of our labour, and the nights and mornings were becoming very cold.

October 15th—When we stopped to take breakfast it was very cold and snowing. We held a council, and it was determined that, as the weather had set in so bad, five men and one boat, with the clerk Charles, should return back to Fort Assiniboine with the Russian packs of otter skins. We were now all obliged to crowd into one boat, the others having gone back; and were frequently obliged to disembark and lighten the boat, owing to the unusual lowness of the river. We had almost continually to drag the boat onwards with a line, the men waist deep in the water. One of them slipped off a log into deep water, and it was with no small difficulty we saved him from being drowned. We had not extricated him from the river five minutes before his clothes were stiff with ice. I asked him if he was not cold, and his reply was characteristic of the hardihood of the Iroquois, of which tribe our party principally consisted, "My clothes are cold, but I am not."

October 16th—The weather had now set in so cold that we began to doubt the possibility of crossing the mountains this season. The line by which the men dragged the boat broke twice to-day in the rapids, and our boat was nearly dashed to pieces among the rocks. Had this misfortune happened, we should have lost all our provisions, and had a great chance of perishing with hunger.

October 17th and 18th—Weather fine. This is the most monotonous river that ever I have met with in my travels. Nothing but point after point appearing, all thickly covered with pine, any extensive view being entirely out of the question. The course of the river, although tortuous, is rapid, but unbroken by falls, running at the rate of six or seven miles an hour on an average.

October 19*th*—We fell in with an Indian hunter and his family. He had two bark canoes; he sold one of them to Colin Frazer, in which he embarked with four men, for the purpose of lightening our boat, and proceeded on in advance of us. We traded with them for some beaver meat and moose noses; the latter is the most delicate eating I ever met with, and is valued amongst the Indians beyond all other food.

October 20*th and* 21*st*—The weather was fine, and we made good progress.

October 22*nd*—The men were in extraordinarily good spirits. I measured a tree lying on the ground, which had been cut down by the beaver; it was seven feet in circumference. We found three bears left *en cache* by Colin Frazer, an old one and two cubs. He told me afterwards that he had killed the two cubs at one shot, while one was climbing over the back of the other to ascend a bank. The cubs proved fine eating, and were much relished, as our fresh provisions had been long exhausted.

October 23*rd*—We passed a camp fire still burning that had been left by Frazer the night previously.

October 24*th*—We passed the Rapids de Mort. The men had great difficulty in getting the boat up; we, of course, had all to walk. All the ponds and still water were frozen hard enough to bear. The rapidity of the current, however, prevented ice forming in the river. A small bag of pemmican made in the usual way, except that it contained Sasketome berries, was stolen, and a search being made for its recovery, a part of it was found in one of the men's bags. The only temptation to the theft could have been that it was more palat-

able than his own. M'Gillveray, being one of the most
powerful men of the party, was called upon to admin-
ister the punishment, which he did by repeatedly knocking the delinquent down. This severity of punishment
was called for by the fact, that the most disastrous consequences might arise on a journey through these
desolate regions, if the most rigid care were not taken
of the provisions.

October 25th to 27th—There was no change in the
general aspect of the country; the same monotonous
scenery still surrounded us.

October 28th—We passed the mouth of the Old
Man's River. The Indians say that an evil spirit once
came down this river—which is so rapid that no canoe
can ascend it—and that having reached its mouth, where
it enters the Athabasca, he made five steps down, leaving
a rapid at every step. These rapids are a mile apart.
After which he returned and went up his own river, and
has not since been heard of. The river now became so
shallow, that we were obliged to make two discharges.

October 29th—The bank of the river being very high,
I ascended it, and saw for the first time the sublime and
apparently endless chain of the Rocky Mountains. The
outline was scarcely perceptible in the distance through
the intervening smoky atmosphere, which is caused by
the almost invariable conflagration of the woods at this
season of the year. M'Gillveray wounded a moose while
out with his gun. The deer took to the water, and swam
across to the opposite side. I took the boat and followed
him, and brought him down at the first shot. He was
a fine large buck. It being nearly night, we encamped
on the spot, and supped heartily off him, carrying his
remains with us next morning.

October 30*th*—We had a fine view of the mountains from the boat for the first time; the men greeted them with a hearty cheer.

October 31*st*—The atmosphere clear but very cold. I made a sketch of the river and the mountains in the distance.

November 1*st*—We entered Jasper's Lake in the morning. This lake is about twelve miles long, and from three to four miles wide, but at this season of the year very shallow, on account of its sources in the mountains being frozen. We had to land three men on the south shore for the purpose of decreasing the draft of our boat; but even then we proceeded with great difficulty. Shortly after we had put them on shore, it began to blow a perfect hurricane, which drove us to the north side, and a snow storm coming on, we were compelled to encamp. This was unfortunate, as it was impossible to communicate with the men whom we had left at the other side, and who were without either provisions or blankets, and we knew from the intense cold that they must be suffering severely.

November 2*nd*—We were now close upon the mountains, and it is scarcely possible to conceive the intense force with which the wind howled through a gap formed by the perpendicular rock called "Miëtte's Rock," 1500 feet high, on the one side, and a lofty mountain on the other. The former derives its appellation from a French voyageur, who climbed its summit and sat smoking his pipe with his legs hanging over the fearful abyss. M'Gillveray and the guide went on to Colin Frazer's, distant about fourteen or fifteen miles, to procure horses, as we found that further progress in the boat was impossible, both on account of the shallowness of the water and the violence of the wind.

November 3rd—The hurricane still continued, accompanied by very heavy snow; indeed, from what I heard, I believe it is always blowing at this place. The forest is composed entirely of very high pine trees, small in circumference, and growing thickly together; these had a very curious appearance in the storm, as they waved in the wind like a field of grain. The immense long roots seemed to be especially provided them by nature to prevent their being blown over; and, as the soil is very light, and upon a rocky foundation, these roots formed a net work near the surface, which was in constant motion, and rocked us to sleep as we lay round our camp fires.

Meanwhile, our guide returned from Jasper's House with several horses. We found our boat blown out of the water, and lying fifteen feet distant from it on the shore although its weight was so great, that the strength of our remaining nine men could not return it to its element.

I selected a horse, and, taking the guide with me, started for the establishment in advance of the rest of the party. After a severe ride of four hours, and having forded the river four times, dangerously crowded with drift ice borne down by a rapid current, sometimes coming over the saddle, I arrived at Jasper's House cold, wet and famished. But I was soon cheered by a blazing fire and five or six pounds of mountain sheep, which I certainly then thought far more delicious than any domestic animal of the same species. About 10 o'clock that evening, to our great joy, the three men whom we had left on the south shore, came in. Their sufferings had been very great, as they had been wandering through the woods for three days without food, endeavouring to find the house which none of them had

been at before.   One of them had not even taken his coat
with him, and it was only by lying huddled together at
night that they escaped being frozen.   Another suffered
dreadfully from the swelled state of his legs, caused by
the strings usually tied round their leggings being too
tight, and which, owing to his benumbed condition, he
did not perceive.   We had some difficulty in cutting
them off, as they were buried in the swollen flesh.

7. Jasper House [Rocky Mountains]
Courtesy of Royal Ontario Museum

November 4th—Mr. Lane and party arrived safe in
the evening with the loaded horses.   Jasper's House
consists of only three miserable log huts.   The dwelling-
house is composed of two rooms, of about fourteen or
fifteen feet square each.   One of them is used by all
comers and goers: Indians, voyageurs, and traders, men,
women, and children being huddled together indiscriminately; the other room being devoted to the exclusive
occupation of Colin and his family, consisting of a Cree

squaw, and nine interesting half-breed children. One of the other huts is used for storing provisions in, when they can get any, and the other I should have thought a dog-kennel had I seen many of the canine species about. This post is only kept up for the purpose of supplying horses to parties crossing the mountains. I made a sketch of the establishment (No. 7).

November 5th—We started with a cavalcade of thirteen loaded horses, but as we did not expect to be able to get the horses across the mountains, I got an Indian to make me a pair of snow-shoes. The Indians about here do not number above fifteen or twenty; they are the Shoo-Schawp tribe, and their chief, of whom I made a sketch, is called "Capote Blanc" by the voyageurs —in their own language it is Assannitchay, but means the same. His proper location is a long distance to the north-east; but he had been treacherously entrapped, whilst travelling with thirty-seven of his people, by a hostile tribe, which met him and invited him to sit down and smoke the pipe of peace. They unsuspectingly laid down their arms, but before they had time to smoke, their treacherous hosts seized their arms and murdered them all except eleven who managed to escape, and fled to Jasper's House, where they remained, never daring to return to their own country through the hostile tribe. Capote Blanc was a very simple, kind-hearted old man, with whom I became very friendly.

We left this inhospitable spot about noon, and crossed the river in a small canoe, to where the men were waiting for us, with the horses, which they had swum across the river in the morning. We rode on till 4 o'clock, and encamped in a small prairie, of which I made a sketch.

November 6th—We made but few miles of progress to-day, being obliged to encamp at La Row's Prairie in order to pasture our horses, our next stopping place being too distant to reach that evening.

November 7th—We made a *long day;* our route lay sometimes over almost inaccessible crags, and at others through gloomy and tangled forest; as we ascended, the snow increased in depth, and we began to feel the effects of the increasing cold and rarefaction of the atmosphere.

November 8th—We saw two mountain goats looking down on us from a lofty and precipitous ledge of rock, not exceeding, to all appearance, a few inches in width. One of the Indians who accompanied us from Jasper's House to take back the horses, started to attain a crag above them, as these animals cannot be approached near enough to shoot them from below, their gaze being always directed downwards. They chanced, however, to see him going up, and immediately escaped to an inaccessible height.

November 9th—Finding the snow so deep, and knowing, not only that we were late, but that our further progress must be slow, we became apprehensive that the party who should be waiting for us with boats and provisions from Fort Vancouver, at the other side of the mountains, would give up all hopes of meeting us and might leave. This would have entailed the most fearful hardships upon us, if it did not produce actual destruction, as we should have had to recross the mountains with scarcely any or no provisions. We, therefore despatched the guide and M'Gillveray, to hasten on to Boat Encampment. We encamped at the "Grand Batteur," where we found some snow-shoes, which had been hidden by the party that had come out in the spring.

November 10*th*—We had not proceeded far before the horses stuck fast in the snow, and we were obliged to encamp on the spot to give those men who were unprovided, time to make snow-shoes, without which they could not proceed. We remained here all day, and sent the horses back with everything we could dispense with, our provisions and blankets being quite as much as the men could carry; and some of the new hands, who had only come into the country that year, were now so knocked up by their long and fatiguing voyage from Montreal, which they had left in the spring, as to be quite useless.

November 11*th*—We sent two experienced men in advance to beat the track for the new beginners, and made our first essay on snow-shoes. Some of our men succeeded but indifferently in the attempt, having never used them before; and the shoes, which we made the day before not being of the best description, materially impeded our progress. The shoes which the Indian had made for me at Jasper House were particularly good ones, and I found little difficulty in their use. Mrs. Lane had also taken the precaution to bring a pair with her, and as she had been accustomed to them from her childhood at Red River, where they are a great deal used, she proved one of our best pedestrians. We encamped early, making for the first time what is called a regular winter encampment. This is only made where the snow is so deep that it cannot be removed so as to reach the ground. The depth to which the snow attains can be calculated by the stumps of the trees cut off at its former level for previous camp fires; some of these were twelve or fifteen feet above us at the present time, and the snow was

nine or ten feet deep under us. Some of the old voyageurs amused themselves by telling the new hands or
Mangeurs du Lard, that the Indians in those parts were
giants from thirty to forty feet high, and that accounted
for the trees being cut off at such an unusual height.

It is necessary to walk repeatedly with snow-shoes
over the place chosen for the encampment until it is
sufficiently beaten down to bear a man without sinking
on its furface. Five or six logs of green timber, from
eighteen to twenty feet long, are laid down close together, in parallel lines, so as to form a platform. The
fire of dry wood is then kindled on it, and pine branches
are spread on each side, on which the party, wrapped in
their blankets, lie down with their feet towards the fire.
The parallel logs rarely burn through in one night, but
the dropping coal and heat form a deep chasm immediately under the fire, into which the logs are prevented
from falling by their length. Into this hole an Iroquois,
who had placed himself too near the fire, rolled a depth
of at least six or seven feet, the snow having melted from
under him while asleep. His cries awoke me, and after
a hearty laugh at his fiery entombment, we succeeded
in dragging him out.

November 12*th*—To-day we attained what is called
the Height of Land. There is a small lake at this
eminence called the Committee's Punch-bowl; this forms
the head waters of one branch of the Columbia River on
the west side of the mountains, and of the Athabasca
on the east side. It is about three quarters of a mile in
circumference, and is remarkable as giving rise to two
such mighty rivers; the waters of the one emptying into
the Pacific Ocean, and of the other into the Arctic Sea.
We encamped on its margin, with difficulty protecting
ourselves from the intense cold.

November 13th—The lake being frozen over to some depth, we walked across it, and shortly after commenced the descent of the grand côte, having been seven days continually ascending. The descent was so steep, that it took us only one day to get down to nearly the same level as that of Jasper's House. The descent was a work of great difficulty on snow-shoes, particularly for those carrying loads; their feet frequently slipped from under them, and the loads rolled down the hill. Some of the men, indeed, adopted the mode of rolling such loads as would not be injured down before them. On reaching the bottom, we found eight men waiting, whom M'Gillveray and the guide had sent on to assist us to Boat Encampment, and we all encamped together.

November 14th—I remained at the camp fire finishing one of my sketches, the men having made a very early start in order to reach Boat Encampment, where they would get a fresh supply of provisions, ours being nearly exhausted. As soon as I had finished my sketch I followed them, and soon arrived at a river about seventy yards across, and with a very rapid current.

Having followed their tracks in the snow to the edge of the river, and seeing the strength of the current, I began to look for other tracks, under the impression that they might possibly have discovered a way to get round it. But I was soon undeceived by seeing it in the snow on the other side of the path they had beaten down on the opposite bank; nothing, therefore, remained but for me to take off my snow-shoes, and make the traverse. The water was up to my middle, running very rapidly, and filled with drift ice, some pieces of which struck me, and nearly forced me down the stream. I found on coming out of the water my capote and leggings frozen stiff. My difficulties, however, were only beginning, as I was soon obliged to cross again four times, when, my legs becoming completely benumbed, I dared not venture on the fifth, until I had restored the circulation by running up and down the beach. I had to cross twelve others in a similar manner, being seventeen in all, before I overtook the rest of the party at the encampment. The reason of these frequent crossings is, that the only pass across the mountains is the gorge formed by the Athabasca at one side, and the Columbia at the other; and the beds of these torrents can only be crossed in the spring before the thaws commence, or in the fall after the severe weather has set in. During the summer the melting of the mountain snow and ice renders them utterly impracticable.

November 15th—It will be easily imagined with what regret we left a warm fire and comfortable encampment, to plunge at once into one of the deepest crossings we had yet encountered, covered like the preceding with running ice. Here, as in many other of the crossings, our only means of withstanding the force of the current was for all to go abreast shoulder to shoulder, in a line parallel with it, each man being supported by all below him. Mrs. Lane, although it was necesssary to carry her in the arms of two powerful men across the river, acquitted herself in other respects as well as any of us. One of the greatest annoyances accompanying the use of snow-shoes, is that of having to take them off on entering a river, and replacing them over the wet and frozen moccasins on coming out of it.

Before stopping to breakfast this morning, we crossed the river twenty-five times, and twelve times more before camping; having waded it thirty-seven times in all during the day.

The Columbia here makes long reaches, to and fro, through a valley, in some parts three miles wide, and backed with stupendous mountains, rearing their snowy tops above the clouds, and forming here and there immense glaciers, reflecting the rays of the sun with extreme brilliancy and prismatic beauty. The last part of the route lay through a slimy lake or swamp, frozen over, but not with sufficient solidity to bear us, so that we had to wade above our knees in a dense mass of snow, ice, and mud, there being no such thing as a dry spot to afford a moment's respite from the scarcely endurable severity of the cold, under which I thought I must have sunk exhausted.

At length, however, we arrived at Boat Encampment, about 5 P.M., almost perishing with cold and hunger, having tasted nothing since what I have already termed breakfast, which consisted only of a small supply of soup made of pemmican, this being the mode of making the most of a small quantity of it. On our arrival we found a good fire blazing, and some soup made from pork and corn, brought from Fort Vancouver, boiling in the pot, which I attacked with so much avidity, that one of the men, fearing I might take too much in my present exhausted state, politely walked off with the bowl and its contents.

The men had been here waiting our arrival for thirty-nine days, and would have returned to Fort Vancouver the next day, had not the guide and M'Gillveray opportunely arrived in time to prevent them, as they thought we had either been cut off by the Indians, or that we had found it impossible to cross the mountains. In fact, they were clearing the snow out of the boats preparatory to starting. Had our messengers not arrived in time, it would most likely have proved fatal to us all, as we could not have re-crossed the mountains without provisions.

On leaving Boat Encampment, I did not take any sketches, although the scenery was exceedingly grand; the rapidity with which we now travelled, and the necessity for doing so owing to the lateness of the season, prevented me; and as I was determined to return by the same route, I knew that I should then have plenty of time and opportunity. I shall therefore give a mere outline of my rapid journey to Fort Vancouver, a distance of 1200 miles down the Columbia River, which we accomplished in fifteen days, and which afterwards took me four months to ascend.

November 16th—Our two boats were by this time ready; they were formed canoe fashion, with round bottoms of boards, clinker built. On leaving Boat Encampment the scene is exceedingly grand; immense mountains receding further and further in the distance on every side. Few who read this journal, surrounded by the comforts of civilized life, will be able to imagine the heartfelt satisfaction with which we exchanged the wearisome snow-shoe for the comfortable boats, and the painful anxiety of half-satisfied appetites for a well-stocked larder. True it was, that the innumerable rapids of the Columbia were filled with dangers of no ordinary character, and that it required the constant exercise of all our energy and skill to escape their perils, but we now had health and high spirits to help us. We no longer had to toil on in clothes frozen stiff from wading across torrents, half-famished, and with the consciousness ever before us, that whatever were our hardships and fatigue, rest was sure destruction in the cold solitudes of those dreary mountains.

About three hours after our departure, we shot the celebrated "Dalle de Mort." It is about three miles long and is the most dangerous of all the rapids on the Columbia.

November 17th and 18th—We passed through the two lakes, and were obliged to work night and day to avail ourselves of the calm weather, although the snow fell without ceasing.

November 19th—We again entered the current of the river, where the men were enabled to rest for a few hours.

November 20th—About noon we ran through the Little Dalle, which, though short, is a series of dangerous whirlpools, which can only be passed with the greatest precaution, and arrived safe at Colville at 6 o'clock in the evening. Colville is beautifully situated about a mile above the fall of the Chaudière or Kettle Falls; it exceeds in height any other fall on the Columbia, and derives its name from the round holes that the water has hollowed out in the rocks, resembling cauldrons of various sizes. Here we were most hospitably entertained by Mr. Lewis, who was in charge. To avoid this fall we had to carry our boats a distance of two miles over a hill two or three hundred feet high. We remained here three days, during which time the men did little else but eat and sleep. The rapidity with which they changed their appearance was astonishing. Some of them became so much improved in looks, that it was with difficulty we could recognize our voyageurs.

November 23rd—We encamped in the evening a few miles below the falls. During the night some Indians, who had been prowling about, crept into the boats and stole some wearing apparel, which proved very annoying to us, as our wardrobes were rather limited.

November 24*th*—We arrived at the Grand Rapid, which the boats were obliged to run. I, however, preferred getting out to walk, with the object of making some sketches. I had proceeded nearly three miles along the shore, and felt somewhat astonished at not seeing the boats following, when I observed something in the water, which I at first took to be the head of an Indian swimming across. I accordingly prepared my gun in case of an attack, as the Indians about here are considered some of the worst on the Columbia. On close observation, however, I made out the object to be the hood which I had noticed Mrs. Lane to wear in the morning, and soon afterwards I perceived the paddles and oars of one of the boats. I now began to feel alarmed for the safety of some of the party, and immediately returned to the rapid as fast as possible. There I saw one of the boats, in which Mr. and Mrs. Lane were, in a most dangerous situation, having struck in the midst of the rapids upon a rock, which had stove in her side. The conduct of the men evinced great presence of mind. The instant she struck, they had sprung on the gunwale next the rock, and by their united weight kept her lying upon it. The water foamed and raged around them with fearful violence. Had she slipped off, they must all have been dashed to pieces amongst the rocks and rapids below; as it was, they managed to maintain their position, until the crew of the other boat, which had run the rapids safely, had unloaded and dragged the empty boat up the rapids again. They then succeeded in throwing a line to their hapless companions. But there was still considerable danger, lest in hauling the empty boat towards them they might pull themselves off the rock; they at length, however, succeeded by cautious management in getting the boat alongside, and in embarking in safety. In a moment afterwards their own boat slipped from the rock, and was dashed to pieces. Everything that floated we picked up afterwards, but still we lost a great many useful and necessary articles. We had, in consequence of this mishap, to send back overland to Colville for another boat. This detained us until the morning of the 26th. We now continued our journey rapidly and safely, and arrived at Okanagan on the evening of the 28th November. Our provisions had run short, and we were compelled to shoot one of the horses of the establishment, which we roasted, and found very palatable. In our emergency the men partook of it so voraciously that some of them were unable to work the next day.

November 29th—We continued our course, and in four days arrived at Fort Walla-Walla. Here we remained till December 4th, when we entered that part of the country which is annually visited by an almost continuous rain for five months of the year, and during the remainder of our voyage to Fort Vancouver, which we reached on the 8th December, we were exposed in our open boats to an incessant shower. Mr. Douglas and Mr. Ogden, the two chief factors in charge of the fort, came down to the landing, a distance of about half a mile, to welcome us on our arrival, all hopes of which they had given up, and conducted us up to the fort, where we were entertained with the most liberal hospitality.

CHAPTER XII

Fort Vancouver, the Indian name of which is
Katchutequa, or "the Plain," is the largest post in the
Hudson's Bay Company's dominions, and has usually
two chief factors, with eight or ten clerks and 200 voyageurs, residing there. Our society was also enlivened
by the addition of the officers of Her Majesty's ship of
war the "Modeste," which had been on this station for
two years, and lay in the river opposite the establishment.
The buildings are enclosed by strong pickets about sixteen feet high, with bastions for cannon at the corners.
The men, with their Indian wives, live in log huts near
the margin of the river, forming a little village—quite
a Babel of languages, as the inhabitants are a mixture
of English, French, Iroquois, Sandwich Islanders, Crees
and Chinooks.

The Columbia is here, ninety miles from its mouth, a
mile and a quarter wide; the surrounding country is
well wooded and fertile, the oak and pine being of the
finest description. A large farm is cultivated about
eight miles up the river, producing more grain than the
fort consumes; the surplus being sent to the Sandwich
Islands and the Russian dominions. They have immense herds of domestic horned cattle, which run wild in
unknown numbers; and sheep and horses are equally
numerous. When first introduced from California, Dr.
M'Laughlin, the gentleman then in charge, would not
allow any of the horned cattle to be killed for the use of

the establishment until their numbers had reached 600, by which means they have multiplied beyond calculation. During the five months' autumn and winter, it rains almost continuously, with very little frost or snow. The river, however, was frozen over for a short time during the winter I spent there, but it was remarked as the coldest season ever experienced; during the other seven months the weather is dry and sultry.

The Flathead Indians are met with on the banks of the Columbia River, from its mouth eastward to the Cascades, a distance of about 150 miles; they extend up the Walhamette River's mouth, about thirty or forty miles, and through the district between the Walhamette and Fort Astoria, now called Fort George. To the north they extend along the Cowlitz River, and the tract of land lying between that and Puget's Sound. About two-thirds of Vancouver's Island is also occupied by them, and they are found along the coasts of Puget's Sound and the Straits of Juan de Fuca. The Flatheads are divided into numerous tribes, each having its own peculiar locality, and differing more or less from the others in language, customs, and manners. Those in the immediate vicinity of the fort are principally Chinooks and Klickataats, and are governed by a chief called Casanov. This name has no translation, the Indians on the west side of the Rocky Mountains differing from those on the east in having hereditary names, to which no particular meaning appears to be attached, and the origin of which is in many instances forgotten.

Casanov is a man of advanced age, and resides principally at Fort Vancouver. I made a sketch (No. 8) of him while staying at the fort. Previously in 1829 Casanov was considered a powerful chief, and could lead into the field 1000 men, but in that year the Hudson's

Bay Company and emigrants from the United States introduced the plough for the first time into Oregon; and the locality, hitherto considered one of the most healthy, was almost depopulated by the fever and ague. His own immediate family, consisting of ten wives, four

8. Ca-sa-nov [Great Chief of Chinooks and Klickataats,
Fort Vancouver]
Courtesy of Royal Ontario Museum

children, and eighteen slaves, were reduced in one year to one wife, one child, and two slaves. Casanov is a man of more than ordinary talent for an Indian, and he has maintained his great influence over his tribe chiefly by means of the superstitious dread in which they have held him. For many years, in the early period of his life, he kept a hired assassin to remove any obnoxious individual against whom he entertained personal enmity. This bravo, whose occupation was no secret, went by the name of Casanov's scoocoom, or "the Evil Genius." He finally fell in love with one of Casanov's wives, who eloped with him. Casanov vowed vengeance, but the pair for a long time eluded his search; until one day he met his wife in a canoe near the mouth of the Cowlitz River, and shot her on the spot, and at last procured also the assassination of the lover.

A few years before my arrival at Fort Vancouver, Mr. Douglass, who was then in charge, heard from his office the report of a gun inside the gates. This being a breach of discipline he hurried out to inquire the cause of so unusual a circumstance, and found one of Casanov's slaves standing over the body of an Indian whom he had just killed, and in the act of reloading his gun with apparent indifference, Casanov himself standing by. On Mr. Douglass arriving at the spot, he was told by Casanov, with an apology, that the man deserved death according to the laws of the tribe, who as well as the white man inflicted punishment proportionate to the nature of the offence. In this case the crime was one of the greatest an Indian could be guilty of, namely, the robbing the sepulchre canoes. Mr. Douglass, after severely reprimanding him, allowed him to depart with the dead body.

Sacred as the Indians hold their burial places, Casanov himself, a short time after the latter occurrence, had his only son buried in the cemetery of the Fort. He died of consumption—a disease very common amongst all Indians—proceeding no doubt from their constant exposure to the sudden vicissitudes of the climate. The coffin was made sufficiently large to contain all the necessaries supposed to be required for his comfort and convenience in the world of spirits. The chaplain of the Fort read the usual service at the grave, and after the conclusion of the ceremony, Casanov returned to his lodge, and the same evening attempted, as narrated below, the life of the bereaved mother, who was the daughter of the great chief generally known as King Comcomly, so beautifully alluded to in Washington Irving's "Astoria." She was formerly the wife of a Mr. McDougall, who bought her from her father for, as it was supposed, the enormous price of ten articles of each description, guns, blankets, knives, hatchets, etc., then in Fort Astoria. Concomly, however, acted with unexpected liberality on the occasion by carpeting her path from the canoe to the Fort with sea otter skins, at that time numerous and valuable, but now scarce, and presenting them as a dowry, in reality far exceeding in value the articles at which she had been estimated. On Mr. McDougall's leaving the Indian country she became the wife of Casanov.

It is the prevailing opinion of the chiefs that they and their sons are too important to die in a natural way, and whenever the event takes place, they attribute it to the malevolent influence of some other person, whom they fix upon, often in the most unaccountable manner, frequently selecting those the most dear to themselves and the deceased. The person so selected is sacrificed without hesitation. On this occasion Casanov selected the afflicted mother, notwithstanding she had during the sickness of her son been one of the most assiduous and devoted of his attendants, and of his several wives she was the one he most loved; but it is the general belief of the Indians on the west side of the mountains that the greater the privation they inflict on themselves the greater would be the manifestation of their grief, and the more pleasing to the departed spirit. Casanov assigned to me an additional motive for his wish to kill his wife, namely, that as he knew she had been so useful to her son and so necessary to his happiness and comfort in this world, he wished to send her with him as his companion on his long journey. She, however, escaped into the woods, and next morning reached the Fort imploring protection; she was accordingly secreted for several days until her own relations took her home to Chinook Point. In the meantime a woman was found murdered in the woods, and the act was universally attributed to Casanov or one of his emissaries.

I may here mention a painful occurrence which took place on Thompson's River, in New Caledonia, as illustrative of this peculiar superstition.

A chief dying, his widow considered a sacrifice as indispensable, but having selected a victim of rather too much importance, she was unable for some time to accomplish her object; at length the nephew of the chief, no longer able to bear the continual taunts of cowardice which she unceasingly heaped upon him, seized his gun and started for the Company's Fort on the river, about twenty miles distant. On arriving he was courteously received by Mr. Black, the gentleman in charge of the Fort, who expressed great regret at the death of his old friend the chief. After presenting the Indian with something to eat and giving him some tobacco, Mr. Black turned to leave the room, and while opening the door was shot from behind by his treacherous guest and immediately expired. The murderer succeeded in escaping from the Fort, but the tribe, who were warmly attached to Mr. Black, took his revenge upon themselves and hunted him down. This was done more to evince their high esteem for Mr. Black than from any sense of impropriety in the customary sacrifice.

Amongst the Chinooks I have never heard any traditions as to their former origin, although such traditions are common amongst those on the east side of the Rocky

Mountains. They do not believe in any future state of punishment, although in this world they suppose themselves exposed to the malicious designs of the scoocoom, or evil genius, to whom they attribute all their misfortunes and ill luck. The Good Spirit is called the *Hias Soch-a-li-Ti-yah,* that is, the Great High Chief, from whom they obtain all that is good in this life, and to whose happy and peaceful hunting grounds they will all eventually go, to reside for ever in comfort and abundance.

The Chinooks and Cowlitz Indians carry the custom of flattening the head to a greater extent than any other of the Flathead tribes. The process is as follows:— The Indian mothers all carry their infants strapped to a piece of board covered with moss or loose fibres of cedar bark, and in order to flatten the head they place a pad on the infant's forehead, on the top of which is laid a piece of smooth bark, bound on by a leathern band passing through holes in the board on either side, and kept tightly pressed across the front of the head,—a sort of pillow of grass or cedar fibres being placed under the back of the neck to support it. This process commences with the birth of the infant, and is continued for a period of from eight to twelve months, by which time the head has lost its natural shape, and acquired that of a wedge: the front of the skull flat and higher at the crown, giving it a most unnatural appearance.

It might be supposed, from the extent to which this is carried, that the operation would be attended with great suffering to the infant, but I have never heard the infants crying or moaning, although I have seen the eyes seemingly starting out of the sockets from the great pressure. But, on the contrary, when the lashings were removed, I have noticed them cry until they were replaced. From the apparent dulness of the children whilst under the pressure, I should imagine that a state of torpor or insensibility is induced, and that the return to consciousness occasioned by its removal must be naturally followed by the sense of pain.

This unnatural operation does not, however, seem to injure the health, the mortality amongst the Flathead children not being perceptibly greater than amongst other Indian tribes; nor does it seem to injure their intellect. On the contrary, the Flatheads are generally considered fully as intelligent as the surrounding tribes, who allow their heads to preserve their natural shape, and it is from amongst the round heads that the Flatheads take their slaves, looking with contempt even upon the white for having round heads, the flat head being considered as the distinguishing mark of freedom.

The Chinooks, like all other Indians, pluck out the beard at its first appearance. Slavery is carried on to a great extent among them, and, considering how much they have themselves been reduced, they still retain a large number of slaves. These are usually procured from the Chastay tribe, who live near the Umqua, a river south of the Columbia, emptying near the Pacific. They are sometimes seized by war parties, but the children are often bought from their own people. They do not flatten the head, nor is the child of one of them (although by a Chinook father) allowed this privilege. Their slavery is of the most abject description. The Chinook men and women treat them with great severity, and exercise the power of life and death at pleasure. I took a sketch of a Chastay female slave, the lower part of whose face, from the corners of the mouth to the ears and downwards, was tattooed of a blueish colour. The men of this tribe do not tattoo, but paint their faces like other Indians.

I would willingly give a specimen of the barbarous language of this people were it possible to represent by any combination of our alphabet the horrible, harsh, spluttering sounds which proceed from their throats, apparently unguided either by the tongue or lip. It is so difficult to acquire a mastery of their language that none have been able to attain it, except those who have been born amongst them. They have, however, by their intercourse with the English and French traders, succeeded in amalgamating, after a fashion, some words of each of these tongues with their own, and forming a sort of patois, barbarous enough certainly, but still sufficient to enable them to communicate with the traders. This patois I was enabled after some short time to acquire, and could converse with most of the chiefs with tolerable ease; their common salutation is Clak-hoh-ah-yah, originating, as I believe, in their having heard in the early days of the fur trade, a gentleman named Clark frequently addressed by his friends, "Clark, how are you?" This salutation is now applied to every white man, their own language affording no appropriate expression. Their language is also peculiar in containing no oaths, or any words conveying gratitude or thanks.

Their habits are extremely filthy, their persons abounding with vermin, and one of their chief amusements consists in picking these disgusting insects from each other's heads and eating them. On my asking an Indian one day why he ate them, he replied that they bit him and he gratified his revenge by biting them in return. It might naturally be supposed that they are thus beset from want of combs, or other means of displacing the intruders; but this is not the case, as they pride themselves on carrying such companions about them, and giving their friends the opportunity of amusing themselves by hunting and eating them.

The costume of the men consists of a musk-rat skin robe, the size of our ordinary blanket, thrown over the shoulder, without any breech-cloth, moccasins, or leggings. The dress which Casanov is represented as wearing, in the picture, being one that was presented to him by a friend from Walla-Walla. Painting the face is not much practiced amongst them, except on extraordinary occasions, such as the death of a relative, some solemn feast, or going on a war party. The female dress consists of a girdle of cedar-bark round the waist, with a dense mass of strings of the same material hanging from it all round, and reaching almost to the knees. This is their sole summer habiliment. They, however, in very severe weather, add the musk-rat blanket. They also make another sort of blanket from the skin of the wild goose, which is here taken in great abundance. The skin is stripped from the bird with the feathers on and cut in strips, which they twist so as to have the feathers outward. This makes a feathered cord, and is then netted together so as to form a blanket, the feathers filling up the meshes, rendering it a light and very warm covering. In the summer these are entirely thrown aside, not being in any case worn from feelings of delicacy. The men go quite naked, though the women always wear the cedar petticoat.

The country which the Chinooks inhabit, being almost destitute of furs, they have little to trade in with the whites. This, coupled with their laziness, probably induced by the ease with which they procure fish, which is their chief subsistence, prevents their obtaining ornaments of European manufacture, consequently anything of the kind is seldom seen amongst them.

The Chinooks evince very little taste, in comparison with some of the tribes on the eastern side of the Rocky Mountains, in ornamenting either their persons or their warlike or domestic implements. The only utensils I saw at all creditable to their decorative skill were carved bowls and spoons of horn, and baskets made of roots and grass, woven so closely as to serve all the purposes of a pail in holding and carrying water. In these they even boil their fish. This is done by immersing the fish in one of the baskets filled with water, into which they throw red-hot stones until the fish is cooked; and I have seen fish dressed as expeditiously by them in this way, as if done in a kettle over the fire by our own people. The only vegetables in use among them are the camas and wappatoo. The camas is a bulbous root, much resembling the onion in outward appearance, but is more like the potato when cooked, and is very good eating. The wappatoo is somewhat similar, but larger, and not so dry or delicate in its flavour. They are found in immense quantities in the plains in the vicinity of Fort Vancouver, and in the spring of the year present a most curious and beautiful appearance, the whole surface presenting an uninterrupted sheet of bright ultramarine blue, from the innumerable blossoms of these plants. They are cooked by digging a hole in the ground, then putting down a layer of hot stones, covering them with dry grass, on which the roots are placed, they are then covered with a layer of grass, and on the top of this they place earth with a small hole perforated through the earth and grass down to the vegetables. Into this water is poured, which, reaching the hot stones, forms sufficient steam to completely cook the roots in a short time, the hole being immediately stopped up on the introduction of the water. They often adopt the same ingenious process for cooking their fish and game.

There is another article of food made use of amongst them, which, from its disgusting nature, I should have been tempted to omit, were it not a peculiarly characteristic trait of the Chinook Indians, both from its extraordinary character and its use, being confined solely to this tribe. The Whites have given it the name of Chinook olives, and it is prepared as follows:— About a bushel of acorns are placed in a hole dug for the purpose close to the entrance of the lodge or hut, covered over with a thin layer of grass, on the top of which is laid about half a foot of earth. Every member of the family henceforth regards this hole as the special place of deposit for his urine, which is on no occasion to be diverted from its legitimate receptacle. In this hole the acorns are allowed to remain four or five months before they are considered fit for use. However disgusting such an odoriferous preparation would be to people in civilized life, the product is regarded by them as the greatest of all delicacies.

During the season the Chinooks are engaged in gathering camas and fishing, they live in lodges constructed by means of a few poles covered with mats made of rushes, which can be easily moved from place to place, but in the villages they build permanent huts of split cedar boards. Having selected a dry place for the hut, a hole is dug about three feet deep, and about twenty feet square. Round the sides square cedar boards are sunk and fastened together with cords and twisted roots, rising about four feet above the outer level; two posts are sunk at the middle of each end with a crotch at the top, on which the ridge pole is laid, and boards are laid from thence to the top of the upright boards fastened in the same manner. Round the interior are erected sleeping places, one above another, something like the berths in a vessel, but larger. In the centre of this lodge the fire is made, and the smoke escapes through a hole left in the roof for that purpose.

The fire is obtained by means of a small flat piece of dry cedar, in which a small hollow is cut, with a channel for the ignited charcoal to run over; this piece the Indian sits on to hold it steady, while he rapidly twirls a round stick of the same wood between the palms of his hands, with the point pressed into the hollow of the flat piece. In a very short time sparks begin to fall through the channel upon finely frayed cedar bark placed underneath, which they soon ignite. There is a great deal of knack in doing this, but those who are used to it will light a fire in a very short time. The men usually carry these sticks about with them, as after they have been once used they produce the fire more quickly.

The only native warlike instruments I have seen amongst them were bows and arrows; these they use with great precision. Their canoes are hollowed out of the cedar by fire, and smoothed off with stone axes. Some of them are very large, as the cedar grows to an enormous size in this neighbourhood. They are made very light, and from their formation, are capable of withstanding very heavy seas.

The principal amusement of the Chinooks is gambling, which is carried to great excess amongst them. You never visit the camp but you hear the eternal gambling song of he hah ha, accompanied by the beating of small sticks on some hollow substance. Their games are few. The one most generally played amongst them consists in holding in each hand a small stick, the thickness of a goose quill, and about an inch and a half in length, one plain, and the other distinguished by a little thread wound round it, the opposite party being required to guess in which hand the marked stick is to be found. A Chinook will play at this simple game for days and nights together, until he has gambled away everything he possesses, even to his wife. They play, however, with much equanimity, and I never knew any ill feeling evinced by the loser against his successful opponent. They will cheat if they can, and pride themselves on its success; if detected, no unpleasant consequence follows, the offending party being merely laughed at, and allowed to amend his game. They also take great delight in a game with a ball, which is played by them in the same manner as by the Cree, Chippewa, and Sioux Indians. Two poles are erected about a mile apart, and the company is divided into two bands, armed with sticks, having a small ring or hoop at the end, with which the ball is picked up and thrown to a great distance; each party then strives to get the ball past their own goal. There are sometimes a hundred on a side, and the play is kept up with great noise and excitement. At this game they bet heavily, as it is generally played between tribes or villages. The Chinooks have tolerably good horses, and are fond of racing, at which they also bet considerably. They are expert jockeys, and ride fearlessly.

Chapter XIII

I continued at Fort Vancouver for about a month, and left on the 10th of January 1847, with Mr. Mackenlie, a chief trader, for Oregon City, where the company has an establishment. After going down the Columbia about five miles, we entered the mouth of the Walhamette River, and ascended it twenty-five miles to Oregon City, passing two cities that are to be. One of them contained but two houses, and the other was not much more advanced. Oregon City contains about ninety-four houses, and two or three hundred inhabitants. There are a Methodist and a Roman Catholic church, two hotels, two grist mills, three saw mills, four stores, two watchmakers, one gunsmith, one lawyer, and doctors *ad libitum*. The city stands near the Falls of the Walhamette which is here about thirty-two feet high.

The water privileges are of the most powerful and convenient description. Dr. M'Laughlin, formerly a chief factor in the Hudson's Bay Company, first obtained a location of the place, and now owns the principal mills. A great drawback, however, to its prosperity, is, that vessels cannot ascend the river nearer to it than fifteen miles, on account of the rapids. At the head of the navigation a city is building, which must eventually rival, if not eclipse Oregon in commercial prosperity. The morning after our arrival the thermometer stood at 7° below zero. Such intense cold had not been felt by the oldest inhabitants of these regions. It had the effect of killing nearly all the cattle that had become acclimated, as they are never housed. The Columbia, too, was frozen over, an unprecedented circumstance, so that my travels were for a time interrupted. I was, however, very comfortably quartered at Mr. Mackenlie's residence, who amused me in the long winter evenings over a good fire by his interesting tales of Indian life, with which he was well conversant. I will relate a couple of his anecdotes.

While he was in charge of a fort in New Caledonia, which is situated south of the Columbia River, he had a carat of tobacco, or three pounds, stolen from him. It was all that he had at that time, and of course was a serious loss. Supposing it to have been taken by some of the Indians, who were trading in large numbers about the establishment at that time, he requested the chief to call a council of all the tribe, as he had something to say to them. On this they all assembled and squatted down, leaving an open space in the centre, into which he walked with his fowling piece; this he loaded with two balls in the presence of the assembly, after which he related the circumstance of his loss, and stated his belief that some one of the Indians then present had taken it. He then told them that he wished that every one present would place his mouth to the muzzle of the gun, and blow into it, assuring them that it would injure no one innocent of the theft; but, on the other hand, if the guilty party should attempt to do so, it would inevitably kill him. He himself set the example of blowing into the piece, standing muzzle upwards on the ground; the chief followed, as well as the whole tribe, with the exception of one man, who sat hanging down his head, and when called upon by the chief to follow the example of the rest refused, saying, that he would not tempt the Great Spirit, for that he had taken the tobacco, and would return it, which he accordingly did.

Whilst Mr. Mackenlie was in charge of Walla-Walla he exhibited an instance of great presence of mind under very trying circumstances. His clerk had a quarrel and fight with the son of the chief, whom he beat. The Indian thereupon collected a large party of the tribe, and rushed with them into the yard of the fort, and attempted to seize the offender for the purpose of taking his life. Mr. Mackenlie kept them off for some time, but finding he could do so no longer, he ordered one of the men to bring him out a keg of powder, the head of which he knocked in, and taking a flint and steel from his pocket, he stood over it as if about to ignite it, telling the Indians that if they did not immediately depart he would show them how a white chief could die and destroy his enemies. The Indians took the alarm, and fled through the gates, which he immediately barred against them, secretly sending the clerk the next day to another post out of their reach.

After remaining at Mr. Mackenlie's house for about three weeks, I ascended the Walhamette River, in company with Father Acolti, a Jesuit missionary, for about thirty miles. We then disembarked and proceeded on horseback about eight miles to the Roman Catholic mission, where there is a large establishment of religieuses for the purposes of education, as well as a good brick church, situated in a beautiful prairie, surrounded with woods. It has also a nunnery occupied by six Sisters of Charity, who employ themselves in teaching the children, both white and red, amounting to forty-two pupils.

Father Acolti's residence is three miles from here,

the Jesuit mission being distinct from the Roman Catholic; at least they are under separate authorities. Besides this one under Father Acolti, there are three Jesuit missions near the Rocky Mountains, and one in New Caledonia. This part of the country contains the largest tract of good land that is to be met with in Oregon. I enjoyed the hospitality of Père Acolti's establishment for three or four days, when I again returned to the Walhamette; and previously to embarking in the canoe, I ascended a high mountain, and made a sketch of the windings of the river, with the Umqua Mountains, where it takes it rise, in the distance.

After visiting Mr. Mackinlie at Oregon City for a few days, I once more started for Fort Vancouver. About four miles below Oregon the Klackamuss enters the Walhamette; and, seated on the banks at its mouth, I saw a party of Indians of the Klackamuss tribe, and I put ashore for the purpose of taking a sketch of them. They were busy gambling at one of their favourite games. Two were seated together on skins, and immediately opposite to them sat two others, several trinkets and ornaments being placed between them, for which they played. The game consists in one of them having his hands covered with a small round mat resting on the ground. He has four small sticks in his hand, which he disposes under the mat in certain positions, requiring the opposite party to guess how he has placed them. If he guesses right, the mat is handed round to the next, and a stick is stuck up as a counter in his favour. If wrong, a stick is stuck up on the opposite side as a mark against him. This, like almost all the Indian games, was accompanied with singing; but in this case the singing was peculiarly sweet and wild, possessing a harmony I never heard before or since amongst Indians.

This tribe was once very numerous; but owing to their close vicinity to Oregon City, and the ease with which they can procure spirits, they have dwindled down to six or eight lodges.

We arrived late that evening at Fort Vancouver, having paddled on all day through heavy rain and cold. This, however, is thought little of in the Columbia during the rainy seasons, as no one troubles himself with making vain attempts to avoid wet at these periods. I remained here until the 25th of March; and although the weather was very wet, I found plenty of amusement with the officers of the "Modeste," who had built stables, and selected some very good horses. With these we ran races, and chased the wild calves; the object of which latter exercise consisted principally in showing the dexterity of the rider, in stooping from his saddle and throwing the calf heels-over-head by the tail.

These sports we occasionally varied by shooting and fishing, ducks and geese and seal being in great quantities in the neighbourhood of the fort. One day, a tall, large-boned Indian came on board the "Modeste" while I was sitting below with some of the officers. The Indian was dressed, as usual, in full costume, as they would call it in California (where, it is said, a shirt collar and spurs are considered the only clothing indispensably necessary); that is to say, he had his paddle in his hand, and walked about the deck with great gravity, examining the cannon, and other things equally incomprehensible to him, much to the amusement of the idle sailors. The purser, no doubt from a feeling of delicacy, took the Indian below, and gave him an old swallow-tailed coat of his, which was adorned with numerous brass buttons. The Indian, highly delighted, struggled into the garment with the greatest difficulty, as it was

infinitely too small for him, the cuffs reaching but little
below the elbow, and the front not meeting within a
foot.   Having, however, succeeded in getting into it,
he perambulated the deck with tenfold dignity, and the
whole ship's crew yelled with laughter.   The extraordinary noise brought us all on deck, and, amongst
others, the captain came up.   Even his dignity could not
withstand the absurdity of the figure, to which he immediately added, by sending his steward down for an
old cocked hat of his, which was given to the Indian.
When this was mounted the figure was complete; and
seldom has the deck of one of Her Majesty's ships been
the scene of such uproarious and violent laughter.   I
made several efforts to make a sketch of the Indian before I could succeed; and though I at length did so,
yet I fear that the picture would give but a faint idea of
the cause of all our merriment.

March 25th—I started from the Fort for Vancouver's Island in a small wooden canoe, with a couple of
Indians, and encamped at the mouth of the Walhamette.

March 26th—When we arrived at the mouth of the
Kattlepoutal River, twenty-six miles from Fort Vancouver, I stopped to make a sketch of the volcano,
Mount St. Helen's, distant, I suppose, about thirty or
forty miles.   This mountain has never been visited by
either Whites or Indians; the latter assert that it is
inhabited by a race of beings of a different species, who
are cannibals, and whom they hold in great dread; they
also say that there is a lake at its base with a very extraordinary kind of fish in it, with a head more resembling
that of a bear than any other animal.   These superstitions are taken from the statement of a man who, they
say, went to the mountain with another, and escaped the
fate of his companion, who was eaten by the "Skoo-

cooms," or evil genii. I offered a considerable bribe to
any Indian who would accompany me in its exploration,
but could not find one hardy enough to venture. It is
of very great height, and being eternally covered with
snow, is seen at a great distance. There was not a cloud
visible in the sky at the time I commenced my sketch,
and not a breath of air was perceptible; suddenly a
stream of white smoke shot up from the crater of the
mountain, and hovered a short time over its summit; it
then settled down like a cap. This shape it retained for
about an hour and a half, and then gradually disappeared.

About three years before this the mountain was in
a violent state of eruption for three or four days, and
threw up burning stones and lava to an immense height,
which ran in burning torrents down its snow-clad sides.
About ten miles lower down we encamped for the night
near Coffin Rock, much against the inclination of my
men, whose superstition would have led them to avoid
such a place. This rock gets its name from its being
the place in which the Indians deposit\ their dead. I
took a sketch of the rock before the night set in.

There is another rock lower down, on which were
deposited two or three hundred of their burial canoes;
but Commodore Wilkes having made a fire near the
spot, it communicated to the bodies, and nearly the
whole of them were consumed. The Indians showed
much indignation at the violation of a place which was
held so sacred by them, and would no doubt have sought
revenge had they felt themselves strong enough to do so.

March 27th—As usual, the rain came down in torrents. As we neared one of the points on the river, we
perceived a naked Indian watching us; as we came up
he ran away to his lodge, and, to my astonishment, re-

appeared in the cocked hat and purser's coat aforesaid. He received me with great friendship, having recognized me, before landing, as one of the party he had seen on board the "Modeste." He took me to his lodge and gave me some boiled salmon. He seemed to take great care of his uniform; but, unfortunately, the coat would not stretch, and it now burst wide open all the way up the back, which, I have no doubt, added considerably to his comfort. After leaving him we entered the Cowlitz River, and proceeded up about eight miles and encamped on its banks. We saw a family of immigrants winding their toilsome way in quest of a spot to make their home. Their condition appeared miserable in the extreme.

March 28*th*—One of my Indians falling sick here, I procured another Indian and proceeded up the river at a very slow rate, owing to the rapidity of the current. The pine trees here are the largest I have even seen. I measured one, which had drifted down the stream, and which had apparently a third of its length broken off. It was still 180 feet long, and 26 feet in circumference 5 feet from its root.

March 29*th*—We came to another Indian burial ground, which seemed to be highly decorated. I wished my Indians to put ashore, but they would not do so. I was obliged, therefore, to put them out of the canoe on the opposite side of the river, and paddle the canoe over by myself. I have no doubt that they would have opposed my doing so had it not been for the name which I had already acquired amongst the Indians, of being a great medicine-man, on account of the likenesses which I had taken. My power of pourtraying the features of individuals was attributed entirely to supernatural agency, and I found that, in looking at my pictures, they always covered their eyes with their hands and looked

through the fingers; this being also the invariable custom when looking at a dead person.   On arriving at the
place I found it lavishly decorated with numerous
articles, of supposed utility and ornament, for the convenience of the defunct in the journey to the world of
spirits.   These articles consisted of blankets, tin cups,
pots, pans, kettles, plates, baskets, horn bowls, and

9. Burial-Place on the Cowlitz River
Courtesy of Royal Ontario Museum

spoons, with shreds of cloth of various colours.   One
canoe, which was decorated more highly than the rest,
I examined particularly.   All the articles appended to it
were rendered useless for this world by either tearing,
breaking, or boring holes in them, the Indians believing
that they would be made whole again by the Great
Spirit.   On examining the interior of a canoe I found a
great number of ioquas and other shells, together with
beads and rings: even the mouth of the deceased was
filled with these articles.   The body itself was carefully
enveloped in numerous folds of matting made of rushes.

At the bottom of the canoe lay a bow and arrow, a paddle, a spear, and a kind of pick, made of horn, for digging the camas roots; the top of the canoe immediately over the body, had a covering of bark, and holes were bored in the bottom to allow the water to run out. These canoes are always placed on wooden supports, suspended in the branches of trees, or placed upon isolated rocks in the river, to keep them beyond the reach of ravenous animals. Sketch No. 9 represents this burial place.

During my stay the Indians watched me closely from the opposite bank, and, on my return, they examined me as minutely as they well could with their eyes to see that I had not brought anything away with me. Had I been so imprudent as to have done so I should probably have answered for the sacrilege with my life, death being the certain penalty to the most trifling violation of the sanctity of a coffin canoe. I endeavoured to discover who was buried in the richly decorated canoe, but the only information I could get from them was that the deceased was the daughter of a Chinook chief. The Indians here have a superstitious dread of mentioning the name of any person after death, nor will they tell you their own names, which can only be found out from a third party. One of the men asked me if my desire to know his name proceeded from a wish to steal it. It is not an uncommon thing for a chief, when he wishes to pay you a very high compliment, to give and call you by his own name, and adopt some other for himself.

March 30*th*—We landed at the Cowlitz farm, which belongs to the Hudson's Bay Company. Large quantities of wheat are raised at this place. I had a fine view of Mount St. Helen's throwing up a long column of dark smoke into the clear blue sky. Here I remained until the 5th of April, and took the likeness of Kiscox, the chief of the Cowlitz Indians, a small tribe of about 200. They flatten their heads and speak a language very similar to the Chinooks. They were very friendly

10. Flathead Woman and Child
Courtesy of Royal Ontario Museum

to me and I was a good deal amongst them. Sketch No. 10 is Caw-wacham, a woman of the tribe, with her child under the process of having its head flattened. It was with some difficulty that I persuaded her to sit, as she seemed apprehensive that it would be injurious to her. On the 5th April I procured horses to cross to Nasqually at Puget's Sound, and rain poured down in torrents the whole day, making the swamps nearly impassable. We encamped in the evening near a small village of Cowlitz Indians, whom we found unusually kind and civil.

April 6th—We passed over what is called the Mud Mountain. The mud is so very deep in this pass that we were compelled to dismount and drag our horses through it by the bridle, the poor beasts being up to their bellies in mud of the tenacity of bird-lime. This evening we encamped in the Prairie de Bute. This is remarkable for having innumerable round elevations, touching each other like so many hemispheres, of ten or twelve yards in circumference, and four or fire feet in height. I dug one of them open, but found nothing in it but loose stones, although I went four or five feet down. The whole surface is thickly covered with coarse grass. I travelled twenty-two miles through this extraordinary looking prairie.

April 7th—We found some difficulty in crossing the Nasqually River, as the rains had flooded it, and we were obliged to adopt the usual plan where canoes cannot be obtained, that is, swimming at our horses' tails, and floating our things over in skin baskets. A couple of hours brought us to Nasqually, which was established by a company called the Puget's Sound Company, for grazing and farming. When I visited it, it had about 6000 sheep and 2000 horned cattle. Its site is beautiful, on the banks of the eastern end of Puget's Sound. The land is inferior to that in some other parts of the same district, the soil being gravelly; the grass, however, grows luxuriantly, and the mildness of the climate adapts it well for grazing purposes, as it is never necessary to house the animals. The wool, which is good, finds its way to the English market by the Company's ships, and the cattle are slaughtered and salted for the Sandwich Islands and the Russian dominions. The Indians about here are of very large stature; indeed, the largest that I have met with on the continent. The women are particularly large and stout. The tribe numbers between five and six hundred. They flatten their heads, but use a language different from the Chinooks. I made a sketch of Lach-oh-lett, their head chief, and his daughter, who wore a cap made of grass of different colours, much used by the women.

CHAPTER XIV

Fort Victoria—Accidental Clover—Blankets of Dog's Hair—Aprons of Bark—A Chief's Inauguration—Monstrous Sturgeon—Crows which Feed on Fish—The Domestic Institution—The Dead Slave—Frightening a Native—Washing the Dead—The Game of Lehallum—An Expensive Feast—Medicine Caps.

April 8*th*—I left Nasqually this morning with six Indians in a canoe, and continued paddling on the whole day and the following night, as the tide seemed favourable, not stopping till 2 P.M., when we reached Fort Victoria on Vancouver's Island, having travelled ninety miles without stopping. Fort Victoria stands upon the banks of an inlet in the island about seven miles long and a quarter of a mile wide, forming a safe and convenient harbour, deep enough for any sized vessel. Its Indian name is the Esquimalt, or, "Place for gathering Camas", great quantities of that vegetable being found in the neighbourhood. On my arrival I was kindly welcomed by Mr. Finlayson, the gentleman in charge. He gave me a comfortable room, which I made my headquarters during the two months I was occupied in sketching excursions amongst the Indians in the neighbourhood and along the surrounding coasts.

The soil of this locality is good, and wheat is grown in considerable abundance. Clover grows plentifully, and is supposed to have sprung from accidental seeds which had fallen from the packages of goods brought from England, many of which are made up in hay.

The interior of the island has not been explored to any extent except by the Indians, who represent it as badly supplied with water in the summer, and the water obtained from a well dug at the fort was found to be too brackish for use. The appearance of the interior, when seen from the coast, is rocky and mountainous, evidently volcanic; the trees are large, principally oak and pine. The timbers of a vessel of some magnitude were being got out. The establishment is very large, and must eventually become the great depôt for the business of the Company. They had ten white men and forty Indians engaged in building new stores and warehouses. On the opposite side of the harbour, facing the fort, stands a village of Clal-lums Indians. They boast of being able to turn out 500 warriors, armed chiefly with bows and arrows. The lodges are built of cedar like the Chinook lodges, but much larger, some of them being sixty or seventy feet long.

The men wear no clothing in summer, and nothing but a blanket in winter, made either of dog's hair alone, or dog's hair and goosedown mixed, frayed cedar-bark, or wildgoose skin, like the Chinooks. They have a peculiar breed of small dogs with long hair of a brownish black and a clear white. These dogs are bred for clothing purposes. The hair is cut off with a knife and mixed with goosedown and a little white earth, with a view to curing the feathers. This is then beaten together with sticks, and twisted into threads by rubbing it down the thigh with the palm of the hand, in the same way that a shoemaker forms his waxend, after which it undergoes a second twisting on a distaff to increase its firmness. The cedar bark is frayed and twisted into threads in a similar manner. These threads are then woven into blankets by a very simple loom of their own contrivance. A single thread is wound over rollers at the top and bottom of a square frame, so as to form a continuous woof through which an alternate thread is carried by the hand, and pressed closely together by a sort of wooden comb; by turning the rollers every part of the woof is brought within reach of the weaver; by this means a bag is formed, open at each end, which being cut down makes a square blanket. The women wear only an apron of twisted cedar-bark shreds, tied round the waist and hanging down in front only, almost to the knees. They however, use the blankets more than the men do, but certainly not from any feeling of delicacy.

This tribe flatten the head, but their language varies very much from the Chinook; however, the same patois used on the Columbia is spoken by many of them, and I was thus enabled to communicate easily with them. I took a sketch of Chea-clach, their head chief, of whose inauguration I heard the following account from an eye-witness. On his father becoming too old to fulfil the duties of head chief, the son was called upon by the tribe to take his place; on which occasion he left for the mountains for the ostensible purpose of fasting and dreaming for thirty days and nights; these Indians, like all other tribes, placing great confidence in dreams, and believing that it is necessary to undergo a long fast whenever they are desirous of inducing one of any importance. At the end of the period assigned, the tribe prepared a great feast. After covering himself with a thick covering of grease and goosedown, he rushed into the midst of the village, seized a small dog, and began devouring it alive, this being a customary preliminary on such occasions. The tribe collected about him singing and dancing in the wildest manner, on which he approached those whom he most regarded and bit their bare shoulders or arms, which was considered by them as a high mark of distinction, more especially those from whom he took the piece clean out and swallowed it. Of the women he took no notice.

I have seen many men on the north-west coast of the Pacific who bore frightful marks of what they regarded as an honourable distinction; nor is this the only way in which their persons become disfigured. I have myself seen a young girl bleeding most profusely from gashes inflicted by her own hand over her arms and bosom with a sharp flint, on the occasion of losing a near relative. After some time spent in singing and dancing, Chea-clach retired with his people to the feast prepared inside a large lodge, which consisted principally of whale's blubber, in their opinion the greatest of all delicacies, although they have salmon, cod, sturgeon, and other excellent fish in great abundance.

All the tribes about here subsist almost entirely upon fish, which they obtain with so little trouble during all seasons of the year, that they are probably the laziest race of people in the world.   Sturgeon are caught in considerable numbers, and here attain an enormous size, weighing from four to six hundred weight; this is done by means of a long pointed spear handle seventy to eighty feet in length, fitted into, but not actually fastened to, a barbed spear-head, to which is attached a line, with which they feel along the bottom of the river where the sturgeon are found lying at the spawning season. Upon feeling the fish the barbed spear is driven in and the handle withdrawn. The fish is then gradually drawn in by the line, which being very long, allows the sturgeon to waste his great strength, so that he can with safety be taken into the canoe or towed ashore. Most of their fishing lines are formed of a long seaweed, which is often found 150 feet long, of equal thickness throughout the whole length, and about as thick as a black-lead pencil; while wet it is very strong. Their fish-hooks are made of pine-roots, made something in the shape of our ordinary hooks, but attached differently to the line; the barb is made of bone.

Clams are in great plenty, and are preyed on in great numbers by the crows, who seize them in their claws and fly up with them to some height, and then let them drop on the rocks, which of course smashes the shells to pieces. I have watched dozens of them at this singular employment. A small oyster of a fine flavour is found in the bays in great plenty. Seal, wild ducks and geese, are also in great numbers.

The Indians are extremely fond of herring-roe, which they collect in the following manner:—Cedar branches are sunk to the bottom of the river in shallow places by placing upon them a few heavy stones, taking care not to cover the green foliage, as the fish prefer spawning on anything green. The branches are all covered by the next morning with the spawn, which is washed off into their waterproof baskets, to the bottom of which it sinks; it is then squeezed by the hand into small balls and dried, and is very palatable.

The only other vegetable besides the camas and wappatoos that the Indians use, are roots of fern roasted, which here grow to a very large size.

Slavery in its most cruel form exists among the Indians of the whole coast, from California to Behring's Straits, the stronger tribes making slaves of all the others they can conquer. In the interior, where there is but little warfare, slavery does not exist. On the coast a custom prevails which authorizes the seizure and en-slavement, unless ransomed by his friends, of every Indian met with at a distance from his tribe, although they may not be at war with each other. The master exercises the power of life and death over his slaves, whom he sacrifices at pleasure in gratification of any superstitious or other whim of the moment.

One morning while I was sketching, I saw upon the rocks the dead body of a young woman, thrown out to the vultures and crows, whom I had seen a few days previously walking about in perfect health. Mr. Finlayson, the gentleman in charge of Fort Victoria, accompanied me to the lodge she belonged to, where we found an Indian woman, her mistress, who made light of her death, and was doubtless the cause of it. She told us that a slave had no right to burial, and became perfectly furious when Mr. Finlayson told her that the slave was far better than herself. "I," she exclaimed, "the daughter of a chief, no better than a dead slave!" and bridling up with all the dignity she could assume, she stalked out, and next morning she had up her lodge and was gone. I was also told by an eye-witness, of a chief, who having erected a colossal idol of wood, sacrificed five slaves to it, barbarously murdering them at its base, and asking in a boasting manner who amongst them could afford to kill so many slaves.

These Indians also flatten their heads, and are far more superstitious than any I have met with. They believe, for instance, that if they can procure the hair of an enemy and confine it with a frog in a hole, the head from which it came will suffer all the torments that the frog endures in its living grave. They are never seen to spit without carefully obliterating all traces of their saliva. This they do lest an enemy should find it, in which case they believe he would have the power of doing them some injury. They always spit on their blankets, if they happen to wear one at the time.

I was indebted to the superstitious fears which they attached to my pictures for the safety and ease with which I mingled amongst them. One of them gave me a great deal of annoyance by continually following and watching me wherever I went, for the purpose of warning the other Indians against my sketching them, telling them that it would expose them to all sorts of ill luck. I repeatedly requested him to desist, but in vain. At last I bethought me of looking steadily at himself, paper and pencil in hand, as if in the act of taking his likeness; when he became greatly alarmed, and asked me what I was about. I replied, "I am taking a sketch of you." He earnestly begged of me to stop, and promised never to annoy me again.

These Indians have a great dance, which is called "The Medicine Mask Dance;" this is performed both before and after any important action of the tribe, such as fishing, gathering camas, or going on a war party, either for the purpose of gaining the goodwill of the Great Spirit in their undertaking, or else in honour of him for the success which has attended them. Six or eight of the principal men of the tribe, generally medicine-men, adorn themselves with masks cut out of some soft light wood and with feathers, highly painted and ornamented, with the eyes and mouth ingeniously made to open and shut. In their hands they hold carved rattles, which are shaken in time to a monotonous song or humming noise (for there are no words to it) which is sung by the whole company as they slowly dance round and round in a circle.

Among the Clal-lums and other tribes inhabiting this region, I have never heard any traditions as to their former origin, although such traditions are common amongst those on the east side of the Rocky Mountains. They do not believe in any future state of punishment, although in this world they suppose themselves exposed to the malicious designs of the skoocoom, or evil genius, to whom they attribute all their misfortune and ill luck.

The good spirit is called Hias-Soch-a-la-Ti-Yah, that is, the great high chief, from whom they obtain all that is good in this life, and to whose happy and peaceful hunting-grounds they will all eventually go to reside for ever in comfort and abundance. The medicine-men of the tribe are supposed to possess a mysterious influence with these two spirits, either for good or evil. They form a secret society, the initiation into which is accompanied with great ceremony and much expense. The candidate has to prepare a feast for his friends and all who choose to partake of it, and make presents to the other medicine-men. A lodge is prepared for him which he enters, and remains alone for three days and nights without food, whilst those already initiated keep dancing and singing round the lodge during the whole time. After this feast, which is supposed to endue him with wonderful skill, he is taken up apparently lifeless and plunged into the nearest cold water, where they rub and wash him until he revives: this they call "washing the dead." As soon as he revives, he runs into the woods, and soon returns dressed as a medicine-man, which generally consists of the light down of the goose stuck all over their bodies and heads with thick grease, and a mantle of frayed cedar bark, with the medicine rattle in his hand. He now collects all his property, blankets, shells, and ornaments, and distributes the whole amongst his friends, trusting for his future support to the fees of his profession. The dancing and singing are still continued with great vigour, during the division of the property, at the conclusion of which the whole party again sit down to feast, apparently with miraculous appetites, the quantity of food consumed being perfectly incredible.

Their lodges are the largest buildings of any description that I have met with amongst Indians. They are divided in the interior into compartments, so as to accommodate eight or ten families, and are well built, considering that the boards are split from the logs with bone wedges; but they succeed in getting them out with great smoothness and regularity. I took a sketch one day while a party were engaged in gambling in the centre of the lodge. The game is called lehallum, and is played with ten small circular pieces of wood, one of which is marked black; these pieces are shuffled about rapidly by the player between two bundles of frayed cedar bark. His opponent suddenly stops his shuffling, and endeavours to guess in which bundle the blackened piece is concealed. They are so passionately fond of this game that they frequently pass two or three consecutive days and nights at it without ceasing.

Saw-se-a the head chief of the Cowitchins, from the Gulf of Georgia, an inveterate gambler, was engaged at the game. He had come to the Esquimalt on a friendly visit. This chief was a great warrior in his younger days, and received an arrow through the cheek in one of his battles. He took many captives, whom he usually sold to the tribes further north, thus diminishing their chance of escaping back through a hostile country to their own people, the northern tribes making slaves only of those living south of them. He possessed much of what is considered wealth amongst the Indians, and it gradually accumulated from tributes which he exacted from his people. On his possessions reaching a certain amount it is customary to make a great feast, to which all contribute. The neighbouring chiefs with

whom he is in amity are invited, and at the conclusion of
the entertainment, he distributes all he has collected
since the last feast, perhaps three or four years preceding, among his guests as presents. The amount of property thus collected and given away by a chief is sometimes very considerable. I have heard of one possessing as many as twelve bales of blankets, from twenty to

11. Culchillum [Son of Saw-se-a, with medicine cap]
Courtesy of Royal Ontario Museum

thirty guns, with numberless pots, kettles, and pans,
knives, and other articles of cutlery, and great quantities
of beads, and other trinkets, as well as numerous beautiful Chinese boxes, which find their way here from the
Sandwich Islands. The object in thus giving his
treasures away is to add to his own importance in the
eyes of others, his own people often boasting of how

much their chief had given away, and exhibiting with pride such things as they had received themselves from him.

I also took a sketch of his son, No. 11, Culchillum. He had a medicine cap on, to which he attached great importance. It was made of human hair, taken from the heads of persons killed in battle, and ornamented with feathers. This, he told me, he only wore on great occasions, such as his present visit to the Clal-lums. On my expressing a wish to purchase it, he told me that he valued it too highly to part with it; nor would he allow me to take it to my tent to finish this sketch without himself accompanying it, for fear it might be deprived of some of its magical properties.

As I was desirous to coast round the Straits of De Fuca and visit the tribes on its shores, I employed Cheaclach the head chief and four of his people to take me and the interpreter of the fort round the straits in his canoe; and on the morning of the 6th of May we started about 10 o'clock, running up the east side of Vancouver's Island, and crossed the canal De Aro to the main land. On nearing an Indian village, which contained, as I afterwards found, between five and six hundred Indians, they came rushing down to the beach in an attitude apparently hostile, and as the boats of the exploring expedition had been attacked the year before at the same place, we naturally felt some apprehension for our safety.

We had no sooner approached the shore than a dense crowd surrounded us, wading up to their middles in water, and seizing our canoe dragged us all high and dry upon the shore, and inquired what we wanted. I replied, that I would explain my business to their chief, who immediately stepped forward in a friendly manner. Having told him that my business was to visit all the Indians, and to take likenesses of the head chiefs and great warriors, he took me to his lodge, where I seated myself on a mat with him in front of me and commenced my drawing. In a few minutes the place was crowded, and when it could hold no more, the people clambered to the top of the lodge and tore off the mats from the

155

supports, to which they clung, one upon another, like
a swarm of bees, peering down upon us. Look which
way I could it seemed one solid mass of hideous faces,
daubed with red and white mud.

I hastily finished my sketch and hurried away, first
giving the chief a plug of tobacco for his civility. His
name was Chea-clach, chief of the Clallums. On coming over I found the wind so strong that I thought it
advisable to risk an encampment, and pitched my tent
about two hundred yards from the village. We were
soon surrounded by hundreds of Indians, the chief
among the rest. I gave the latter some supper, and all
the news, which he eagerly inquired after, and on my
telling him I was tired and wished to go to sleep, which
I could not do while so many of his people were about,
he instantly arose and desired them to retire, which was
promptly obeyed, he going away with them.

About 10 o'clock at night I strolled into the village,
and on hearing a great noise in one of the lodges I
entered it, and found an old woman supporting one of
the handsomest Indian girls I had even seen. She was
in a state of nudity. Cross-legged and naked, in the
middle of the room sat the medicine-man, with a wooden
dish of water before him; twelve or fifteen other men
were sitting round the lodge. The object in view was
to cure the girl of a disease affecting her side. As soon
as my presence was noticed a space was cleared for me
to sit down. The officiating medicine-man appeared in
a state of profuse perspiration from the exertions he had
used, and soon took his seat among the rest as if quite
exhausted; a younger medicine-man then took his place
in front of the bowl, and close beside the patient.
Throwing off his blanket he commenced singing and
gesticulating in the most violent manner, whilst the

others kept time by beating with little sticks on hollow wooden bowls and drums, singing continually. After exercising himself in this manner for about half an hour, until the perspiration ran down his body, he darted suddenly upon the young woman, catching hold of her side with his teeth and shaking her for a few minutes, while the patient seemed to suffer great agony. He then relinquished his hold, and cried out he had got it, at the same time holding his hands to his mouth; after which he plunged them in the water and pretended to hold down with great difficulty the disease which he had extracted, lest it might spring out and return to its victim.

At length, having obtained the mastery over it, he turned round to me in an exulting manner, and held something up between the finger and thumb of each hand, which had the appearance of a piece of cartilage, whereupon one of the Indians sharpened his knife, and divided it in two, leaving one end in each hand. One of the pieces he threw into the water, and the other into the fire, accompanying the action with a diabolical noise, which none but a medicine-man can make. After which he got up perfectly satisfied with himself, although the poor patient seemed to be anything but relieved by the violent treatment she had undergone.

May 7th—We this morning left our encampment before daylight, without waiting to pay our respects to the chief. In the afternoon we touched at Whitby's Island, which divides the Straits of De Fuca from Puget's Sound. A Catholic mission had been established on the island some few years before, but was obliged to be given up, owing to the turbulent disposition of the Indians, who, though friendly to the Hudson's Bay Company as traders, look with great suspicion upon others who attempt to settle there, fearing that the whites would attempt to dispossess them of their lands.

On approaching the village of Toanichum, we perceived two stout bastions of logs, well calculated for defence in Indian warfare, and built with considerable skill. As our canoe neared the land, I observed them hurrying towards these bastions, and shortly afterwards we heard several shots. Supposing this to be intended as a salute, we drew still nearer, and were astonished at hearing more discharges, and seeing the balls fall near our canoe. My Indians immediately ceased paddling, and it was with the utmost difficulty that I could prevail on them to proceed. Had we shown the least inclination to retreat, I have no doubt that the firing would have been continued, and with better aim. However, on my landing and asking what they meant, they said it was only done for the purpose of letting us know that they were in possession of fire-arms.

They afterwards treated me very hospitably. Lock-hi-num, the chief, offered us all the supplies at his command. It was, however, with the greatest difficulty that I could prevail on him to let me take his likeness; but at last I succeeded, by showing him the likenesses of several other chiefs, and telling him that they were intended to be shown to his Great Mother, the Queen, who no doubt would be much disappointed if his was not amongst the rest. I remained amongst them two or three hours, and sketched the village. I also succeeded in getting a very good-looking woman, the wife of the second chief, to sit for me. She had the flattest head of any I had seen in that vicinity. We then crossed over to the south side of the strait, and encamped for the night.

May 8th—Proceeded up the south side of the straits in our canoe, and encamped on a long sand spit, projecting into the straits three or four miles.

May 9th—Made a portage across the spit, and by the evening reached I-eh-nus, a Clallum village or fort, It was composed of a double row of strong pickets, the outer ones about twenty feet high, and the inner row about five feet, enclosing a space of 150 feet square. The whole of this inner space is roofed in, and divided into small compartments, or pens, for the use of each separate family. There were about 200 of the tribe in the fort at the time of my arrival. Their chief, Yates-sut-soot, received me with great cordiality. I remained with them three days, and all the tribe treated me with kindness, with one solitary exception, proceeding from a superstitious fear that the presence of a white man in a lodge would produce sickness in the family. Yates-sut-soot was very apprehensive of an attack from the Macaw Indians, and believing my powers and influence as a medicine-man to be of much importance, eagerly asked me which side I would take, in the event of their coming. I replied, that as long as they treated me well I would be their friend.

A few months before my arrival a great battle had been fought with the Macaws, in which the Clallums had suffered very severely. It originated in the Clallums having taken possession of the body of a whale which had been killed by the Macaws, but had got away, and was drifted by the current to the village. The Macaws demanded a share of the spoil, and also the return of their spears, some fifteen or twenty in number, which were sticking in the carcase; both demands were refused, and a feeling of animosity sprang up between the tribes.

There are few whales now caught on the coast, but the Indians are most enthusiastic in the hunt, and the blubber is highly prized amongst them; it is cut into strips about four inches wide and two feet long, and eaten generally with dried fish.

Their manner of catching the whale is ingenious, and from the description which I received of the hunt must be very exciting. Upon a whale being seen blowing in the offing, they rush down to their large canoes, and push off with ten or twelve men in each. Each canoe is furnished with a number of strong seal-skin bags filled with air, and made with great care and skill, capable of containing about ten gallons each. To each bag is attached a barbed spear-head, made of bone or iron, when they can get it, by a strong string, eight or nine feet long, and in the socket of the spear-head is fitted a handle, seven or eight feet in length. Upon coming up with the whale, the barbed heads with the bags attached are driven into him and the handles withdrawn. The attack is continually renewed, until the whale is no longer able to sink from the buoyancy of the bags, when he is despatched and towed ashore. They are sometimes led twenty or thirty miles out to sea in the chase, but such is the admirable construction of their canoes, and so skilfully are they managed, that an accident rarely happens.

A few months after the quarrel about the whale the brother of Yellow-cum, the head chief of the Macaws, went to Fort Victoria to trade for ammunition and other necessaries, and on his return was attacked by the Clallums. He and one of his men were killed, but three others escaped, and succeeded in getting to Cape Flattery, where Yellow-cum resided. Immediately upon hearing of the death of his brother, Yellow-cum fitted out twelve of his largest canoes, with twenty warriors in each, and made a sudden descent upon I-eh-nus; but he soon perceived that he had little chance of success while the Clallums remained within their enclosure completely protected by the logs, while his men were exposed without any shelter to the galling fire which was kept up through the openings between the pickets. He accordingly sent some of his party to the westward side of the fort, who set fire to the grass and wood, which soon communicated with the buildings, while he and the rest of his party kept watch to prevent any from escaping. The Clallums were soon forced to rush out and cover the retreat of their women and children into the mountains. Yates-sut-soot and Yellow-cum fought with great bravery hand to hand, with nothing but their knives, until they were separated in the mêlée. I saw one of the Clallums who had been shockingly gashed in the battle, having had to run through a long line of the Macaws, each of whom made a cut at him as he passed. The buildings were only partly consumed. Yellow-cum took eighteen prisoners, mostly females, who were made slaves, and he had eight heads stuck on poles placed in the bows of the canoes on his return. These heads are carried to their village, and placed in front of the lodge of the warriors who had killed them as trophies. These Indians do not scalp their enemies.

Near the village are numerous singular graves with different erections over them, on which the Indians place the offerings for the dead.

May 12*th*—We left with the intention of returning to Vancouver's Island, but the wind being very violent we had to put back to the shore, which coasted for twelve or fourteen miles, until we came to the mouth of a river. The land to the south of us rises

in one continuous range of high mountains far as the
eye can reach, the peaks of many of which are covered
with snow, even at this period of the year. We ascended
the river about a mile to an Indian fishing station called
Suck. The whole breadth of the stream is obstructed
by stakes and open work of willow and other branches,
with holes at intervals leading into wicker compartments, which the fish enter in their way up the river
from the sea. Once in they cannot get out, as the holes
are formed with wicker work inside shaped something
like a funnel or a wire mouse-trap. In this preserve
they are speared without trouble when required, and the
village has thus a constant supply of food. They were
catching great quantities at the time of my arrival, and
we obtained an abundant supply for a small piece of
tobacco.

These Indians also take a great many ducks by
means of a fine net stretched between two posts about
thirty feet high, and fifty or sixty feet apart. This is
erected in a narrow valley through which the ducks fly
in the evening. A smoky fire is made at the bottom of
the net, which prevents the ducks from seeing it, and
when they fly against it they become confused and fall
down, when they are seized by the Indians.

The wind being still too strong for us to venture,
we remained until the 14th. Chaw-u-wit, the chief's
daughter, allowed me to take her likeness. Whilst she
was sitting a great many of the Indians surrounded us,
causing her much annoyance, as their native bashful-
ness renders all squaws peculiarly sensitive to any public
notice or ridicule. She was, perhaps, about the best-
looking girl I had seen in the straits, which is certainly
no very high compliment to the rest of the female population.

Chea-clack considering that our canoe was too small, succeeded in changing it for a larger one, and at 3 o'clock A.M. we embarked and proceeded to make a traverse of thirty-two miles in an open sea. When we had been out for about a couple of hours the wind increased to a perfect gale, and blowing against an ebb tide caused a heavy swell. We were obliged to keep one man constantly baling to prevent our being swamped.

The Indians on board now commenced one of their wild chants, which increased to a perfect yell whenever a wave larger than the rest approached; this was accompanied with blowing and spitting against the wind as if they were in angry contention with the evil spirit of the storm. It was altogether a scene of the most wild and intense excitement: the mountainous waves roaming round our little canoe as if to engulph us every moment, the wind howling over our heads, and the yelling Indians, made it actually terrific. I was surprised at the dexterity with which they managed the canoe, all putting out their paddles on the windward side whenever a wave broke, thus breaking its force and guiding the spray over our heads to the other side of the boat.

It was with the greatest anxiety that I watched each coming wave as it came thundering down, and I must confess that I felt considerable fear as to the event. However, we arrived safely at the fort at 2 P.M., without further damage than what we suffered from intense fatigue, as might be expected, from eleven hours' hard work, thoroughly soaked and without food; but even this soon passed away before the cheerful fire and "hearty" dinner with which we were welcomed at Fort Victoria. One of the Indians told me he had no fear during the storm, except on my account, as his brethren

could easily reach the shore by swimming, even should
the distance have been ten miles.

A couple of days after·my arrival at the fort, I was
engaged in taking the likeness of an Indian. The door
of my room was suddenly thrown open, and an Indian
entered of a very plain and unprepossessing appearance.
As I was unwilling to be disturbed, I rather unceremon-
iously dismissed the intruder, and closed the door on
him, supposing him to be some common Indian; for were
I to admit all comers, I should have been annoyed from
morning till night. About half an hour afterwards, Mr.
Finlayson came in, and told me that the great Yellow-
cum, the head chief of the Macaws at Cape Flattery,
had arrived at the fort. I had heard so much of this
chief, both from his enemies, the Clallums at I-eh-nus,
and the Indians at Fort Vancouver, that I had determined to go to Cape Flattery, a distance of sixty miles, to
see him. I was therefore very glad of his coming, as it
would save me the journey; and I immediately went out
in search of him, and was not a little astonished and
vexed to find in him the visitor I had so rudely sent out
of my room. I of course apologized, by stating my
ignorance of who he was, and told him how anxious I
had been to see him, and of my intention of going to Cape
Flattery for that purpose. He said that he willingly
acquitted me of any intentional insult; but he had felt
extremely mortified at being treated so before so many
Indians.

He accompanied me to my room, where I made a
sketch of him, and had from him a recital of much of his
private history. Yellow-cum's father was the pilot of
the unfortunate "Tonquin," the vessel sent out by John
Jacob Astor to trade with the Indians north of Vancouver's Island, mentioned in Washington Irving's

"Astoria." He was the only survivor who escaped from the vessel previous to her being blown up, the rest of the unfortunate crew having been butchered on board or blown up with the ship. It was impossible to obtain a clear narrative of this melancholy event, as no white man lived to tell the tale.

Yellow-cum is the wealthiest man of his tribe. His property consists principally of slaves and ioquas, a small shell found at Cape Flattery, and only there, in great abundance. These shells are used as money, and a great traffic is carried on among all the tribes by means of them. They are obtained at the bottom of the sea, at a considerable depth, by means of a long pole stuck in a flat board about fifteen inches square. From this board a number of bone pieces project, which, when pressed down, enter the hollow ends of the shells, which seem to be attached to the bottom by their small ends. The shells stick on the pieces, and are thus brought to the surface. They are from an inch and a half to two inches in length, and are white, slender, and hollow, and tapering to a point; slightly curved, and about the size of an ordinary tobacco-pipe stem. They are valuable in proportion to their length, and their value increases according to a fixed ratio, forty shells being the standard number to extend a fathom's length; which number, in that case, is equal in value to a beaver skin; but if thirty-nine be found large enough to make the fathom, it would be worth two beavers' skins; if thirty-eight, three skins; and so on, increasing one beaver skin for every shell less than the standard number.

Yellow-cum presented me with a pair of ear ornaments of these shells, consisting of seventy or eighty shells in each. His wealth also partly consisted of sea otter skins, which are the most valuable fur found on the North American coast, their usual value in the tariff being twelve blankets; two blankets being equal to a gun; tobacco and ammunition and other things in porportion. The blanket is the standard by which the value of all articles on the north-west coast is calculated. Independent of his wealth, he possesses vast influence over all the tribes, and has become head chief from his own personal prowess and ability, and not from any hereditary claim to that dignity. It may be adduced, as a proof of the courage of this chief, and of his personal confidence, that I saw him at the fort surrounded by, and in cheerful conversation with, several of the chiefs of the Clallums, with whom he had often been engaged in deadly conflict. His prudence, however, led him to remain inside the fort after nightfall.

I visited the lodges of the Eus-ā-nich Indians, who were on a visit. The chief was very rich, and had eight wives with him. I made him understand, by showing him some sketches, that I wished to take his likeness. This was, however, opposed so violently by his ladies that I was glad to escape out of reach of their tongues, as they were all chattering together, while he sat like a Grand Turk, evidently flattered by the interest they showed for his welfare. A few days afterwards I met the chief some distance from his camp, and alone, when he willingly consented to let me take his likeness upon my giving him a piece of tobacco.

In one of my daily excursions I was particularly struck by the ugliness of an Indian whom I met. Upon inquiry, I found he was Shawstun, the head chief of the Sinahomas. He inquired very earnestly if my sketching him would not involve the risk of his dying; and after I had finished the sketch, and given him a piece of tobacco, he held it up for some moments, and said it was a small recompense for risking his life. He followed me afterwards for two or three days, begging of me to destroy the picture; and at last, to get rid of him, I made a rough copy of it, which I tore up in his presence, pretending that it was the original.

I remained on Vancouver's Island until the 10th of June; and perhaps it would be as well, before my taking leave of it, to give a general summary of the information I acquired, from personal observation, and from the gentlemen of the Hudson's Bay Company, respecting the characteristics of the different tribes inhabiting these regions.

The Indians south of the Columbia River tattoo themselves below the mouth, which gives a light blue appearance to the countenance. Those at the mouth of the Columbia, and for a hundred miles up it, as well as those at Puget's Sound, and the Straits of De Fuca, and at the southern part of Vancouver's Island, have their heads flattened down in their infancy, as represented in the sketches of the Chinook tribe. Those inhabiting the north part of the island have their heads compressed into a conical shape during infancy. This is done by means of a bandage, which is wound round the forehead, and gradually tightened, until the head becomes of the required shape.

The next tribe lying north of these on the continent are called by the voyageurs "Babines," or Big-lips, from the fact of the females having their under lips enlarged by the insertion of a piece of wood. A small, slender piece of bone is inserted through the under lip of the infant, from below upwards, and is gradually enlarged, until a flat piece of wood three inches long and an inch and a half wide has caused the lip to protrude to a frightful extent, the protrusion increasing with age.

Great importance is attached to the size of the lip, as it constitutes the standard of female beauty; it also marks the difference between native free women and their slaves.

When the stick is removed on any occasion the lip drops down to the chin, presenting one of the most disgusting spectacles imaginable.

The men sometimes wear a ring through the nose, formed of bone, or brass if they can get it; but the practice is not universal. They wear a cap made of the fibres of cedar-bark, woven very finely together, and a blanket made from the wool of the mountain sheep; they are very valuable, and take years in making. For one which I procured with great difficulty I had to pay five pounds of tobacco, ten charges of ammunition, one blanket, one pound of beads, two check shirts, and one ounce of vermilion.

The next tribes, still more north than the last, insert beads of various colours, two-thirds of their depth, into the whole length of the upper lip, giving it the appearance of so much bead work.

In the interior of New Caledonia, which is east of Vancouver's Island and north of the Columbia, among the tribe called "Taw-wa-tins," who are also Babines, and also among other tribes in their neighbourhood, the custom prevails of burning the bodies, with circumstances of peculiar barbarity to the widows of the deceased. The dead body of the husband is laid naked upon a large heap of resinous wood, his wife is then placed upon the body and covered over with a skin; the pile is then lighted, and the poor woman is compelled to remain until she is nearly suffocated, when she is allowed to descend as best she can through the smoke and flames. No sooner, however, does she reach the ground than she is expected to prevent the body from becoming distorted by the action of the fire on the muscles and sinews; and whenever such an event takes place she must, with her bare hands, restore the burning corpse to its proper position; her person being the whole time exposed to the scorching effects of the intense heat. Should she fail in the due performance of this indispensable rite, from weakness or the intensity of her pain, she is held up by some one until the body is consumed. A continual singing and beating of drums is kept up throughout the ceremony, which drowns her cries. Afterwards she must collect the unconsumed pieces of bone and ashes and put them into a bag made for the purpose, which she has to carry on her back for three years; remaining for the time a slave to her husband's relations, and being neither allowed to wash nor comb herself for the whole time, so that she soon becomes a most disgusting object. At the expiration of the three years, a feast is given by her tormentors, who invite all the friends and relations of her and themselves. At the commencement they deposit, with great ceremony, the remains of the burnt dead in a box, which they affix to the top of a high pole and dance around it. The widow is then stripped naked and smeared from head to foot with fish oil, over which one of the bystanders throws a quantity of swan's down, covering her entire person. She is then obliged to dance with the others. After all this is over she is free to marry again, if she have the inclination and courage enough to venture on a second risk of being roasted alive and the subsequent horrors.

It has often happened that a widow who has married a second husband, in the hope perhaps of not outliving him, committed suicide in the event of her second husband's death, rather than undergo a second ordeal. I was unable to learn any explanation of the motive for these cruel rites, and can only account for them in the natural selfishness, laziness, and cruelty of the Indians, who probably hope by these means to render their wives more attentive to their personal ease and comfort; whilst, at the same time, it secures them from assassination either by a jealous or an errant spouse.

June 9th—The Company's vessel which annually
brings out goods and despatches for the interior having
arrived, Mr. Finlayson was anxious to forward the letters on, and, knowing that I was soon to start on my
return, he asked me if I would take them to Fort Vancouver. I was very anxious to do anything in my power
in return for the hospitality and kindness I had received,
and accordingly commenced my preparations for starting on the following morning. An old Nasqually chief
had come down to the coast to look for a favourite wife
who had been carried off by some of his predatory neighbours, and, as he supposed, had been sold somewhere in
Vancouver's Island. But, not being successful in his
search, he was now returning, and I engaged to go with
him. He was very glad of my company, as my being
the bearer of despatches would be a certain protection
for the whole party from whatever Indians we might
meet. I asked him how he had managed to escape on
coming down, and he showed me an old piece of news-
paper, which he said he held up whenever he met with
strange Indians, and that they, supposing it to be a
letter for Fort Victoria, had allowed him to pass without molestation.

The gentlemen in charge of the various posts have
frequent occasion to send letters, sometimes for a considerable distance, when it is either inconvenient or

impossible for them to fit out a canoe with their own men
to carry it. In such cases the letter is given to an Indian,
who carries it as far as suits his convenience and safety.
He then sells the letter to another, who carries it until
he finds an opportunity of selling it to advantage; it is
thus passed on and sold until it arrives at its destination,
gradually increasing in value according to the distance,
and the last possessor receiving the reward for its safe
delivery. In this manner letters are frequently sent with
perfect security, and with much greater rapidity than
could be done otherwise.

June 10*th*—Early in the morning I embarked with
the chief, a wife he had brought with him, and two slaves;
we paddled on all day, and made good progress. In the
evening we encamped under a high rock, where we found
some goose eggs, of which we made a hearty supper.

June 11*th*—We came to a rocky island, which was
covered with thousands of seal, playing and basking in
the sun. We shot several of them, as the Indians highly
prize the blubber as food; but it was far too oily for my
stomach. I, however, shot a white-headed eagle and
roasted him for my supper, and found him particularly
good eating.

June 12*th*—In the evening we arrived at an Indian
village, where we stopped for the night; the whole surface of the water at this place seemed to be alive with
the gambols of a small silvery fish, dancing and glisten-
ing in the rays of the setting sun. This fish is about the
size of our sardines, and is caught in immense numbers;
it is called there ulé kun, and is much prized on account
of its delicacy and extraordinary fatness. When dried
this fish will burn from one end to the other with a clear,
steady light like a candle.

There were several canoes out fishing in the evening, and they caught them with astonishing rapidity: this is done by means of an instrument about seven feet long, the handle is about three feet, into which is fixed a curved wooden blade about four feet, something the shape of a sabre, with the edge at the back.   In this edge, at the distance of about an inch and a half, are inserted sharp bone teeth, about an inch long.   The Indian stands in the canoe and, holding it as he would a paddle, draws it edgeways with both hands rapidly through the dense mass of fish, which are so thick that every tooth will strike a fish.   One knock across the thwarts safely deposits them in the bottom of the canoe.   This is done with such rapidity that they never use nets for this description of fishing.

June 13*th*—To-day as we neared the shore we perceived two deer grazing, which the Indians were anxious to go after, but as we had already lost some time on the way I was more anxious to proceed.   While at a very long distance I fired my double-barrelled gun at them, more in the hope of driving them away than of killing them, when, much to the astonishment of both myself and the Indians, one of them fell dead.   The chief looked very hard at me and then examined the gun, apparently in doubt whether the magic was in the gun or myself.   I said nothing, but took it all as a matter of course, whilst the Indians evidently looked upon me as a person not to be trifled with.   We had a splendid supper that evening on our venison, and I took good care not to test the qualities of my gun again before them, although they often asked me.

June 14*th*—Whilst passing an isolated rock, standing six or seven feet high above the water, and a little more than four feet in circumference, the old chief asked

me if I knew what it had originally been. On my replying in the negative, he told me the following legend:—

"It is many moons since a Nasqually family lived
near this spot. It consisted of a widow with four sons,—
one of them was by her first husband, the other three by
the second. The three younger sons treated their elder
brother with great unkindness, refusing him any share
of the produce of their hunting and fishing; he, on the
contrary, wishing to conciliate them, always gave them
a share of his spoils. He, in fact, was a great medicine-
man, although this was unknown to them, and, being
tired of their harsh treatment, which no kindness on his
part seemed to soften, he at length resolved to retaliate.
He accordingly one day entered the lodge where they
were feasting and told them that there was a large seal
a short distance off. They instantly seized their spears
and started in the direction he pointed out, and, coming
up to the animal, the eldest drove his spear into it. This
seal was 'a great medicine,' a familiar of the elder
brother, who had himself created him for the occasion.
The foremost of them had no sooner driven in his spear
than he found it impossible to disengage his hand from
the handle, or to draw it out; the two others drove in
their spears with the like effect. The seal now took to
the water, dragging them after it, and swam far out to
sea. Having travelled on for many miles they saw an
island in the distance, towards which the seal made. On
nearing the shore they found, for the first time, they
could remove their hands from their spears. They
accordingly landed, and, supposing themselves in some
enemy's country, they hid themselves in a clump of
bushes from observation. While lying concealed they
saw a diminutive canoe coming round a point in the distance, paddled by a very little man, who, when he came

opposite to where they were, anchored his boat with a
stone attached to a long line, without perceiving them.
He now sprang over the side and, diving down, remained
a long time under water. At length he rose to the surface, and brought with him a large fish, which he threw
into the boat: this he repeated several times, each time
looking in to count the fish he had caught. The three
brothers, being very hungry, one of them offered to swim
out while the little man was under water and steal one
of the fish. This he safely accomplished before the
return of the fisherman; but the little fellow no sooner
returned with another fish than he discovered that one
of those already caught was missing, and, stretching out
his hand, he passed it slowly along the horizon, until it
pointed directly to their place of concealment. He now
drew up his anchor and paddled to the shore, and immediately discovered the three brothers, and, being as
miraculously strong as he was diminutive, he tied their
hands and feet together, and, throwing them into his
canoe, jumped in and paddled back in the direction from
whence he had come. Having rounded the distant point,
where they had first descried him, they came to a village
inhabited by a race of people as small as their captor,
their houses, boats, and utensils being all in proportion
to themselves.

"The three brothers were then taken out and thrown,
bound as they were, into a lodge, while a council was
convened to decide upon their fate. During the sitting
of the council an immense flock of birds, resembling
geese, but much larger, pounced down upon the inhabitants and commenced a violent attack. These birds had
the power of throwing their sharp quills like the porcupine, and, although the little warriors fought with great
valour, they soon became covered with the piercing

darts, and all sank insensible on the ground. When all
resistance had ceased the birds took to flight and disappeared.

"The brothers had witnessed the conflict from their
place of confinement, and with much labour had succeeded in releasing themselves from their bonds, when
they went to the battle ground and commenced pulling
the quills from the apparently lifeless bodies; but no
sooner had they done this than all instantly returned to
consciousness. When all of them had become well
again they wished to express their gratitude to their
preservers, and offered to grant whatsoever they should
desire. The brothers requested to be sent back to their
own country. A council was accordingly called to decide
on the easiest mode of doing so, and they eventually
determined upon employing a whale for the purpose.
The brothers were then seated on the back of the monster, and proceeded in the direction of Nasqually. However, when they had reached about half way the whale
began to think what a fool he was for carrying them
instead of turning them into porpoises and letting them
swim home themselves. Now, the whale is considered
as a 'Soch-a-li-ti-yah,' or Great Spirit, although not the
same as the 'Hias-Soch-a-li-ti-yah,' or Great High
Spirit, possessing greater powers than all other animals
put together, and no sooner had he thought upon the
matter than he carried it into effect. This, accordingly,
is the way that the porpoises first came into existence,
and accounts for their being constantly at war with the
seals, one of which species was the cause of their misfortunes. After the three brothers had so strangely
disappeared, their mother came down to the beach and
remained there for days, watching for their return and
bewailing their absence with tears. Whilst thus engaged

one day the whale happened to pass by and, taking pity on her distress, turned her into that stone."

I could not observe any very special peculiarity in the formation of this rock while paddling past it in a canoe; and, at least from the points of observation presented to my eye, no resemblance to the human figure, such as the conclusion of the legend might lead us to anticipate, appeared to be traceable. Standing, however, as this rock does, entirely isolated, and without any other being visible for miles around, it has naturally become an object of special note to the Indians, and is not uncalculated, from its solitary position, to be made the scene of some of the fanciful creations of their superstitious credulity.

June 15th—We arrived at Nasqually, where I procured horses to take me to the Cowlitz River. I again crossed Prairie de Bute and Mud Mountain, and arrived at my old friend Kiscox's lodge on the evening of the third day; but, to my astonishment, I found him and his family unusually distant in their manners, and the children even running away from me and hiding. At last he asked if I had not taken the likeness of a woman when last amongst them. I said that I had, and mentioned her name, Caw-wacham, alluding to the portrait of a woman and child, No. 10, page 141; a dead silence ensued, nor could I get the slightest answer to my inquiries. Upon leaving the lodge, I met a half-breed, who told me that Caw-wacham was dead, and that I was supposed to be the cause of her death. The silence was occasioned by my having mentioned a dead person's name, which is considered disrespectful to the deceased, and unlucky.

I immediately procured a canoe, and started for Fort Vancouver, down the river, paddling all night, well

knowing the danger that would result from my meeting
with any of her relations, and arrived safely at Fort
Vancouver on the 20th of June, with my budget of news
from the civilized world. Here I had to remain until the
1st of July, waiting for the boats, which were daily
arriving from New Caledonia and the Upper Columbia
with furs, and reloading again with their winter outfits
for their posts in the interior.   During this time I
amused myself in hunting and sketching. I took a sketch
of a Chinook boy with a singular headdress of beads;
the design seemed to be entirely original with him, as I
had never before met with any resembling it.

July 1st—The nine boats composing the brigade had
now completed their outfit, and were all prepared for
their different destinations. Mr. Lewis was to command
until he arrived at his own post, Colville; but we had
great difficulty in collecting the men, between sixty and
seventy in number: some wanted their allowance of
rum, or regale, before they started, given to the Company's men only preparatory to a long voyage.   Others
were bidding farewell to their Indian loves, and were
hard to be found; in fact, all hesitated to give up the
life of idleness and plenty in which they had been luxuriating for the last two or three weeks for the toils and
privations which they well knew were before them.
However, towards evening we succeeded in collecting
our crews, and Mr. Lewis promised them their regale on
the first fitting opportunity. The fort gave us a salute
of seven guns, which was repeated by the Company's
ship lying at the store-house. The occupants of the fort
crowded round us; and at last, amidst cheers and hearty
wishes for our safety, we pushed off. Owing to the lateness of the hour at which we started, we only got to the
Company's mills, eight miles from the fort, that evening.

July 2nd—We started very early this morning, and the men plied their oars with unusual vigour, as they were to get their regale this evening. By 2 o'clock P.M. we had reached the Prairie de Thé, a distance of twenty-eight miles. Here we landed to let the men have their customary debauch. In the Hudson's Bay Company's service no rations of liquor are given to the men, either while they are stopping in fort or while travelling, nor are they allowed to purchase any; but when they are about commencing a long journey, the men are given what is called a regale, which consists of a pint of rum each. This, however, they are not allowed to drink until they are some distance from the post, where those who are entitled to get drunk may do so without interfering with the resident servants of the establishment.

Immediately on landing, the camp was made, fires lit, and victuals cooked; in short, every preparation for the night was completed before the liquor was given out. As soon as the men got their allowance, they commenced all sorts of athletic games: running, jumping, wrestling, etc. We had eight Sandwich Islanders amongst the crews, who afforded great amusement by a sort of pantomimic dance, accompanied by singing. The whole thing was exceedingly grotesque and ridiculous, and elicited peals of laughter from the audience; gradually, as the rum began to take effect, the brigades, belonging to different posts, began to boast of their deeds of daring and endurance. This gradually led on to trying which was the best man. Numberless fights ensued; black eyes and bloody noses became plentiful, but all terminated in good humour. The next day the men were stupid from the effects of drink, but quite good-tempered and obedient; in fact, the fights of the previous evening seemed to be a sort of final settlement of all old grudges

and disputes. We did not get away until 3 o'clock P.M.,
and only made a distance of about fourteen miles. We
encamped at the foot of the Cascades, where the first
portage in ascending the Columbia commences.

July 4th and 5th—We were engaged both days in
carrying the parcels of goods across the portage, and
dragging the empty boats up by lines. This is a large
fishing station, and immense numbers of fish are caught
by the Hudson's Bay Company and the Cascade
Indians, who congregate about here in great numbers at
the fishing season, which happened at the time of our
passing. They gave us a good deal of trouble and
uneasiness, as it was only by the utmost vigilance that we
could keep them from stealing. On the evening of the
5th we got over the portage; and, although the men were
tired, we proceeded seven miles further up the river
before we encamped, so as to get clear of the Indians.

In strolling about while the men were engaged in
carrying the goods across the Cascades, I discovered a
large burying-ground of Flatheads, and I was very
anxious to procure a skull. To do this, however, I had
to use the greatest precaution, and ran no small risk, not
only in getting it but in having it in my possession afterwards; even the voyageurs would have refused to travel
with me had they known that I had it in my collection,
not only on account of the superstitious dread in which
they hold these burial-places, but also on account of the
danger of discovery, which might have cost the lives of
the whole party. I, however, took advantage of the men
being busy watching the Indians to keep them from
stealing, and the Indians being equally busy in watching for an opportunity to steal, and succeeded in getting
a very perfect skull smuggled in among my traps without the slightest suspicion.

At the place where we encamped on the evening of the 5th, there were a great many stumps of trees standing in the river; it is supposed to be a landslip. I made a sketch of it.

During the night, two of our Sandwich Islanders deserted. A boat was immediately unloaded and sent back, with the view of intercepting them at the Cascades. They had received 10l. sterling each in goods as their outfit, and, in passing the Cascades, had hid their bags in the woods, and hoped to get back again to the coast with their booty. Their pursuers, however, discovered their track, and found the goods, though they did not find the men; but, knowing they must be near the place, they got Tomaquin to look after them. The next morning Tomaquin, with three of his tribe, brought them in: each of the Indians, while paddling, carried his knife in his mouth, ready to strike should the Islanders make any resistance. It appeared that they had visited his camp in the night, on which he assembled his tribe and surrounded them; when the Islanders, thinking they were going to be killed, surrendered and begged for mercy. Tomaquin was rewarded with four blankets and four shirts. The next thing was to punish the deserters, and very little time was wasted in either finding a verdict or carrying it out. Our guide, a tall, powerful Iroquois, took one of them and Mr. Lewis seized the other, as they stepped from the canoe: the punishment consisted in simply knocking the men down, kicking them until they got up, and knocking them down again until they could not get up any more, when they finished them off with a few more kicks. Mr. Lewis, although a very powerful man, had only his left hand, a gun having exploded in his right, shattering it so dreadfully that he was obliged to have it cut off at the wrist; but the operation having

been performed in the roughest backwoods fashion, it
often pained him, and the doctors wanted him to let
them cut it off again, so as to make a good stump, but
he would not let them. On this stump he usually wore
a heavy wooden shield, but, luckily for the poor Islanders, it was not on when they landed, or, as he said himself, he might have killed them. The punishment of
those men must, of course, appear savage and severe to
persons in civilized life, but it is only treatment of this
kind that will keep this sort of men in order; and deser-
tion or insubordination, on journeys through the interior, is often attended by the most dangerous consequences to the whole party.

July 6th—It rained heavily all day, and the wind
became so high, that we were obliged to put ashore,
although the ground was very low and swampy, and
the mosquitoes were in myriads.

July 7th—Passed a Methodist mission, and came to
the Portage of the Dalles. We employed the Indians
here to make the portage, thirty to each boat, for which
each man receives five balls and powder. The Indians
at the Dalles do not distort the head. The country
begins to look barren and is entirely destitute of wood.
Salmon in great abundance is caught in these rapids.

July 8th—Arrived at the Chutes: we found no difficulty as to the carriage of our boats, as the Indians were
very numerous and willing to be employed. In former
times these people were more troublesome than any
other tribes on the Columbia River. In making this
portage, it was then necessary to have sixty armed men
for the protection of the goods. It was here that the
man with the tin box was shot, mentioned in Washington Irving's "Astoria." We were on the present occasion obliged to buy wood from the Indians to cook our

supper, not a tree nor even a bush being visible in any direction. The Indians, who obtain drift-wood for their own use when the river is high and brings it within their reach, of course prize it highly from its scarcity. The Indians who reside and congregate about the Chutes for

12. Man-ce-muckt [Chief of Indians of the Dalles, Columbia River]
Courtesy of Royal Ontario Museum

the purpose of fishing are called the Sheen tribe; they do not flatten their heads, and appear to be a hardy, brave people, at this time particularly friendly to the Hudson's Bay Company people, and at peace with their Flathead neighbours. The Indians hereabouts catch a few deer and some other game, out of whose skins they make whatever dresses they wear, which are, however, very scanty. I give, in sketch No. 12, the likeness of Mancemuckt, the chief; he wore a fox-skin cape and a leather deerskin skirt at the time.

July 9th—Left the Chutes with a strong, fair wind running up the rapids under sail, while the water curled over the bows of the boats, which we only prevented from filling by shortening the sail. We encamped in the neighbourhood of a very thievish tribe of Indians, according to report, and were obliged to make use of one of the burial canoes for fuel, taking the boxes out and depositing them carefully near some of the others. We had not got our pot to boil, before some of the tribe made their appearance and gave us to understand that we had destroyed the grave of the relative of one of the men. After a great deal of arguing and trouble, and our party being too strong for the Indians to attack in open violence, this man consented, at last, to receive tobacco, ammunition and other little presents, as an indemnity for our sacrilege. This we willingly gave him, as, had we not done so, in all probability they would have killed the first white man they could have laid their hands on, with impunity; having, however, received compensation for the insult, there was no fear of anything further being done about it.

July 10th—Saw great quantities of rattlesnakes to-day, some few of which we killed; the men, while tracking (that is, hauling the boats along the edge of the shore by a line, in places where the river is too rapid to row), were in great dread of them, as they had no shoes, but, fortunately, no one was bitten. It is said by the Indians that salt applied plentifully and immediately to the wound will effect a cure; also that drinking copiously of ardent spirits, as soon as the bite has been inflicted, will avert the danger. I have, however, never seen either of them tried, and should much suspect the latter cure to be merely a piece of Indian cunning to overcome the great difficulty of getting liquor, on any terms, from the Company's servants and officers.

July 11*th*—Many Indians followed us for a long distance on horseback along the shore. I obtained one of their horses and, accompanied by an Indian, took a gallop of seven or eight miles into the interior, and found the country equally sterile and unpromising as on the banks of the stream. The bend in the river which the boats were obliged to follow enabled me to go up with them a very few miles further; the ride, although uninteresting as regarded landscape—for not a tree was visible as far as the eye could reach—was still a delightful change to me from the monotony of the boats. As we approached the place where the Walla-Walla debauches into the Columbia River, we came in sight of two extraordinary rocks projecting from a high steep cone or mound about 700 feet above the level of the river. These are called by the voyageurs the Chimney Rocks, and from their being visible from a great distance they are very serviceable as landmarks. Sketch No. 13 represents one of them and the cone, but, owing to the position in which I stood while taking the sketch, the other rock or chimney is not visible, being immediately in rear of the one represented.

The Walla-Walla Indians call these the "Rocks of the Kye-use girls," of which they relate the following legend, which was told to me by an Indian whilst I was sketching this extraordinary scene. It must be borne in mind that all Indian tribes select some animal to which they attribute supernatural or, in the language of the country, *medicine* powers: the whale, for instance, on

the north-west coast; the kee-yeu, or war eagle, on the
east side of the Rocky Mountains, supposed to be the
maker of thunder; and the wolf, on the Columbia River.
Now, the great medicine wolf of the Columbia River—
according to the Walla-Walla tradition the most cunning and artful of all manitous—having heard that a

13. Chimney Rocks [Columbia River]
Courtesy of Royal Ontario Museum

great medicine grasshopper was desolating the whole of
the country which of right belonged to himself, and was
especially under his protection, immediately resolved to
trace him out, and have a personal encounter with him.
With this view, he proceeded down the banks of the
river, and soon fell in with the object of his search. Each
of these formidable manitous thought it best to resort to
stratagem to overcome his opponent. Being afraid of
each other's "medicine" powers, they accordingly commenced by exchanging civilities, and then, with a view of

terrifying each other, began boasting of their wonderful exploits, and the numbers they had killed and eaten. The grasshopper said to the wolf that the best way to ascertain who had devoured the largest numbers would be to vomit up the contents of their respective stomachs, and he who threw up the most hair—that being an indigestible substance—by showing who had swallowed the most animals, should be considered as the superior. To this proposal the wolf consented, and they commenced retching and vomiting up all in their stomachs. The grasshopper, in the violence of his exertions, naturally closed his eyes, and the wolf, perceiving this, adroitly drew a great part of his opponent's share over to his own side without being detected. The grasshopper, when he perceived how much larger the pile before the wolf was than his own, gave up the contest, and proposed to the wolf an exchange of shirts in token of amity and forgiveness. To this also the wolf consented, but requested the grasshopper to take off his shirt first as he was the first proposer; but the grasshopper refused, and wished the wolf to commence the ceremony.

The wolf finally even agreed to this and striking himself suddenly on the breast, his shirt immediately flew off; the grasshopper was greatly astonished, and, not being possessed of any charm by which he could strip himself so expeditiously, was obliged to take off his shirt in the common way of drawing it over his head; the wolf now watched his opportunity, and while the grasshopper had his head and arms entangled in the shirt he killed him.

The wolf, having thus got rid of his troublesome and dangerous rival, commenced his return home. On arriving within a few miles of the Walla-Walla, he saw three beautiful Kye-use girls, with whom he fell desperately in love; they were engaged in carrying stones into the river, in order to make an artificial cascade or rapid, to catch the salmon in leaping over it. The wolf secretly watched their operations through the day, and repaired at night to the dam and entirely destroyed their work: this he repeated for three successive evenings. On the fourth morning he saw the girls sitting weeping on the bank, and accosted them, inquiring what was the matter: they told him they were starving, as they could get no fish for want of a dam. He then proposed to erect a dam for them, if they would consent to become his wives, to which they consented sooner than perish from the want of food. A long point of stones running nearly across the river is to this day attributed to the magic of the wolf-lover.

For a long time he lived happily with the three sisters (a custom very frequent amongst Indians, who marry as many sisters in a family as they can, and assign as a reason that sisters will naturally agree together better than strangers); but at length the wolf became jealous of his wives, and, by his supernatural power, changed two of them into the two basalt pillars, on the south side of the river, and then changed himself into a lark rock, somewhat similar to them, on the north side, so that he might watch them for ever afterwards. I asked the narrator what had become of the third sister. Said he: "Did you not observe a cavern as you came up?" I said that I had. "That," he replied, "is all that remains of her!"

Chapter XVII

Fort Walla-Walla—Salmon the Staff of Life—Burrows for the Winter—Ride to see a Cataract—Splendid Fall of Water—Desert of Burning Sand—A Jealous Spouse—Respect to a Dead Chief.

July 12*th*—I arrived at Walla-Walla. It is a small fort, built of *dobies,* or blocks of mud baked in the sun, which is here intensely hot. Fort Walla-Walla is situated at the mouth of the river of the same name, in the most sandy and barren desert that can be conceived, and is about 500 miles from the mouth of the Columbia. Little or no rain ever falls here, although a few miles lower down the river it is seen from hence to pour down in torrents. Owing to its being built at the mouth of a gully, formed by the Columbia River through high, mountainous land leading to the Pacific Ocean, it is exposed to furious gales of wind, which rush through the opening in the hills with inconceivable violence, and raise the sand in clouds so dense and continuous as frequently to render travelling impossible. I was kindly received by Mr. M'Bain, a clerk in the Hudson's Bay Company's service, who, with five men, had charge of the fort. The establishment is kept up solely for trading with the Indians from the interior, as those about the post have few or no peltries to deal in.

The Walla-Walla Indians live almost entirely upon salmon throughout the whole year. In the summer season they inhabit lodges made of mats of rushes spread on poles. Owing to the absence of trees in their vicinity they have to depend for the small quantity of fuel which they require upon the drift-wood, which they collect from the river in the spring. In the winter they dig a large circular excavation in the ground, about ten or

189

twelve feet deep and from forty to fifty feet in circumference, and cover it over with split logs, over which they
place a layer of mud collected from the river. A hole is
left at one side of this roofing large enough for one
person to enter at a time. A stick with notches reaches
to the bottom of the excavation, and serves as a ladder,
by means of which they ascend and descend into the
subterranean dwelling. Here twelve or fifteen persons
burrow through the winter, having little or no occasion
for fuel; their food of dried salmon being most frequently eaten uncooked, and the place being excessively
warm from the numbers congregated together in so
small and confined a space. They are frequently obliged,
by the drifting billows of sand, to close the aperture,
when the heat and stench become insupportable to all
but those accustomed to it. The drifting of the sand is
a frightful feature in this barren waste. Great numbers
of the Indians lose their sight, and even those who have
not suffered to so great an extent have the appearance
of labouring under intense inflammation of these organs.
The salmon, while in the process of drying, also become
filled with sand to such an extent as to wear away the
teeth of the Indians, and an Indian is seldom met with
over forty years of age whose teeth are not worn quite
to the gums.

July 13*th*—Procured three horses and a man, and
left for the Pelouse or Pavilion River; traversed a sandy
country, where we could find no water until we arrived
at the Fouchay River, when we met with Pere José, a
Jesuit missionary, who had left Walla-Walla on the
night before, on the way to his mission of the Cœur de
Laine. Here we encamped.

July 14*th*—Started at five o'clock in the morning.
Weather intensely hot, and no water procurable all day.

Found some Indians, who ferried ourselves and baggage in a canoe over the Nezperees River, which is here about 250 yards wide. We swam our horses at the mouth of the Pelouse River, where it empties itself into the Nezperees. The Chief of this place is named Slo-ce-ac-cum. He wore his hair divided in long masses, stuck together with grease. The tribe do not number more than seventy or eighty warriors, and are called Upputuppets. He told me that there was a fall up the Pelouse that no white man had ever seen, and that he would conduct me up the bed of the river, as it was sufficiently shallow for our horses. I accepted his proposal, and rode eight or ten miles through a wild and savage gorge, composed of dark brown basaltic rocks, heaped in confusion one upon another to the height of 1,000 and 1,500 feet, sometimes taking the appearance of immense ruins in the distance. At one place the strata assumed the circular form, and somewhat the appearance, of the Colosseum at Rome. Our path, at the bottom of this gorge, was very difficult, as it lay through masses of tangled brush and fallen rocks.

The chief now halted, and refused to go further unless I gave him a blanket in payment; but as this was unreasonable I urged on my horse, desiring my own man, who accompanied me, to follow with the jaded nag. I had not advanced more than a mile when the chief came up to us and guided us to the falls through one of the boldest and most sublime passes the eye ever beheld. At the foot of the falls we made our encampment, and our guide left us, quite satisfied with his present of tobacco and ammunition. The water falls in one perpendicular sheet of about 600 feet in height, from between rocks of a greyish-yellow colour, which rise to about 400 feet above the summit of the fall. The water tumbles into a rocky basin below, with a continuous hollow, echoing roar, and courses with great velocity along its bed, until it falls into the Nezperees. There was a constant current of air around our encampment, which was delightfully cool and refreshing. When I was there it was low water, and the Indian told me that during the rainy season the falls were much increased in volume and, of course, in grandeur of effect.

July 15*th*—Having finished my sketches of this magnificent scene, we left our encampment for a fall fifteen or twenty miles higher up the river, and it was necessary for us to leave the bed of the river and attain the top of the banks, which, being at least 1,000 feet above us, would have been impracticable had we not found a ravine, which, although steep and difficult, we managed to lead our horses up. In this hollow we found great quantities of wild currants, of delicious flavour, which proved most refreshing.

At length we gained the summit. The country around, as far as the eye could reach, seemed to be a per-fect desert of yellow, hot sand, with immense masses of broken rock jutting up abruptly here and there over the surface. No trees or shrubs of any kind relieved the monotony of the barren waste. A few patches of tuft-grass, thinly scattered here and there, were the only representatives of vegetation, whilst animal life seemed to be entirely extinct, and during my whole journey through this place I never met with an animal or bird,—not even a mosquito or a snake.

We now followed the course of the river, and encamped at the upper fall, where I remained until the 17th, sketching, much gratified with the surrounding magnificent scenes. The fall of water is only about fif-teen feet. Along the margin of the river high bushes and grass grow. whose bright green contrasts vividly with the high hills of yellow sand which enclose them.

I was anxious to have remained in this neighbour-hood for a week or ten days longer, to have made some more sketches of the curious and strange region in which I found myself, but the half-breed whom I had with me became so anxious to return, and so importunate and sulky about it, that he made me quite uncomfortable, and I consented to return. I found out afterwards that it was on account of his wife, of whom he was jealous, being left at the fort. Had I known this sooner I would have chosen another man; as it was, it was with great regret that I commenced retracing my steps down the river on the 17th, and in the evening again encamped on the banks of the Nezperees.

During the day we saw a large band of fine horses running wild; they had belonged to a chief who was much honoured by his tribe, and as a mark of respect, at his death, they determined not to use or touch his horses, which had, accordingly, kept increasing in numbers. I took a sketch of the Nezperees, near the mouth of the Pelouse River, showing the singular formation of the basaltic rocks.

July 18*th*—Started for Dr. Whitman's mission, a
distance of sixty miles, neither myself nor my man knowing anything of the road. I inquired of one of the
Indians here: he pointed out the direction, but told us
that we would be sure to die before we reached it for
want of water; nor could we prevail on any of them to
guide us. However, we started in the direction pointed
out: the weather was intensely hot, and we had nothing
to shelter us from the scorching rays of the sun, which
were reflected back by the hot yellow sand. Towards
the middle of the day we observed a bush in the distance,
and in our line of march; we eagerly rushed forward,
hoping to find water, for want of which both ourselves
and our horses were now suffering severely; but had the
mortification to find the stream dried up, if ever there
had been one there. Our only hope now was to struggle
on as fast as possible, but our horses soon began to fail,
and we were obliged to lead them many a weary mile,
tottering with exhaustion, before we arrived at the mission house. This we at length accomplished about 6
o'clock in the evening, and I was received very kindly by
the missionary and his wife.

Dr. Whitman's duties included those of superintendent of the American Presbyterian missions on the
west side of the Rocky Mountains. He had built himself
a house of unburnt clay, for want of timber, which, as

stated above, is here extremely scarce. He had resided at this locality, on the banks of the Walla-Walla River, upwards of eight years, doing all in his power to benefit the Indians in his mission. He had brought forty or fifty acres of land in the vicinity of the river under cultivation, and had a great many heads of domestic cattle, affording greater comfort to his family than one would expect in such an isolated spot. I remained with him four days, during which he kindly accompanied me amongst the Indians. These Indians, the Kye-use, resemble the Walla-Wallas very much. They are always allies in war, and their language and customs are almost identical, except that the Kye-use Indians are far more vicious and ungovernable.

Dr. Whitman took me to the lodge of an Indian called To-ma-kus, that I might take his likeness. We found him in his lodge sitting perfectly naked. His appearance was the most savage I ever beheld, and his looks, as I afterwards heard, by no means belied his character. He was not aware of what I was doing until I had finished the sketch. He then asked to look at it, and inquired what I intended doing with it, and whether I was not going to give it to the Americans, against whom he bore a strong antipathy, superstitiously fancying that their possessing it would put him in their power. I in vain told him that I should not give it to them; but, not being satisfied with this assurance, he attempted to throw it in the fire, when I seized him by the arm and snatched it from him. He glanced at me like a fiend and appeared greatly enraged, but before he had time to recover from his surprise I left the lodge and mounted my horse, not without occasionally looking back to see if he might not send an arrow after me.

Usually, when I wished to take the likeness of an Indian, I walked into the lodge, sat down, and commenced without speaking, as an Indian under these circumstances will generally pretend not to notice. If they did not like what I was doing they would get up and walk away; but if I asked them to sit they most frequently refused, supposing that it would have some injurious effect upon themselves. In this manner I went into the lodge of Til-au-kite, the chief, and took his likeness without a word passing between us.

Having enjoyed the kind hospitality of Dr. Whitman and his lady for four days, on

July 22nd I left for Walla-Walla, after breakfast, taking with me, at the Doctor's desire, a dog belonging to Mr. M'Bain. The weather continued intensely hot, and I had not ridden more than an hour when I observed the poor animal in a state of such extreme exhaustion that I requested my man to place him on his horse, but the man, feeling inconvenienced by him, put him down on the ground, and in a few minutes afterwards the poor brute lay down and died, actually scorched to death by the burning sand.

On the day after my arrival at the fort, a boy, one of the sons of Peo-peo-mox-mox, the chief of the Walla-Wallas, arrived at the camp close to the fort. He was a few days in advance of a war party headed by his father, and composed of Walla-Walla and Kye-use Indians, which had been absent eighteen months, and had been almost given up by the tribes. This party, numbering 200 men, had started for California for the purpose of revenging the death of another son of the chief, who had been killed by some Californian emigrants; and the messenger now arrived bringing the most disastrous tidings, not only of the total failure of the expedition, but also of their suffering and detention by sickness. Hearing that a messenger was coming in across the plains, I went to the Indian camp and was there at his arrival. No sooner had he dismounted from his horse than the whole camp, men, women, and children, surrounded him, eagerly inquiring after their absent friends, as they had hitherto received no intelligence, beyond a report, that the party had been cut off by hostile tribes. His downcast looks and silence confirmed the fears that some dire calamity must have happened, and they set up a tremendous howl, whilst he stood silent and dejected with the tears streaming down his face. At length, after much coaxing and entreaty on their part, he commenced the recital of their misfortunes.

After describing the progress of the journey up to the time of the disease (the measles) making its appearance, during which he was listened to in breathless silence, he began to name its victims one after another. On the first name being mentioned, a terrific howl ensued, the women loosening their hair and gesticulating in a most violent manner. When this had subsided, he, after much persuasion, named a second and a third, until he had named upwards of thirty. The same signs of intense grief followed the mention of each name, presenting a scene which accustomed as I was to Indian life, I must confess, affected me deeply. I stood close by them on a log, with the interpreter of the fort, who explained to me the Indian's statement, which occupied nearly three hours. After this the excitement increased, and apprehensions were entertained at the fort that it might lead to some hostile movement against the establishment. This fear, however, was groundless, as the Indians knew the distinction between the Hudson's Bay

Company and the Americans. They immediately sent messengers in every direction on horseback to spread the news of the disaster amongst all the neighbouring tribes, and Mr. M'Bain and I both considered that Dr. Whitman and his family would be in great danger. I, therefore, determined to go and warn him of what had occurred. It was six o'clock in the evening when I started, but I had a good horse, and arrived at his house in three hours. I told him of the arrival of the messenger, and the excitement of the Indians, and advised him strongly to come to the fort, for a while at least, until the Indians had cooled down; but he said he had lived so long amongst them, and had done so much for them, that he did not apprehend they would injure him. I remained with him only an hour, and hastened back to the fort, where I arrived at one o'clock A.M. Not wishing to expose myself unnecessarily to any danger arising from the superstitious notions which the Indians might attach to my having taken some of their likenesses, I remained at Fort Walla-Walla four or five days, during which the war party had returned, and I had an opportunity of taking the likeness of the great chief Peo-Peo-mox-mox, or "the Yellow Serpent," who exercises great influence not only over his own people, but also among the neighbouring tribes.

While at the fort one of the gentlemen of the establishment, who had been amongst the Indians for forty years, and who had resided for the most part of that time amongst the Walla-Wallas, related to me the following story, which I shall introduce, as nearly as possible, in the manner in which it was told to me; as it is strongly illustrative of the Indian character, of their love for their children, and the firmness with which they meet the approach of death, and their belief in a future state.

Several years back when the Walla-Wallas used to go in annual buffalo hunts, and herds of these immense animals frequented the west side of the mountains, though now rarely seen, the tribe was governed by a chief adored by his own people, and respected and feared by all the surrounding tribes for his great wisdom and courage. This chief had many sons, who, in childhood, all promised to resemble their father both in mind and body, but one by one, as they arrived at manhood, and as the proud father hoped to see them take their place amongst the warriors and leaders of the tribe, they withered and sank into untimely graves, and as each loved one passed away, the stern chief soothed his silent sorrow with hopes of those still left. At last his hair grew white with sorrow and with age, and he had but one boy left—his youngest—but apparently the strongest, the bravest, and the best; at least to the old warrior's heart he was all this; for in him still seemed to live all the most cherished virtues of his dead brothers.

The old man now devoted his whole time to the instruction of this boy: he taught him to hunt the buffalo and the moose, to snare the lynx and trap the bear, to draw the bow and poise the spear with unerring aim. Young as the boy was, he yet made him head the warriors of his tribe, and led him on himself, the foremost to surprise the enemy and secure the bloody trophies of victory; already had he become the theme of the war-chant, and his name was known far and wide for all the virtues that could adorn an Indian brave.

But the Great Spirit took this one too; and the lonely and desolate father shut himself up in the solitude of his lodge, and no one saw him nor spoke to him, nor was there any sound of wailing or of grief heard from that sad abode. At length the appointed day arrived upon which the body was to be laid in its last resting-place, where the chief had ordered a large grave to be made; and the funeral procession being formed, the chief came forth and placed himself at their head, but, to the astonishment of all, instead of being dressed in the shabby garments indicative of mourning, he came forth arrayed in full war costume, fully equipped as if for some distant hostile excursion, painted with the most brilliant war paints, and hung round with the trophies of his many bloody and successful wars.

Calmly and sternly he marched to the grave, and the body of his loved son having been laid in it, with all the Indian treasures supposed to be useful to him in the next world, the bereaved father stood on the verge, and addressed his tribe: "From my youth upwards I have ever sought the honour and welfare of my tribe, and have never spared myself either in the battle or the chase. I have led you from victory to victory, and, instead of being surrounded by hostile tribes, you are now feared by all, and your friendship is sought, and your enmity dreaded, wherever the hunters of the tribe may roam. I have been a father to you, and ye have been as children to me, for more moons than I am able to count, until my hairs have become as hoar frost upon the mountains. You have never withheld your obedience from me, nor will you deny it to me now. When the Great Spirit was pleased to call my children one by one, to His blessed hunting grounds, I saw them borne to the sepulchre of their fathers without murmuring against His will, so long as one was left. I toiled on for him, taking pride in his pride, glorying in his glory, and living in his life, fondly hoping that when I should go to join his loved brothers in the other world that I should leave him to perpetuate my deeds amongst you; but the

Great Spirit hath called him also,—this last prop of my declining years,—this hope of my old age,—endeared to me by so many fond recollections of his worth, his manly strength, his courage, skill, and prowess in war. Alas! he lies in the cold ground, and I am left alone, like the sapless trunk of a tree whose branches have been scathed by the lightning. I tracked that loved form, now cold, from its childhood's gambols to its manly acts of daring. I it was who first placed in his hands the bow and the tomahawk, and taught him how to use them; and often have you witnessed and praised his skill and courage in wielding them. And shall I now forsake him, and leave him alone and unaided, to take the long and toilsome journey in the Spirit's hunting grounds? No! his spirit beckons me to follow, and he shall not be disappointed; the same grave shall contain us, the same earth shall cover us; and as in this world, his father's arm was ever near to assist him in every toil and danger, so shall his spirit find him by his side in the long and toilsome journey to the plenteous and everlasting hunting grounds of the Great Spirit. You, my people, have never disobeyed me, and will not fail to fulfil my last commands. I now leave you, and when I lie extended at his side, heap the earth over us both; nothing can change my purpose." He then descended into the grave, and clasped the corpse in his arms. His people, after in vain endeavouring to change his resolution, obeyed his commands, and buried the living and the dead. A stick, with a piece of ragged red cloth, was the only monument erected over the warriors, but their names will form the theme of many an Indian *talk* as long as the Walla-Walla tribe exists.

July 29*th*—I had determined to go to Colville by the Grand Coulet: this, from the appearance of the two extremities, seemed to have been a former bed of the Columbia River, but no person could tell me anything about it, nor could I hear of any one, either Indian or White, who had penetrated any considerable distance up it; the place was, however, so much talked of as the abode of evil spirits and other strange things, that I could not resist the desire of trying to explore it. I accordingly sent on everything by the boats, except what I usually carried about my own person, but I could not get an Indian guide, as none of them would venture an encounter with the evil spirits.

At last a half-breed, called Donny, although ignorant of the route, agreed to accompany me. We procured two riding horses, and one to carry our provisions, consisting of two fine hams, which had been sent to me from Fort Vancouver, and a stock of dried salmon, cured by the Indians. About ten miles from the fort, we swam our horses across the Nezperees River, where it enters the Columbia, and then proceeded along the banks of the Columbia, about ten miles further, where we encamped for the night.

During the day we passed a large encampment of Nezperees, who were very kind to us, but stole a tin cup (a valuable article in that part of the world) I suppose as a souvenir of my visit. I took a sketch of a man, and might have frightened the chief into getting the cup restored to me by means of this sketch, but I had been so warned of the treachery and villany of these Indians, that I considered it too dangerous an experiment.

July 30*th*—Proceeded along the shore for eight or ten miles, when I discovered that I had left my pistols and some other articles at our last night's encampment. I had, therefore, to send my man back for them, whilst I sat by the river, with horses and baggage, under a burning sun, without the slightest shelter. Whilst sitting there, a canoe approached with four Indians, streaked all over with white mud (the ordinary pipe-clay). On landing, they showed much surprise, and watched very cautiously at a distance, some creeping close to me, and then retreating. This continued for about three hours, during which not a sound broke through the surrounding stillness. I had commenced travelling very early, and this, combined with the heat and silence, made me intensely drowsy. Even the danger I was in scarcely sufficed to keep my eyes open, but the Indians were evidently at fault as to what to make of me.

As I sat upon the packs taken from the horse, nodding in silence, with a fixed stare at them whichever way they turned, my double-barrelled gun cocked, across my knees, and a large red beard (an object of great wonder to all Indians) hanging half way down my breast, I was, no doubt, a very good embodiment of their idea of a scoocoom, or evil genius. To this I attributed my safety, and took good care not to encourage their closer acquaintance, as I had no wish to have my immortality tested by them.

At length my man returned with the missing articles, and the Indians hastily took to their canoe and crossed the river. We now continued our course along the river until evening, when we encamped, and as we were very hungry, and expected a hard journey next day, we determined upon attacking one of our hams. I accordingly seized hold of the bone to pull it from the bag with which it was covered, when, alas! the bare bone slipped out, leaving a living mass of maggots, into which the heat had turned the flesh, behind. Upon examination, we found the other in the same state, and had to satisfy our hunger on the salmon, which, as usual, was full of sand.

Chapter XIX

The Horrors of Thirst—The Lake of Pelicans—A Queer Bedfellow—Steering by the Sun—Sweet Water at Last—Rather a Hardy Horse—Losing Each Other—Wonderful Natural Walls—The Grand Coulet—A Great Treat—The River Columbia—Indians Again.

July 31*st*—Owing to the great bend which the Columbia takes to the northward, I thought I should save a considerable distance by striking across the country, and intersecting the Grand Coulet at some distance from its mouth. We accordingly left the river early in the morning, and travelled all day through a barren, sandy desert, without a drop of water to drink, a tree to rest under, or a spot of grass to sit upon. Towards evening, we saw in the distance a small lake, and to this we accordingly pushed forward: as soon as our horses perceived it, wearied and exhausted as they were, they rushed forward and plunged bodily into the water. No sooner, however, had they tasted it, than they drew their heads back, refusing to drink. On alighting, I found the water was intensely salt, and never shall I forget the painful emotion which came over me, as it became certain to my mind that I could not satisfy my thirst. Our horses were too weary, after our long and rapid ride, to proceed further; and though it was tantalizing to look at the water which we could not drink, the vegetation which surrounded it was refreshing to the horses, and we remained here all night, though we enjoyed scarcely any sleep owing to our thirst.

August 1*st*—We started at 4 o'clock this morning, and travelled steadily on without getting water, until about noon, when we fell in with a narrow lake, about a mile long, very shallow, and swarming with pelicans,

whose dung had made the water green and thick. Bad
as this was, added to its being also rather salt, yet our
thirst was so great, that we strained some through a
cloth and drank it. Leaving this Lake of Pelicans, we
now entered upon a still more discouraging route: the
country, as far as the eye could reach, was covered with
loose fine sand, which the violent winds of this region
had drifted into immense mounds, varying from 80 to
120 feet in height. This was very toilsome to us, as our
horses had become so exhausted that we were obliged
to lead them, and we sank deep at every step in the hot
sand. Had the wind risen while we were crossing this
place, we must have been immediately buried in the sand.
Towards evening we arrived at a rock, and in a small
cleft we discovered three or four gallons of water almost
as black as ink, and abounding in disgusting animalcula.
The horses no sooner saw it, than they made a spring
towards it, and it was with the greatest difficulty we
drove them back, fearing that they would drink all, and
leave us to our misery. After satisfying our thirst, we
strained a kettleful for our supper, and allowed the
horses to drink up the remainder, which they did to the
last drop, showing how necessary was the precaution we
had taken. Here we passed the night.

August 2nd—I awoke in the morning, and felt
something cold and clammy against my thigh, and on
throwing off my blanket, perceived a reptile of the lizard
species, eight or ten inches long, which had been my
companion during the night. I cannot say whether it
was venomous or not, but I found no ill effects from it.
We proceeded on, and about noon emerged from these
mountains of sand; the country was still sandy and
barren, but here and there we found tufts of grass sufficient to support our horses. The country was inter-

sected with immense walls of basaltic rock, which continually threw us out of our direct course, or rather the course I had determined on, for of the actual route I had no information. These interruptions added considerably to our difficulties, as I had no compass, and it was only by noticing the sun at mid-day by my watch, and fixing on some distant hill, that I guided my course. We still suffered from the want of water, and my man was getting disheartened at our wandering thus almost at random through this trackless desert.

August 3rd—After riding a few hours, we came to an immense gully of dried-up water-courses crossing our route. The banks rose seven or eight hundred feet high from the bottom on each side, and its width was nearly half a mile. At first it seemed impossible to pass it; however, after many difficulties, we succeeded in leading our horses to the bottom, which we crossed, and clambered up the rocks on the opposite side for about 200 feet, when we came to one of the most beautiful spots that can well be conceived: at least, it appeared to us all that was beautiful, amongst the surrounding desolation.

It was a piece of table land, about half a mile in circumference, covered with luxuriant grass, and having in its centre a small lake of exquisitely cool fresh water. The basaltic rock rose like an amphitheatre, from about three-quarters of its circuit to the height of about 500 feet, while the precipice up which we had toiled sank down at the other side. We remained here three hours, luxuriating in the delicious water, so sweet to us after suffering the torments of thirst for so long. My man seemed as if he never could have enough of it, for when he could swallow no more, he walked in, clothes and all, and actually wallowed in it, the horses following his example. How much longer we might have been tempted to stay here, it is impossible to say, but we accidentally set fire to the grass and were obliged to decamp; this was accomplished with considerable difficulty, and in getting up the precipitous rocks, the pack-horse lost his footing and fell to the bottom, but pitching, fortunately, on his back with the packs under him, he escaped with a few cuts on his legs only. Had he been anything but an Indian horse, he would doubtless have paid the forfeit of his life for the insecurity of his feet.

As soon as I arrived at the level of the country once more, I saw in the distance another vast wall of rock, and leaving my man to bring up the unfortunate pack-horse, I rode briskly forward to endeavour to find a passage over this formidable barrier, considering it to be like many others that we had already passed, an isolated wall of basalt. I therefore rode backwards and forwards along its front, exploring every part that presented any opening, but without finding one that our horses could traverse. At last I came to the conclusion that we must go round it, but my man not having come up, it was necessary for me to return and seek him, which proved for several hours unavailing, and I began to fear that he and my provisions were inevitably lost; however, after riding a long way back, I fell upon his track, which I followed up with care.

I soon perceived that he had taken a wrong direction. After some time, I saw him mounted on a high rock in the distance, shouting and signalling with all his might till I got up to him. He was very much frightened, as he said that if he had lost me he never could have got on. Though the day was by this time pretty far advanced, we succeeded in making a circuit of the basaltic wall, and struck a deep ravine which in the distance so much resembled the banks of the Columbia, that I at first thought I had missed my way, and had come upon the river.

When we reached the edge, I saw that there was no water at the bottom, and that there could be no doubt of my having at last arrived at the Grand Coulet. With great difficulty we descended the bank, 1000 feet; its width varies from one mile to a mile and a half; and there can be no doubt of its having been previously an arm of the Columbia, which now flows four or five hundred feet below it, leaving the channel of the Coulet dry, and exposing to view the bases of the enormous rocky islands that now stud its bottom, some of them rising to the elevation of the surrounding country.

This wonderful gully is about 150 miles long, and walled-in in many places with an unbroken length twenty miles long of perpendicular basalt 1000 feet high. The bottom of this valley is perfectly level, and covered with luxuriant grass, except where broken by the immense rocks above mentioned: there is not a single tree to be seen throughout its whole extent, and scarcely a bush; neither did we see any insects, reptiles, or animals. Having found a beautiful spring of water gushing from the rocks, we encamped near it. After we had rested ourselves, we commenced an examination of our provisions of dried salmon, for we saw no chance of adding anything to our larder, and of course what we had was of great importance. Much to our regret, we found that it was perfectly alive with maggots, and every mouthful had to be well shaken before eating; so full of life indeed had the fish become, that my man proposed tying them by the tails to prevent their crawling away. Bad as the salmon was, our prospects were made still more gloomy by the fact that there was but

a very small supply left, and that we had a long and
unknown road to travel before we could hope for any
help. A thunderstorm came on during the night, and
in the whole course of my life I never heard anything
so awfully sublime as the endless reverberations amongst
the rocks of this grand and beautiful ravine. There is
hardly another spot in the world that could produce so
astounding an effect.

August 4th—We followed the course of the Coulet,
lost in admiration of its beauty and grandeur assuming
a new aspect of increased wildness and magnificence at
every turn. I shot the first bird we had seen since leaving Walla-Walla, except the pelicans, which are never
eaten, even by the Indians, who are far from particular.
This bird proved to be what is here called a wild turkey,
but resembling in nothing the wild turkeys of the south.
Its plumage resembles that of a pheasant, it is not larger
than a domestic hen, and its flesh, though very white, is
dry and unpalatable; to us, however, it proved a great
treat, as we were enabled to make one meal without the
usual accompaniments of sand and maggots. Our
journey now would have been delightful, if we had had
anything like good food. We had plenty of grass of the
best quality for our horses, delicious springs gushing
from the rocks at every mile or two, and camping
grounds which almost tempted us to stay at the risk of
starvation.

August 5th—Towards evening we began to see trees,
principally pine, in the heights and in the distance, and
I concluded that we were now approaching the Columbia River. I pressed forward and before sundown
emerged from the gorge of this stupendous ravine, and
saw the mighty river flowing at least 500 feet below us,
though the banks rose considerably more than that

height above us on each side. This river exceeds in grandeur any other perhaps in the world, not so much from its volume of water, although that is immense, as from the romantic wildness of its stupendous and ever-varying surrounding scenery, now towering into snow-capped mountains thousands of feet high, and now sinking in undulating terraces to the level of its pellucid waters.

Two Indians were floating down the river, on a few logs tied together. They were the first we had encountered for many days; and on our hailing them, they landed, and climbed up to us. They told me we were ten days' journey from Colville. This I did not believe, although I could not tell why they wished to deceive me. I gave them a little tobacco, and hoped to get some provisions from them, but they said they had none, so we were obliged to make our supper on the salmon as usual. We descended the bank, and camped for the night on the margin of the river.

Chapter XX

A Dangerous Path—Incredible Sagacity—Levying Black Mail—Fort Colville—Hiding-Places of the Indians—Indian Baptism—The Kettle Falls—Tilting at the Ring—Chief of the Waters—Dead Salmon by Thousands—Dislike to Salt Meat—A Widow's Consolation—A Wife for the Woods.

August 6th—We continued along the shore for twelve or fifteen miles, under the rocky banks, which towered over our heads fourteen or fifteen hundred feet. In some places, immense ledges hung over our path, seemingly ready to crush all beneath them. At length we came to a high perpendicular rock jutting out into the river; and as the water was too deep and too rapid to allow us to wade round its base, we attempted to ascend the bank over loose rocks and stones that slipped from under us at every step, and rolled thundering to the bottom. Having led our horses up about three hundred feet, I stopped, and sent Donny a-head on foot to seek for an opening to the top. The pack-horse could with difficulty preserve his footing under his load. One of the other horses, with incredible sagacity, now walked up past me, until he reached his burdened companion; and putting his shoulder, under one side of the load actually assisted him in sustaining it, until the man's return. Finding that we could not possibly ascend, we were obliged to turn back, and we did not find a practicable place to ascend until we had nearly reached the place from which we had started in the morning.

At last, with great difficulty, we succeeded in gaining the upper bank, and entered upon a wild and romantic district, studded here and there with small clumps of trees, which gradually increased in thickness, until we became surrounded with dense woods, having made a circuit of about twenty-five miles, traversing gullies of prodigious depth and steepness. We again struck the river opposite the mouth of a small stream, on whose banks we saw a couple of Indians. As soon as we were perceived, they sent a canoe over to us, offering to assist in swimming the horses across, as they assured us that the shortest and best route to Colville was on the other side. We accepted their friendly offer, and camped alongside them on the other side. Both Donny and myself were dreadfully fatigued from the length of our day's travel, the labour we had gone through, and the weakness under which we suffered from the want of sufficient food. These Indians, as I afterwards learned, were generally very unfriendly to the whites, and had often given trouble to small parties passing, generally levying a pretty heavy toll for a free passage through their territory. But to me they were all kindness, presenting me with plenty of fresh salmon and dried berries, which were most acceptable, after the disgusting fare on which we had been so long struggling to support life; and one of them proposed to accompany me as a guide to Colville. My last day's experience made me gladly accept of this offer; and long before darkness set in, I found myself as sound asleep as the most weary of dyspeptic patients could wish himself to be.

August 7th—Started very early in the morning with the guide, and made, what is called in those parts, a long day. We were continually ascending and descending, and found it very fatiguing. It was quite dark when we encamped on the banks of the river.

August 8th—Started again very early for the purpose of reaching Colville before night. Came to a high

hill overlooking the Columbia for many miles of its
course, and sat down on its summit to enjoy the magnificent prospect, and give a short rest to the horses. As
I was lying under the trees, the wind sprang up, and,
much to my astonishment, I felt the whole sod moving
under me. At first I imagined it to be an earthquake,
and expected to see the whole hillside move off; but on
examination, I found that it proceeded from the roots
of the immense trees being interlaced one within another
in the shallow soil. This alone prevented their being
blown over, as the rocks are everywhere close to the surface; and as the wind bends the tops of the trees, the
roots rise and fall with the surface in a rolling motion
like a dead swell. We proceeded on until we were within a mile of Kettle Falls, where we swam across in the
usual way, holding on by the tails of our horses; and just
at dusk we were kindly received by Mr. Lewis.

Fort Colville stands in the middle of a small prairie,
about one mile and a half wide by about three miles long,
surrounded by high hills. This little prairie is extremely
valuable for agricultural purposes, as it is, in fact, an
island of fertility surrounded by barren rocks, sandy
plains, and arid mountains, to the distance of three or
four hundred miles along the river, the Spokan valley
to the south being the nearest land fit for cultivation. I
remained here until the 9th of September, when I made
an excursion of sixty miles, accompanied by Mr. Lewis,
to Walker and Eales' Presbyterian mission, where I
was most hospitably received by these worthy people.

Each of the missionaries has a comfortable log-
house, situated in the midst of a fertile plain, and, with
their wives and children, seem to be happily located.
There are numerous Indian *caches* of dried salmon in
the vicinity, which are very seldom robbed, although left

in isolated spots for months without any person in charge. I enjoyed for a week the kind hospitality of my hosts, who were most attentive in accompanying me in my visits to the Spokan River and the Indians in the vicinity.

The Spokan Indians are a small tribe, differing very little from the Indians at Colville either in their appearance, habits, or language. They all seemed to treat the missionaries with great affection and respect; but as to their success in making converts, I must speak with great diffidence, as I was not sufficiently acquainted with the language to examine them, even had I wished to do so. I have no doubt that a great number have been baptized; but I also am aware that almost all Indians will take a name from a man whom they esteem, and give him one in return; and the more ceremony there is about the transaction, the more importance will be attached to it, and the greater the inducement to others to be equally honoured. No influence, however, seems to be able to make agriculturists of them, as they still pursue their hunting and fishing, evincing the greatest dislike to anything like manual labour.

On the 17th of September I returned again to Colville. The Indian village is situated about two miles below the fort, on a rocky eminence overlooking the Kettle Falls. These are the highest in the Columbia River. They are about one thousand yards across, and eighteen feet high. The immense body of water tumbling amongst the broken rocks renders them exceedingly picturesque and grand. The Indians have no particular name for them, giving them the general name of Tumtum, which is applied to all falls of water. The voyageurs call them the "Chaudière," or "Kettle Falls," from the numerous round holes worn in the solid rocks by loose boulders. These boulders, being caught in the inequalities of rocks below the falls, are constantly driven round by the tremendous force of the current, and wear out holes as perfectly round and smooth as in the inner surface of a cast-iron kettle. The village has a population of about five hundred souls, called, in their own language, Chualpays. They differ but little from the Walla-Wallas. The lodges are formed of mats of rushes stretched on poles. A flooring is made of sticks, raised three or four feet from the ground, leaving the space beneath it entirely open, and forming a cool, airy, and shady place, in which to hang their salmon to dry.

These people are governed by two chiefs, Allam-mak-hum Stole-luch, "the Chief of the Earth," and See-pays "the Chief of the Waters." The first exercises great power over the tribe except as regards the fishing, which is under the exclusive control of the latter. Allam-mak-hum Stole-luch dispenses justice strictly, and punishes with rigour any cheating or dis-honesty among his subjects. He opposes the gambling propensities of his tribe to the utmost, even depriving the victorious gamblers of their share of the fish received annually from the Chief of the Waters; but still the passion for gambling continues, and an instance occurred during my stay here of a young man committing suicide by shooting himself, having lost everything he possessed by indulging in this habit. I may here remark that suicide prevails more among the Indians of the Columbia River than in any other portion of the continent which I have visited.

A curious case occurred, about a year before my visit, of two sisters, wives of one man, each jealous of the other, who went into the woods and hung themselves, as was supposed, unknown to each other, as they were found dead a long distance apart.

The principal game played here is called Al-kol-lock, and requires considerable skill. A smooth level piece of ground is chosen, and a slight barrier of a couple of sticks placed lengthwise, is laid at each end of the chosen spot, being from forty to fifty feet apart and only a few inches high. The two players, stripped naked, are armed each with a very slight spear about three feet long, and finely pointed with bone; one of them takes a ring made of bone, or some heavy wood, and wound round with cord; this ring is about three inches in diameter, on the inner circumference of which are fastened six beads of different colours at equal distances, to each of which a separate numerical value is attached. The ring is then rolled along the ground to one of the barriers, and is followed at the distance of two or three yards by the players, and as the ring strikes the barrier and is falling on its side, the spears are thrown, so that the ring may fall on them. If only one of the spears should be covered by the ring, the owner of it counts according to the coloured bead over it. But it generally happens, from the dexterity of the players, that the ring covers both spears, and each counts according to the colour of the beads above his spear; they then play towards the other barrier, and so on until one party has attained the number agreed upon for the game.

No one is allowed to catch fish without the permission of See-pays. His large fishing basket or trap is put down a month before anyone is allowed to fish for themselves. This basket is constructed of stout willow wands woven together, and supported by stout sticks of timber, and is so placed that the salmon, in leaping up the falls strike against a stick placed at the top, and are thrown back into the confined space at the bottom of the trap, which is too narrow to allow them to attempt another jump.

The salmon commence their ascent about the 15th of July, and continue to arrive in almost incredible numbers for nearly two months; in fact, there is one continuous body of them, more resembling a flock of birds than anything else in their extraordinary leap up the falls, begining at sunrise and ceasing at the approach of night. The chief told me that he had taken as many as 1700 salmon, weighing on an average 30 lbs. each, in the course of one day. Probably the daily average taken in the chief's basket is about 400. The chief distributes the fish thus taken during the season amongst his people, everyone, even to the smallest child, getting an equal share.

By the time the salmon reach the Kettle Falls, after surmounting the numerous rapids impeding their journey from the sea, a distance of between 700 and 800 miles, they become so exhausted, that in their efforts to leap these falls, their strength often proves unequal to the task, and striking against the projecting rocks they batter their noses so severely, that they fall back stunned and often dead, and float down the river, where they are picked up some six miles below by another camp of Indians, who do not belong to the Salmon Chief's jurisdiction, and of course have no participation in the produce of his basket. None of these salmon coming up from the sea ever return, but remain in the river and die by thousands; in fact, in such numbers that in our passage down the river in the fall, whenever we came to still water, we found them floating dead or cast up along the shore in such vast numbers as literally to poison the atmosphere.

The young fish return to the sea in the spring. Strange to say, nothing has ever been found in the stomachs of the salmon caught in the Columbia River; and no angler, although frequent trials have been made by the most expert in the art has yet succeeded in tempting them to take any description of fly or other bait.

After the expiration of one month, the Salmon Chief abandons his exclusive privilege, as the fish are then getting thin and poor, and allows all who wish it to take them. For this purpose some use smaller baskets made like the chief's; others use the spear, with which they are very expert, and an ordinary spearsman will take easily as many as 200 in a day; others use a small hand-net in the rapids, where the salmon are crowded together and near the surface. These nets are somewhat like our common landing-nets, but ingeniously contrived, so that when a fish is in them, his own struggles loosen a little stick which keeps the mouth of the net open while empty; the weight of the salmon then draws the mouth close like a purse, and effectually secures the prey.

Salmon is almost the only food used by the Indians on the Lower Columbia River, the two months' fishing affording a sufficient supply to last them the whole year round. The mode in which they cure them is by splitting them down the back, after which each half is again split, making them sufficiently thin to dry with facility, a process occupying in general from four to five days.* The salmon are afterwards sewed up in rush mats, containing about ninety or one hundred pounds, and put up on scaffolds to keep the dogs from them. Infinitely greater numbers of salmon could be readily taken here,

* I have never seen salt made use of by any tribe of Indians for the purpose of preserving food, and they all evince the greatest dislike to salt meat.

if it were desired; but, as the chief considerately remarked to me, if he were to take all that came up, there
would be none left for the Indians on the upper part of
the river; so that they content themselves with supplying their own wants.

A few days before leaving Colville I was informed
that the Chualpays were about to celebrate a scalp dance,
and accordingly I took my sketch-book and went down
to their encampment, where I learned that a small party
had returned from a hunting expedition to the mountains, bringing with them, as a present from a friendly
tribe, the scalp of a Blackfoot Indian. This to them
was a present of inestimable value, as one of their tribe
had been killed by a Blackfoot Indian two or three years
before, and they had not been able to obtain any revenge
for the injury. This scalp, however, would soothe the
sorrows of his widow and friends. Accordingly, it was
stretched upon a small hoop, and attached to a stick as
a handle, and thus carried by the afflicted woman to a
place where a large fire was kindled: here she commenced
dancing and singing, swaying the scalp violently about
and kicking it, whilst eight women, hideously painted,
chanted and danced round her and the fire. The remainder of the tribe stood round in a circle, beating
drums, and all singing.

Having witnessed the performance for about four
or five hours, seeing no variation in it, nor any likeli-
hood of its termination, I returned, deeply impressed
with the sincerity of a grief which could endure such
violent monotony for so long a period. My kind host,
Mr. Lewis, was now obliged to give up rambling about
with me, as he had to see the preparations for the
further progress of the return brigade. Both himself
and his Cree wife were most attentive in adding every

little thing to my outfit which they could supply. Mrs. Lewis was a most excellent wife for a trader, possessing great energy and decision, combined with natural kindness of disposition. Several years before I became acquainted with her she had amputated her husband's arm, a little below the elbow, with a common knife, and tied it up so well, that he soon recovered without any other assistance. Her surgical aid had been called in requisition by the accidental discharge of his gun, which had shattered the limb so much that it was hopeless to try and save it.

September 21*st*—This evening two men arrived
from Walla-Walla, and my grief and horror can be well
imagined when they told me the sad fate of those with
whom I had so lately been a cherished guest. It appears
that the war party before mentioned had brought the
measles back with them, and that it spread with fearful
rapidity through the neighbouring tribe, but more particularly among the Key-uses. Dr. Whitman, as a
medical man, did all he could to stay its progress; but
owing to their injudicious mode of living, which he could
not prevail on them to relinquish, great numbers of them
died. At this time the doctor's family consisted of himself, his wife, and a nephew, with two or three servants,
and several children whom he had humanely adopted,
left orphans by the death of their parents who had died
on their way to Oregon, besides a Spanish half-breed
boy, whom he had brought up for several years. There
were likewise several families of emigrants staying with
him at the time, to rest and refresh themselves and cattle.

The Indians supposed that the doctor could have
stayed the course of the malady had he wished it; and
they were confirmed in this belief by the Spanish half-
breed boy, who told some of them that he had overheard
the doctor say to his wife after they had retired for the

night, that he would give them bad medicine, and kill all the Indians, that he might appropriate their land to himself. They accordingly concocted a plan to destroy the doctor and his wife, and all the males of the establishment. With this object in view, about sixty of them armed themselves and came to his house. The inmates having no suspicion of any hostile intention, were totally unprepared for resistance or flight. Dr. and Mrs. Whitman and their nephew, a youth about seventeen or eighteen years of age, were sitting in their parlour in the afternoon, when Til-au-kite, the chief, and To-ma-kus entered the room, and, addressing the doctor, told him very coolly that they had come to kill him. The doctor, not believing it possible that they could entertain any hostile intentions towards him, told them as much; but while in the act of speaking, To-ma-kus drew a tomahawk from under his robe and buried it deep in his brain. The unfortunate man fell dead from his chair. Mrs. Whitman and the nephew fled up stairs, and locked themselves into an upper room.

In the meantime Til-au-kite gave the war whoop, as a signal to his party outside to proceed in the work of destruction, which they did with the ferocity and yells of so many fiends. Mrs. Whitman, hearing the shrieks and groans of the dying, looked out of the window, and was shot through the breast by a son of the chief, but not mortally wounded. A party then rushed up stairs, and, despatching the nephew on the spot, dragged her down by the hair of her head, and, taking her to the front of the house, mutilated her in a shocking manner with their knives and tomahawks.

There was one man who had a wife bedridden. On the commencement of the affray he ran to her room, and, taking her up in his arms, carried her, unperceived by the Indians, to the thick bushes that skirted the river, and hurried on with his burden in the direction of Fort Walla-Walla. Having reached a distance of fifteen miles, he became so exhausted, that, unable to carry her further, he concealed her in a thick hummock of bushes on the margin of the river, and hastened to the fort for assistance. On his arrival, Mr. M'Bain immediately sent out men with him, and brought her in. She had fortunately suffered nothing more than fright. The number killed, including Dr. and Mrs. Whitman, amounted to fourteen. The other females and children were carried off by the Indians, and two of them were forthwith taken as wives by Til-au-kite's son and another. A man, employed in a little mill, forming a part of the establishment, was spared to work the mill for the Indians.

The day following this awful tragedy, a Catholic priest, who had not heard of the massacre, stopped, on seeing the mangled corpses strewn round the house, and requested permission to bury them, which he did with the rites of his own church. The permission was granted the more readily as these Indians are friendly towards the Catholic missionaries. On the priest leaving the place, he met, at a distance of five or six miles, a brother missionary of the deceased, a Mr. Spalding, the field of whose labours lay about a hundred miles off, at a place on the River Coldwater. He communicated to him the melancholy fate of his friend, and advised him to fly as fast as possible, or in all probability he would be another victim. He gave him a share of his provisions, and Mr. Spalding hurried homeward full of apprehensions for the safety of his own family; but unfortunately his horse escaped from him in the night, and, after a six days' toilsome march on foot, having lost his way, he at

length reached the banks of the river, but on the opposite side to his own house.

In the dead of the night, and in a state of starvation,
having eaten nothing for three days, everything seeming to be quiet about his own place, he cautiously embarked in a small canoe and paddled across the river.
But he had no sooner landed than an Indian seized him
and dragged him to his house, where he found all his
family prisoners, and the Indians in full possession.
These Indians were not of the same tribe with those who
had destroyed Dr. Whitman's family, nor had they at
all participated in the outrage; but having heard of it,
and fearing that the whites would include them in their
vengeance, they had seized on the family of Mr. Spalding for the purpose of holding them as hostages for their
own safety. The family were uninjured, and he was
overjoyed to find that things were no worse.

Mr. Ogden, the chief factor of the Hudson's Bay
Company on the Columbia, immediately on hearing of
the outrage, came to Walla-Walla, and, although the
occurrence took place in the territory of the United
States, and of course the sufferers could have no further
claim to the protection of the Company than such as
humanity dictated, he at once purchased the release of
all the prisoners, and from them the particulars of the
massacre were afterwards obtained. The Indians, in
their negotiations with Mr. Ogden, offered to give up
the prisoners for nothing, if he would guarantee that the
United States would not go to war with them; but this,
of course, he could not do.

On the 22nd of September our two boats, with their
crews of six men each, being all ready, we bade farewell to our kind host and his family and again embarked
on the river. As usual, on leaving a fort, we did not

start till evening, and stopped again for the night at
ten miles distant, at Day's Encampment. We had no
regale, as these men were not going into the interior.
They only carried the express to Boat Encampment,
where they exchanged boxes with the express from the
east side of the mountains, with whom I was to recross.

September 23rd—To-day we succeeded in getting
past the Little Dalles in safety. They are about twenty
miles from Kettle Falls, and are the narrowest part of
the Columbia River for full one thousand miles. It is
here contracted into a passage of one hundred and fifty
yards by lofty rocks, on each side, through which it
rushes with tremendous violence, forming whirlpools in
its passage capable of engulphing the largest forest trees,
which are afterwards disgorged with great force. This
is one of the most dangerous places that the boats have
to pass.   In going up the river the boats are all emptied,
and the freight has to be carried about half a mile over
the tops of the high and rugged rocks. One man remains
in each boat with a long pole to keep it off from the rocks,
whilst the others drag it by a long tow-rope up the torrent.

Last year a man, who was on the outside of the rope,
was jerked over the rocks by some sudden strain, and
was immediately lost. In coming down, however, all
remain in the boats; and the guides in this perilous pass,
display the greatest courage and presence of mind at
moments when the slightest error in managing the frail
bark would hurl its occupants to certain destruction.
On arriving at the head of the rapids, the guide gets out
on to the rocks and surveys the whirlpools. If they are
filling in "or making," as they term it, the men rest on
their paddles until they commence throwing off, when
the guides instantly re-embark, and shove off the boat,

and shoot through this dread portal with the speed of lightning. Sometimes the boats are whirled round in the vortex with such awful rapidity that it renders the management impossible, and the boat and its hapless crew are swallowed up in the abyss.

September 24th—We had fine weather and made good progress. I shot the largest wolf to-day I had ever seen; he was swimming away from us across the river.

September 25th—The morning broke dark and cloudy, and soon turned to heavy rain; but the wind was fair, so we hoisted our sail, and soon scudded into an open lake, about three miles wide and twelve long.

September 26th—It continued raining heavily all night, and heavy mists hung over us during the day; but we continued our journey and got into what is called another lake.

September 27th—Still in the lakes. The day was clearer, and we could distinguish the surrounding scenery, which seemed to consist of immense mountains, towering peak on peak above the clouds. The land appeared barren and unfit for cultivation. The cedars are of enormous magnitude, some of them measuring not less than thirty or forty feet in circumference. I was told of one fifty feet, but did not see it. I attempted to reach the upper side of one which had been uprooted and lay on the ground, with the end of my gun stretched out at arm's length, and could but just attain it.

September 28th—We had an exciting chase after a mountain goat, which showed himself in the distance, on a point of land jutting out into the lake. Putting the boat ashore, I started in pursuit, accompanied by three or four Indians, and after a long hunt succeeded in killing him. He afforded us a most delicious repast. In size and shape he somewhat resembled the domestic goat, but was covered with white wool resembling that of a sheep; the horns are straight, small, pointed, and black.

September 29th—Got through the lakes by 5 o'clock P.M., and again entered into what may be more properly called the river. The rain was pouring heavily on us almost all day, whilst in the distance we could see the tops of the mountains becoming white with snow down to a well-defined line, where it seemed to change to rain.

September 30th—Started at 6 A.M., during a pouring rain, which soon soaked us to the skin. We stopped here to make some paddles, in a forest abounding with birch, the only wood fit for this purpose, and which is not met with lower down the Columbia; large cedar-trees were also very abundant.

October 1st—The morning was fine and clear, and the temperature was agreeable: I was enabled to leave the boat for a walk for a few miles along the shore, much to the relief of my legs. The place is a sandbank, extending for miles in a direction parallel with the shore, and generally but a few furlongs from it; it is called the "Grand Batteur." The steepness of the banks of the river, and the density of the under-brushwood, had confined us to the boats for the last three days; it was therefore no wonder that I should enjoy a walk. We saw some very large piles of drift-wood, called by the Canadians "Aumbereaux." These piles consist of trees of all sizes, but usually very large, which are drifted down the river, and are piled high up upon one another by the force of the ice when they meet with any obstruction. I amused myself by setting fire to some of them *en passant,* and leaving an immense fire burning, the smoke of which we could see for days in our rear.

October 2nd—It again rained heavily all day. Towards the evening we encamped. It is difficult to imagine the pleasure of an encampment round a large fire, after sitting in an open boat on the Columbia River, with the rain pouring down in torrents all day; but though the rain may not have ceased, yet the cheerful warmth of the fire dispels all the annoyance of mere moisture in this uncivilized state of life. We passed the Upper Little Dalle, a very long and rapid shoot of three or four miles. One of the Indians brought in some white berries, which he ate eagerly, but which I found very nauseous. I never saw any berry in the course of my travels which the Indians scruple to eat, nor have I seen any ill effect result from their doing so.

October 3rd—Saw four cariboos, a species of deer of the ordinary size, which we followed, but without success, as they got the wind of us before we could approach them within gunshot. We fell in with the Indian chief of the lakes, and procured some bear's and deer's meat from him, of which he seemed to possess a plentiful supply. A small species of dog was tied to the bushes near his lodge, to prevent them from hunting on their own account, and driving away all the deer. The chief told me that when disposed to hunt with them, he had only to find a fresh deer-track, set his dogs on it and lie down to sleep, as they never fail to find the deer, and turn them back to the place where they had left him lying. We saw some of these dogs, apparently on the track of some deer, full twelve or fifteen miles from the chief's lodge.

October 4th—The chief, with wife and daughter, accompanied us in their canoe, which they paddled with great dexterity, from ten to fifteen miles. They make their canoes of pine bark, being the only Indians who use this material for the purpose; their form is also peculiar and very beautiful. These canoes run the

rapids with more safety for their size, than those of
any other shape. The chief and his ladies breakfasted
with us, and then bid us good-bye.

We camped at night below the "Dalle des Morts,"
or the Rapid of the Dead, so called from the following
circumstance. About twenty-five or thirty years ago,
an Iroquois, a half-breed, and a French Canadian,
having charge of a boat, had to descend this frightful
rapid. Fearful of running it they affixed a long line
to the bow, and being themselves on the shore, they
attempted to lower her gradually by means of it down
the foaming torrent. The boat took a sheer and ran
outside of a rock, and all their efforts to get her back,
or reach the rock themselves through the boiling surge
were unavailing. The rope, chafing on the sharp edge
of the rock, soon broke, and she dashed down amongst
the whirling eddies, and broke to pieces, with their whole
stock of provisions on board.

They then continued to follow on foot, along the
rugged and difficult banks of the river, without food,
guns, or ammunition; nor had they been able to save
even a blanket to protect them from the inclement
weather. At night they encamped in a shivering and
famishing condition, not having been able to surmount
more than three miles of the obstacles that obstructed
their passage at every step along the banks. The next
day they proceeded with no better success. They well
knew that if they constructed a raft it would not live
an hour in this part of the Columbia River, owing to
the quick succession of rapids that here beset the navigation. In this starving condition they continued their
slow progress till the third day, when the half-breed,
fearing his companions would kill him for their food,
left them, and was never after heard of, falling in all

probability, a prey to the wolves. The other two lay down, and the Iroquois watching his opportunity, got up at night, and beat his companion's brains out with a stick, and going to work in a methodical manner, after first satisfying his craving hunger with a portion of the body, cut the remainder into thin slices and dried them in the sun, after the manner in which buffalo meat is prepared. Here he remained three days drying his meat, which he made into a pack, and continued his journey with it down the river bank, until he came to the commencement of the Upper Lake, where he made a raft, on which he placed his dried meat, and covered it over with pine-bark, seating himself upon it, and paddling down the lake.

He had not proceeded very far, before he met a canoe, which had been sent from one of the forts below, on the Spokan River, in quest of them, owing to their long absence. The new comers immediately inquired what had become of his two companions; he replied, that they had deserted him, giving at the same time an account of the loss of the boat. They took him on board their canoe, and one of the men seeing the bark on the raft, and desirous of getting it to place under him in the canoe, the Iroquois shoved off the raft, with evident signs of confusion, on which the man, who noticed his embarrassment, paddled up to it, and lifting the bark, discovered the dried meat beneath it, among which was a human foot. He was asked how he had obtained the dried meat, and replied, that he had killed a wolf, swimming across the river.

The foot with the meat was slyly deposited in a bag, belonging to one of the men, but not without the act being perceived by the murderer, who, while they were asleep during the night, threw the bag and its

contents into the river. Appearing not to notice its
loss, they went on to Fort Spokan, and delivered him
up to Mr. McMullan, the person in charge, detailing
particulars. The Indian was shortly afterwards sent
to a distant post in New Caledonia, both as a punishment, and also in order to get rid of him, as no voyageur will willingly associate with anyone known to
have eaten human flesh. I had previously travelled
several hundreds of miles with the son of this very man,
who always behaved well, although there certainly was
something repulsive in his appearance, which would
have made me dislike to have had him for a companion
in a situation such as above described.

October 5th—It rained so hard throughout the day
and night, and the river was swollen so much, that we
despaired of hauling the boats up the rapids, and therefore remained until the following morning at our encampment.

October 6th—It was a lovely morning. Saw some
cariboos, but could not approach them near enough
for a shot. We had a magnificent view of the Rocky
Mountains in the distance, in all their azure grandeur.
The flood soon subsided sufficiently to allow our ascending the rapids, although it took us the whole day to
haul the boats up—the distance is not more than three
miles—but the boats were so strained and tossed about
in the operation, that we were obliged to haul them
ashore and grease their bottoms with the resin which
exudes from the pine.

Whilst the men were engaged in these operations,
I took advantage of the delay, and made a sketch, looking down the rapids. As I was sketching, our steersman, who was present at the time, told me a melancholy occurence, which took place at this spot, and which

I will give as nearly as possible in his own words. "About four years ago," said he, "I crossed the Rocky Mountains with a party of forty. When we got to Boat Encampment, we embarked in two boats; the one which I was steering had twenty-two on board, amongst whom was a gentleman sent into the interior for the purpose of botanical research. On his way to Saskatchewan, he had fallen in with a young lady, a half-breed, who was travelling to cross the mountains and go down the Columbia on a visit to some of her friends. They had not travelled far, before a mutual attachment induced them to become man and wife, at Edmonton, though few couples, I think, in the world would choose a trip across the mountains for a honeymoon excursion; but they bore all their hardships and labours cheerfully, perfectly happy in helping each other, and being kind to their companions.

"We had two or three other women with us, and I had my own daughter, about ten years old, whom I was taking home to my wife at Fort Vancouver. I had left her two or three years before, on the east side of the mountains, with some of her relations, as I was unable to bring her over at the time I had come with my wife. We had also a young man of the name of McGillveray, belonging to the Company, with a small dog; the remainder were principally voyageurs.

"When I came to the head of the rapids, I found that the other boat, which contained the principal guide, had passed on, and I thought, therefore, that the rapids were in a proper state for running them, that is, that the whirlpools were throwing out and not filling, which they do alternately. I therefore went on without stopping, and when in the midst of the rapids, where there was no possibility of staying the downward course of

the boat, I discovered to my dismay that the whirlpools
were filling.   One moment more and the water curled
over the sides of the boat, immediately filling her.   I
called out for all to sit still and hold on steadily to the
seats, as the boat would not sink entirely owing to the
nature of the cargo, and that I could guide them to
shore in this state.   We ran more than a mile in safety,
when the boat ran close by a ledge of rocks.   The
botanist, who held his wife in his arms, seeing the boat
approach so near the rock, made a sudden spring for
the shore; but the boat filled with water, yielded to the
double weight of himself and wife, and they sank clasped in each other's arms.   The boat was suddenly turned
completely bottom upwards; but I and another man
succeeded in getting on the top of her, and were thus
carried down safely.   We thought we heard some noise
inside the boat, and the man who was with me, being a
good swimmer, dived under, and soon, to my unexpected joy, appeared with my little daughter, who almost miraculously had been preserved by being jammed in amongst the luggage, and supported by the
small quantity of air which had been caught by the
boat when she turned over.   We soon got ashore: Mc-
Gillveray and four others saved themselves by swimming, the remaining fourteen were drowned; we immediately commenced searching for the bodies, and soon
recovered all of them, the unfortunate botanist and his
wife still fast locked in each other's arms,—an embrace
which we had not the heart to unclasp, but buried them
as we found them, in one grave.   We afterwards found
McGillveray's little dog thrown up dead on the sandbank, with his master's cap held firmly between his
teeth."

October 7th—We embarked in the morning, and continued our journey through a continual drizzle of rain, which was anything but pleasant.

October 8th—The weather cleared up, and we saw cariboos in great numbers; but, as usual, they were too wary for us to get a shot at them.   Passed the rapids of St. Martin before night.

October 9th—Travelled but a short distance to-day, having to cut our way through the numerous fallen trees which, projecting into the stream, obstructed the course close to the shore, which we were obliged to take owing to the violence of the current in mid-channel.

October 10th—In the forenoon we perceived tracks of human feet in the sand on the shore, which astonished us very much, as no Indians come near these parts; and on approaching Boat Encampment, which we did about 2 p.m., we perceived smoke rising, which made us hope that the brigade from the east with the express had arrived, but were much disappointed at finding that it was only my old friend Capote Blanc, the Sho-shawp chief from Jasper's House, and two Indians who had come over to hunt.   Here we made a suitable encampment, and hauled up our boats high and dry on the sand. Capote Blanc had been very successful in his hunt, and had a large stock of dried moose meat and beaver's tails, with which he supplied us abundantly, receiving a few small articles and ammunition in exchange.

We now had nothing to do but to try and pass the time pleasantly as we could under the circumstances, until the arrival of the brigade from the east side of the mountains.   The men spent the day principally in gambling, and performing charms which they supposed would hasten the arrival of the brigade, such as erecting crosses, with one of the arms pointing to the direc-

tion from which it was expected. They also prepared
what they call a "lob-stick." For this purpose a high
tree is chosen which has thick branches at the top, and
all the lower limbs are carefully trimmed off; a smooth
surface is then cut on one side of the tree, on which
the person in whose honour it has been trimmed is invited to cut his name; this being done, three rounds of
blank charges are fired, and three cheers given, and the
spot afterwards bears the name of his encampment.
On this occasion I had the honour of carving my name
upon the "lob-stick." We had almost constant rain,
accompanied by immense snow-flakes, which obscured
our view of the mountains nearly the whole time of our
remaining here. I, however, managed to pick out
some few bright hours for sketching.

We found very little game about here; the men
only succeeded in trapping a few martens, and we began to be very uneasy, fearing that some disaster must
have befallen the brigade which was to meet us. I
endeavoured to prevail on some of the men to accompany me across the mountains; but they would not go
with me, so that I was forced to stay with the rest.
Boat Encampment derives its name from its being the
head of the navigable water. Three rivers here unite,
forming the commencement of the north branch of the
Columbia, so that the enlargement of the river is very
sudden.

October 28*th*—About three o'clock in the afternoon
a clerk in the company's service arrived, and announced
that he had come in advance of the eastern brigade,
which would arrive next day under the command of
Mr. Low. This was indeed joyful news to us, as we
were all heartily tired of our gloomy situation.

October 29*th*—Mr. Low and party arrived this morning with between fifty and sixty horses loaded with provisions, and the furs destined for Russia. They had been nine days crossing from Jasper's House. Mr. Low seemed doubtful about our being able to recross with the horses; but I cared little whether we had horses or not, so that I got away, for I was completely wearied with my long inaction. My provisions, too, were getting short, and the person in charge did not offer to replenish my stock, so that I had no choice but to cross as quickly as possible.

October 30*th*—This day Mr. Low left for Fort Vancouver with the boats which had brought me up, leaving me with four Indians who had accompanied him from the east side for the purpose of taking the horses back, and of guiding me over the mountains.

October 31*st*—It was a beautiful morning, and we started about ten o'clock, after loading fifteen horses out of the fifty-six which Mr. Low had brought with him, and got the first day as far as the Grande Batteur, where we encamped.

November 1*st*—We passed through the Pointe des Bois, a distance of ten miles, by about the worst road I had ever travelled, it being cut up by so many horses having passed it a short time previously. My horse stuck in a mud hole until he sank up to his head, and it was with the greatest difficulty that one of the men and myself extricated him alive. What with the horses sticking in the mud, the packs falling off, the shouting to the animals in Cree, and swearing at them in French, there being no oaths in the Indian language, I never passed such a busy, tiresome, noisy, and disagreeable day in my life. This was in a great measure owing to having so few men to look after so large a number of horses, which would not keep the road, but ran helter skelter through the thick woods. At last we arrived at the bottom of the Grande Côte, and there encamped for the night, thoroughly wearied out and disgusted with horse-driving.

November 2nd—We started an hour before daybreak to ascend the stupendous Grande Côte, and soon found the snow becoming deeper at every step. One of our horses fell down a declivity of twenty-five to thirty feet with a heavy load on his back, and, strange to say, neither deranged his load nor hurt himself. We soon had him on the track again as well as ever, except that he certainly looked a little *bothered*. The snow now reached up to the horses' sides as we slowly toiled along, and reached the summit just as the sun sank below the horizon; but we could not stop here, as there was no food for the horses; we were therefore obliged to push on past the Committee's Punch Bowl, a lake I have before described.

It was intensely cold, as might be supposed, in this elevated region. Although the sun shone during the day with intense brilliancy, my long beard became one solid mass of ice. It was long after dark before we arrived at the Campment de Fusei, having met with no other place which afforded any food for the horses, and even here they had to dig the snow away with their hoofs to enable them to get at it.

A distressing occurrence took place here some years previously. Whilst a party were ascending this mountain, a lady, who was crossing to meet her husband, was in the rear, and it was not noticed until the party had encamped that she was not come up. Men were instantly sent back to seek her. After some hours' search, they found her tracks in the snow, which they followed until they came to a perpendicular rock overhanging a roaring torrent; here all traces of her were lost, and her body was never found, notwithstanding every exertion was made to find it. Little doubt, however, could exist but that she had lost her way, and had fallen over the precipice into the torrent, which would have quickly hurried her into chasms where the foot of a man could not reach.

November 3rd—Last night was the coldest (according to my feelings) that I had ever experienced; but not having a thermometer with me, I do not know what was the intensity. I am, however, confident that it was colder on that night than it was on a subsequent night, when the spirit thermometer indicated 56° below zero, a temperature at which mercury would have become frozen and useless. I endeavoured to thaw myself by melting some snow over the fire; but the water froze upon my hair and beard, although I stood as close as I well could to a blazing fire, and I actually had to scorch my face before I could thaw the ice out. We now passed through the Grande Batteur, and, much to our relief, found the snow decreasing in depth as we descended. We succeeded in reaching the Campment de Regnalle in the evening, and camped there for the night.

November 4th—We got our breakfast and started long before day. We made good progress until about noon, when we came to a wild tract of country which appeared to have been visited years before by some terrible hurricane, which had uprooted the whole forest for miles around, not leaving a tree standing; a younger growth of trees were now pushing their heads up through the fallen timber of the ancient forest. We all got so hungry with our violent exercise in such a cold clear atmosphere, that we could not resist the temptation of stopping and cooking something to eat, before we entered the tangled maze before us. This was the first time we had done so, as daylight was too valuable to be wasted in sitting down, and the danger of being caught in one of the tremendous snowstorms, which are so frequent in these regions, was too imminent for us not to push on to the utmost of our power. The snow often lies here to the depth of twenty or thirty feet, and one storm might have caused us the loss of the horses and baggage at least, even if we had been able to save ourselves by making snowshoes. It was, therefore, no slight temptation which could induce the men who knew the country to stop for dinner; but hunger is a good persuader, and carried the question. After dinner we pushed on with renewed strength; but it was with great difficulty that we were enabled to get the horses through the fallen and tangled woods, and it was not until after nightfall that we reached the "Grand Traverse," where we found three men, who had been sent out to meet us and assist in driving in our sixty horses, which were as yet all safe.

November 5th—In the morning we found the Athabasca River in a flooded state, and a heavy snowstorm had set in; we, however, proceeded to ford the rapid stream, although the snow was driving with such fury in our faces that we could not distinguish the opposite bank. The water almost covered the backs of the horses, and my pack, containing sketches and curiosities, &c., had to be carried on the shoulders of the men riding across, to keep them out of the water. After fording the river we crossed La Rouge's Prairie, and encamped on the very spot that I had slept at exactly a year previously, to the very day.

November 6th—The wind blew intensely cold, and
we had to pass along the margin of a frozen lake, seven
or eight miles long, over which the snow drifted furiously in our faces. It became so cold that we could
no longer sit on the horses, but were obliged to dismount
and drive them on before us. My beard, the growth
of nearly two years, gave me much trouble, as it became
heavy with ice from the freezing of my breath; even
my nostrils became stopped up, and I was forced to
breathe through my mouth.

Fortunately I fell in with an Indian lodge, and had
an opportunity of thawing myself, so that I rode the
remainder of the way to Jasper's House with compara-
tive comfort. There we soon forgot our trouble over
a good piece of mountain sheep, which is really delicious, even when not seasoned by such hardships as we
had undergone.

This place is completely surrounded by lofty
mountains, some of them close to the house, others many
miles distant, and is subject to violent tornadoes, which
sweep through the mountain gorges with terrific fury.
A great number of mountain sheep had been driven
down into the valleys by the intensity of the cold, which
had set in this winter with unusual severity. I have
counted as many as five large flocks of these animals
grazing in different directions from the house at one
time, and the Indians brought them in every day, so
that we fared most sumptuously. These sheep are those
most commonly called the "big horn."

I made a sketch of a ram's head of an enormous
size; his horns were similar in shape to those of our
domestic ram, but measured forty-two inches in length.
They are considerably larger than our domestic sheep;
their coat somewhat resembles in texture and colour

the red deer, but a little darker. We were now
obliged to set our men to work to make snowshoes, as
our further journey had to be made over deep snow.
The birch wood of which they are made does not grow
near Jasper's House, and the men had to go twenty
miles off to get it. At last, by the 14th, our snowshoes
and a sledge were completed, and with much difficulty
I obtained two wretched dogs from the Indians, and one
Mr. Colin Frazer lent me, to drag the sledge with my
packs, provisions, and blankets. I had two men, one
an Indian, the other a half-breed. They had come with
Mr. Low from Edmonton, with seven others, and ought
to have waited for me; but we had been so long coming,
and the weather had got so cold, that the seven got
afraid of waiting any longer, and departed without me.
Had these two followed the example of their companions, I should have been obliged to spend a most dreary
winter in the wretched accommodation which Jasper's
House afforded.

November 15*th*—Early in the morning we equipped
ourselves for the journey, putting on snowshoes between five and six feet long,—the pair I wore were exactly my own height, five feet eleven inches. Owing
to our having so few dogs, we could not carry many
provisions, but trusted to our guns to provide more on
the way.

About fifteen or sixteen miles from Jasper's House,
we came to an Indian's lodge, which we found tenanted
by a woman and her five children, her husband being out on a hunt. She was so civil and kind, and
the lodge was so comfortable, that we were induced
to stop, particularly as it was our first day on snow
shoes, and stopping there saved us the trouble of making a camp for ourselves. The hunter returned late

in the evening, having killed four sheep, one of which he brought home on his back.   This we all set to work to cook, the squaw boiling as much as her kettle would hold, and the men sticking the rest upon sticks and roasting it.   The whole party then set resolutely to work, and ate the whole sheep, and it was not a small one either.   The hunter told us that he had seen thirty-four sheep that day, and that he never remembered a winter in which so many sheep had come down from the mountains.   He proved a most agreeable host, and entertained me with stories of his hunting exploits during the whole evening.   My kind hostess prepared me a bed of sheep skins for the night, the most comfortable bed I had slept in for many months.

November 16*th*—At an early hour before daylight we got our breakfast and harnessed our dogs, and made our way through some very thick woods.   We entered on Jasper's Lake, twelve miles long, the wind blowing a perfect hurricane, as it always does here when it blows at all.   Fortunately the wind always comes from the mountains; had it been otherwise, we should not have been able to pass along the lake on the glare of ice against such a storm of wind and sleet; as it was, we were blown along by the wind, and could only stop ourselves by lying down; our sledge sometimes flying in front of the dogs, while we were enveloped in a cloud of snow that prevented our seeing more than a few yards before us.

When we were about half way over the lake, we perceived two Indians, who were making their way across in a course intersecting our own route, and evidently had hard work to keep in the right direction. On coming up to them, we all sat down and had a smoke.   The Indians, when they come to ice or hard frozen snow, where the snowshoe has to be taken off, always take off their moccasins also, and travel barefooted; by this means they preserve their moccasins, and when they sit down they put them on dry and wrap their feet in their furs.   This walking barefooted on the ice in such intense cold would seem dangerous to the inexperienced, but, in fact, the feet of those who are accustomed to it suffer less in this way than they do from the ice which always forms on the inside of the moccasin in long and quick travelling, as the ice thus formed cracks into small pieces and cuts the feet. After we had crossed the lake, we proceeded about five miles down the river, and encamped.

November 17*th*—The night had been intensely cold, but we all felt well and in high spirits when we started in the morning.   These feelings were, however, soon damped by the painful difficulties which we soon encountered.   Where the river is rapid, the ice becomes rough, craggy, and unsafe, and is raised in hillocks to a considerable height, by the masses being forced by the current on the top of each other. Some of those hillocks we met were so formidable, that we at first doubted the possibility of surmounting them; even in the hollows we were obliged to move slowly, feeling our way with long sticks, to ascertain if the ice was solid. This was rendered necessary by the frequent occurrence of flat fields of ice, which, being formed high above the usual level of the water, and having nothing to support them underneath, easily give way, and the traveller falls either into the torrent far below, or upon another layer of ice.   These dangerous places are formed by the large masses of ice getting jammed together against the rocks, or in some bend of the river, and damming the water up, on the top of which a thin coating is formed. As soon as the weight of water becomes too heavy for the dam, it is carried away, and the water sinks, leaving the coat formed on the top without support from underneath, which, when covered with snow, it is impossible to distinguish from good ice, except by feeling it with a stick.

We had not proceeded very far, before one of the men fell through one of these places; luckily he did not come to water, and we soon got him out. Our dogs were now almost useless, as they were unable to drag the sledge over the uneven surface, and we were obliged to push the sledge after them with our poles, and often to lift the dogs, sledge, and baggage up and down the perpendicular ice ridges (or *bourdigneaux,* as the voyageurs call them) with which our path was constantly intersected. At this place it was impossible to leave the river, as the ground on both sides was so broken, and the forest was so dense and tangled, that we should have starved long before we could have made our way through it. About an hour before sundown I unfortunately broke through, and it was with the utmost difficulty that I saved myself from being carried under by the current, which here ran with the velocity of a mill race; happily, I neither lost my pole nor my presence of mind, so the men had time to come up and help me out; but the moment I was out of the water my clothes became perfectly stiff, and we were obliged to make a fire and encamp for the night.

November 18*th*—Our trials seemed now to be increasing at every step, but the struggle was not optional now; so cheering ourselves with the idea that none know what they can bear until they are tried, we prepared for an early start. Our first trouble was that the dog Mr. Frazer lent me (the best dog we had) was gone; he had gnawed the cord asunder with which he was tied, and bolted off home. This was a serious loss, as besides his use in drawing the sledge, we did not know but that we might want to eat him, our provisions were getting so scarce, and we met with very few rabbits, the only thing to be found on the route at this season.

Our next difficulty was to pass the Grand Rapid, where we found the river obstructed for nearly four miles by bourdigneaux, from ten to fourteen feet high. Over this continuous mass of icy pinnacles we scrambled with incredible labour, our limbs bruised with repeated falls, and our feet wounded and cut by treading on the sharp edges of fractured ice. At last, overpowered by fatigue and pain, we made our camp for the night, almost disheartened with our slow progress, as we had not made more than ten or twelve miles through the whole day.

During the night we were awoke by a tremendous roaring amongst the masses of ice, caused by a rising in the river. I could not help feeling apprehensive lest we should be crushed amongst it, from our camp being so near; but the men were with them; so we slept on.

November 19*th*—When we got up in the morning, we found that the water had overflowed the ice, and we were compelled to make a circuit through the woods. We found the brush and fallen timber so thick, that we had to cut a road through it to enable our two dogs and the sledge to get along. It took us three hours to make an advance of one mile, before we again got back to the bourdigneaux, glad even to get to them, in preference to the tangled and almost impassable growth of trees and underwood which follows the course of the river through its whole length. This day I suffered a great deal; my feet were so severely cut by the frozen strings of my snowshoes, that I left a track of blood behind me on the snow at every step.

At night, when we encamped, it became so cold that we could only sleep for a few minutes at a time; no matter how large we made the fire, it would only keep that part warm which was immediately next to it, so that we were obliged to keep turning round and round to save ourselves from freezing.

November 20*th*—This morning I found I had what the voyageurs call *mal de racquet*. This complaint attacks those who are unaccustomed to the use of snow shoes, if they walk far on them at first. It is felt at the instep. I do not know how to convey an idea of the intense pain, except by saying that it feels as if the bones were broken, and the rough edges were grinding against each other at every motion.

November 21*st*—In the morning we found that the river had become dammed up a short distance below our encampment, and was throwing the ice up in mountainous heaps with tremendous noise. This forced us again to make a short détour through the woods, which we effected with a great deal of trouble. By the time we got to the river again it snowed very hard, and continued without intermission all day; notwithstanding all this, and the *mal de racquet,* from which I suffered very severely, we pushed on, and, impelled by the dire necessity, for our supply of food was fast diminishing, we made rather a good day's journey. We had, up to this, always given our dogs food every day, but my guide advised us not to do so any more, as he had known dogs to travel twenty days without food, and every ounce we now had was too precious to give to them, even if they died; so the poor brutes were tied up supper-

less, and we tried to content ourselves with about half
of what was our usual allowance.

November 22nd—The snow still continued, and
was getting very deep and light, adding considerably
to the labour of our journey; but we toiled on man-
fully, and succeeded in getting across Baptiste River
before we stopped for the night, which did not seem
to me as cold as usual, I suppose on account of the falling snow and stillness of the atmosphere.

November 23rd—The snow had ceased falling, but
lay very deep and feathery on the ground, so that it
fell over on to the snowshoes, adding to their weight.
This to me became very distressing, after two or three
hours' walking, owing to the state of my ankles; but
the weather was clear and fine, and the bright sun,
while it lasted, seemed to cheer us on, so that at night,
when we stopped, we calculated that we had made at
least thirty-five miles. Not having met with any rabbits, we were obliged to stint ourselves in food, and
starve our dogs.

November 24th—To-day we again came to open
water, and had to make another détour through the
woods of about a mile and a half, but it was not such
a bad place as we had encountered before, the woods
being a little more open. When we came to the river
again, we found ourselves on the top of a high bank,
down which we lowered our sledge and baggage, and
then pitched the poor dogs after. As for ourselves,
we scrambled at the commencement of the descent, then
rolled a little by way of variety, and fell the rest of the
way; however, the snow was so deep, that we did not
get hurt, and after some trouble in unburying ourselves
at the bottom, we continued our route along the river.

November 25th—We had not travelled more than twenty miles, when we came to a part of the river in which the current was so rapid, that the ice was all tumbling about in broken masses. On each side we were encompassed by high banks rising into hills, which it was impossible for us to ascend; and as it is a rule, in travelling in the interior, never to go back, we had nothing for it but to encamp under the shelter of the hill, in hopes that the intense cold of the night would sufficiently unite the masses of ice to enable us to cross in the morning.

After our camp was made, the men, seeing me suffer so much from the *mal de racquet,* recommended me to scarify my insteps, and kindly offered to perform the operation, which is done with a sharp gun-flint; but I was afraid of the frost getting into the wounds, and refused, although I had every confidence in their knowledge of what would be the best remedy in a case like mine. We had not succeeded in shooting a single animal on our route, and it was with melancholy forebodings we looked at our diminished stock of provisions. Our poor dogs looked so savage and starved, that we had to tie their heads close up to the trees, fearing lest they might gnaw the strings, and make off.

November 26th—In the morning we found the ice sufficiently strong to induce us to proceed, but we had to use great caution, as it was still very weak. Our long snowshoes covering such a large surface, supported us safely; but the ice was so thin, that the dogs and sledge went through, and we should have lost everything we had, had not the Indian held a string fastened to the sledge, and by this means hauled them up. When we surmounted this difficulty, we found the ice better than usual, and were enabled to make in all forty miles before we encamped.

November 27th—We got on to-day very well till about noon, when the *mal de racquet* became so painful to me, that I thought I would try to walk without my snowshoes.   But I had not waded through the snow very far before I fell through the ice.   Luckily, I got out easily enough, but I was wet through; and as our provisions were nearly all gone, and we were hungry, I pushed on in my wet clothes, trusting to the violent exercise to keep me warm.   I certainly did not suffer from cold, but the freezing of my leathern trousers chafed my legs and made me very uncomfortable.   We encamped after a hard day's work, and as we were in great hopes of reaching Fort Assiniboine next day, we finished the last of our provisions.

November 28th—We started early in the morning, about three o'clock; this was an hour earlier than we usually got away, but we had nothing to cook and no breakfast to eat.   I began to feel that my hardships were telling seriously on me.   The *mal de racquet* tortured me at every step; the soles of my feet were terribly cut and wounded from the ice, which formed inside of my stockings as much as an eighth of an inch thick every day, occasioned by the freezing of the perspiration.   It breaks in small pieces, and is like so much sharp gravel in the shoes; and I was weak from the want of food; but the hope of reaching a place of safety kept me up, and I toiled on over the bourdigneaux, which were very numerous to-day, steadily but slowly. At last, overcome with fatigue and weakness we had to encamp still far from the fort.   We had a long consultation over our camp fire, as to whether we should eat the dogs or not, but their thinness saved them—the two would not have furnished us with a sufficient meal; besides, they could draw the sledge still, and that was a great consideration to us in our weak state; and we knew that if we met with no accident, we must reach the fort next day; still, if the dogs had been young, and in anything like condition, they would most assuredly have gone into the pot.

November 29*th*—We again started very early in the morning, hunger waking us up earlier than usual. It is the general rule of travelling in these northern regions, to start as soon as awake, and to continue until fagged out. Daylight is of such short duration (not more than four or five hours) at this time of the year, that it is taken little into account, the light of the snow and the Aurora enabling the traveller to see at all hours. Our way was not very bad, in comparison with what we had come over; still we had to move on slowly from weakness, and it was not until four o'clock P.M., that we arrived at Fort Assiniboine, having travelled 350 miles in fifteen days.

No sooner had we arrived, than all hands set to work cooking; luckily for us, this post is plentifully supplied with white fish—indeed, it is almost the only thing they ever have to eat here—which are caught in immense numbers in a small lake near the fort, called McLeod's Lake. I never saw such large ones as those caught here. They average six and seven pounds; and one of them which I saw weighed had actually attained to the enormous weight of eighteen pounds.

Whether it was the hunger from which I was suffering, or the real goodness of the fish, I know not now; but certainly they seemed to be the most delicious I had ever tasted, and the memory of that feast hung over me, even in my dreams, for many a day afterwards.

One of the women devoted herself to the rather arduous task of satisfying my appetite, whilst my two men cooked on their own account, thinking that nobody else would do it quick enough; and no cook who cared for his reputation would have dished-up fish in the raw state in which they devoured the first two or three. I, however, controlled myself, and gave the woman a little time to prepare mine. Having wrapped my feet up in clean pieces of blanket (the only stockings worn in the interior) and put on a pair of clean dry moccasins, I bethought me of the poor dogs, and taking down some raw fish, went out to feed them. It was almost miraculous to see the big lumps of fish which they gulped down, without even an attempt at mastication. Their appearance after the repast was singularly ridiculous, as their bellies were paunched out like full bladders, whilst the rest of their bodies retained still all the scraggy symptoms of prolonged hunger.

On returning from my charitable errand, I found that the good woman had lost no time, and soon, seated on a pile of buffalo skins before a good fire, I commenced the most luxurious repast of which it had ever been my fate to partake. I had no brandy, spirits, nor wine, neither had I tea, or coffee—nothing but water to drink. I had no Harvey's sauce, or catsup, or butter, or bread, or potatoes, or any other vegetable. I had nothing but fish; no variety, save that some were broiled on the hot coals and some were boiled. But I had been suffering for days from intense cold, and I now had rest; I had been starving, and I now had food; I had been weary and in pain, without rest or relief, and I now had both rest and ease. But, to sum up all, I had come through a long and serious peril, where for days I had been haunted with the idea that

I must camp alone in that solitary forest, and let the men go on, with no food to support me but what I might obtain by the chance snaring of rabbits. It was, in fact, the dread of this almost hopeless alternative, that urged me to exertions upon which I cannot look back except with wonder, and thus brought me at last to the safety and comfort in which I now luxuriated. How many fish the men ate, I do not know; but having satiated themselves, they all lay down to sleep. In the middle of the night they woke me up, to ask me if I would not join them in another feast, but I did not; much to their astonishment, as the woman had told them that she was afraid I was sick, as I only ate four fish out of the seven she had prepared for me. However, in the morning, about five o'clock, I commenced again, and made another hearty meal; and then how happy I was when I lay down and slept again, instead of clambering over the rugged bourdigneaux!

November 30*th and December* 1*st*—I remained at
Fort Assiniboine to allow my feet to recover, which they
did rapidly, as I did little but sleep before the fire and
eat fish. On the evening of the 1st we all felt so well
that we prepared to proceed next morning to Edmonton, which we calculated to reach easily in four days.

December 2*nd*—We started early in the morning
on snowshoes, taking with us very little provisions, as
we were assured that we should find plenty of rabbits
on the road. Our route lay through the woods, which
were very thick and encumbered with fallen trees: this
rendered our progress slow and very fatiguing; but our
renewed strength, and the certainty of a good supper
when we stopped kept up our spirits and enabled us
to make a very good day's journey. When we encamped for the night, we set to work cooking the rabbits
which we had killed on the way, of which we had more
than enough. The whole evening they were running
across our path. This year they were much more
numerous than had been remembered for a long time
previously, and the woods were filled with traps set by
the Indians, from which we might have helped ourselves if we pleased; but this would not have been considered right as long as we had our guns to shoot them.
These snares are fastened to the tops of young saplings
in such a manner as to spring up when the rabbit is

caught, and so suspend him in the air; if this was not done, the wolves and the lynxes, who always follow the rabbits in great numbers, and whose tracks we perceived all round us, would eat them as fast as they were caught.

The lynx is caught by a slip noose made of sinew, simply fastened to a small movable log, which the ensnared animal can drag with difficulty after him. Strange to say, they never attempt to gnaw the string which holds them, although, from the shape of their teeth, they evidently could do so with the greatest ease.

December 3rd, 4th and 5th—Our route was mostly through woods, but the weather was pleasant, and we had abundance of rabbits, so that the journey seemed like a mere pleasure trip in comparison with what we had gone through.

On the evening of the 5th we arrived at Fort Edmonton, where I was most kindly received by Mr. Harriett, and provided with a comfortable room to myself—a luxury I had not known for many months. This was to be my headquarters for the winter; and certainly no place in the interior is at all equal to it, either in comfort or interest. All the Company's servants, with their wives and children, numbering about 130, live within the palings of the fort in comfortable log-houses, supplied with abundance of firewood.

Along the banks of the river in the vicinity of the fort, about twenty feet below the upper surface, beds of hard coal are seen protruding, which is, however, not much used, except in the blacksmith's forge, for which purpose it seems to be admirably adapted. The want of proper grates or furnaces in those distant regions, where iron is at present so scarce, prevents its general use as fuel.

Provisions are in the greatest plenty, consisting of
fresh buffalo meat, venison, salted geese, magnificent
whitefish, and rabbits in abundance, with plenty of good
potatoes, turnips and flour.   The potatoes are very
fine, and the turnips do well here. Of wheat, they can
of course have only one crop; but with very indifferent
farming they manage to get from twenty to twenty-
five bushels per acre.   The crop, however, is sometimes
destroyed by early frost.   The corn is ground in a wind-
mill, which had been erected since my last visit, and
seemed to make very good flour.   Indian corn has been
tried, but it did not succeed, owing to the very short
summer.

Outside, the buffaloes range in thousands close to
the fort; deer are to be obtained at an easy distance;
rabbits run about in all directions, and wolves and
lynxes prowl after them all through the neighbouring
woods.   As for seeing aborigines, no place can be more
advantageous.   Seven of the most important and warlike tribes on the continent are in constant communication with the fort, which is situated in the country of
the Crees and Assiniboines, and is visited at least twice
in the year by the Blackfeet, Sar-cees, Gros-Vents,
Pay-gans, and Blood Indians, who come to sell the
dried buffalo meat and fat for making pemmican which
is prepared in large quantities for the supply of the
other posts.

The buffaloes were extremely numerous this winter,
and several had been shot within a few hundred yards
of the fort.   The men had already commenced gathering their supply of fresh meat for the summer in the
ice-pit.   This is made by digging a square hole, capable of containing 700 or 800 buffalo carcases.   As
soon as the ice in the river is of sufficient thickness, it

is cut into square blocks of uniform size with saws; with
these blocks the floor of the pit is regularly paved, and
the blocks cemented together by pouring water in between them, and allowing it to freeze solid.   In like
manner, the walls are solidly built up to the surface of
the ground.   The head and feet of the buffalo, when
killed, are cut off, and the carcase, without being skinned, is divided into quarters, and piled in layers in the
pit as brought in, until it is filled up, when the whole
is covered with a thick coating of straw, which is again
protected from the sun and rain by a shed.   In this
manner the meat keeps perfectly good through the
whole summer and eats much better than fresh killed
meat, being more tender and better flavoured.

Shortly after my arrival, Mr. Harriett, myself, and
two or three gentlemen of the establishment, prepared
for a buffalo hunt.   We had our choice of splendid
horses, as about a dozen are selected and kept in stables
for the gentlemen's use from the wild band of 700 or
800, which roam about the fort, and forage for themselves through the winter, by scraping the snow away
from the long grass with their hoofs.   These horses
have only one man to take care of them, who is called
the horsekeeper; he follows them about and encamps
near them with his family, turning the band should he
perceive them going too far away.   This would appear
to be a most arduous task; but instinct soon teaches
the animals that their only safety from their great
enemies, the wolves, is by remaining near the habita-
tions of man; and by keeping in one body they are
enabled to fight the bands of wolves, which they often
drive off after severe contests.   Thus they do not stray
far away, and they never leave the band.   These horses
are kept and bred there for the purpose of sending off

the pemmican and stores to other forts during the summer; in winter they are almost useless, on account of the depth of snow.

In the morning we breakfasted most heartily on white fish and buffalo tongues, accompanied by tea, milk, sugar, and *galettes,* which the voyageurs consider a great luxury. These are cakes made of simple flour and water, and baked by clearing away a place near the fire; the cake is then laid on the hot ground, and covered with hot ashes, where it is allowed to remain until sufficiently baked. They are very light and pleasant, and are much esteemed. We then mounted our chosen horses, and got upon the track the men had made on the river by hauling wood. This we followed for about six miles, when we espied a band of buffaloes on the bank; but a dog, who had sneaked after us, running after them, gave the alarm too soon, and they started off at full speed, much to our disappointment. We caught the dog, and tied his legs together, and left him lying in the road to await our return.

After going about three miles further, we came to a place where the snow was trodden down in every direction, and on ascending the bank, we found ourselves in the close vicinity of an enormous band of buffaloes, probably numbering nearly 10,000. An Indian hunter started off for the purpose of turning some of them towards us; but the snow was so deep, that the buffaloes were either unable or unwilling to run far, and at last came to a dead stand. We therefore secured our horses, and advanced towards them on foot to within forty or fity yards, when we commenced firing, which we continued to do until we were tired of a sport so little exciting; for, strange to say, they never tried either to escape or to attack us.

Seeing a very large bull in the herd, I thought I would kill him, for the purpose of getting the skin of his enormous head, and preserving it. He fell; but as he was surrounded by three others that I could not frighten away, I was obliged to shoot them all before I could venture near him, although they were all bulls, and they are not generally saved for meat. The sport proving rather tedious, from the unusual quietness of the buffaloes, we determined to return home, and send the men for the carcases, and remounted our horses. But, before we came to the river, we found an old bull standing right in our way, and Mr. Harriett, for the purpose of driving him off, fired at him and slightly wounded him, when he turned and made a furious charge. Mr. Harriett barely escaped by jumping his horse on one side. So close, indeed, was the charge, that the horse was slightly struck on the rump. The animal still pursued Mr. Harriett at full speed, and we all set after him, firing ball after ball into him, as we ranged up close to him, without any apparent effect than that of making him more furious, and turning his rage on ourselves. This enabled Mr. Harriett to re-load, and plant a couple more balls in him, which evidently sickened him. We were now all close to him, and we all fired deliberately at him. At last, after receiving sixteen bullets in his body, he slowly fell, dying harder than I had ever seen an animal die before.

On our return, we told the men to get the dog-sledges ready to go in the morning to bring in the cows we had killed, numbering twenty-seven, with the head of the bull I wanted; whereupon the squaws and half-breed women, who have always this job to do, started off to catch the requisite number of dogs. About the fort there are always two or three hundred who forage for themselves like the horses, and lie outside. These dogs are quite as valuable there as horses, as it is with them that everything is drawn over the snow. Two of them will easily draw in a large cow; yet no care is taken of them, except that of beating them sufficiently before using them, to make them quiet for the time they are in harness.

It would be almost impossible to catch these animals, who are almost as wild as wolves, were it not for the precaution which is taken in the autumn of catching the dogs singly by stratagem, and tying light logs to them, which they can drag about. By this means the squaws soon catch as many as they want, and bring them into the fort, where they are fed—sometimes—before being harnessed. This operation is certainly (if it were not for the cruelty exhibited) one of the most amusing scenes I had witnessed. Early next morning I was aroused by a yelling and screaming that made me rush from my room, thinking that we were all being murdered; and there I saw the women harnessing the dogs. Such a scene! The women were like so many furies with big sticks, thrashing away at the poor animals, who rolled and yelled in agony and terror, until each team was yoked up and started off.

During the day the men returned, bringing the quartered cows ready to be put in the ice-pit, and my big head, which, before skinning, I had put in the scales, and found that it weighed exactly 202 lbs. The skin of the head I brought home with me.

The fort at this time of the year presented a most pleasing picture of cheerful activity; every one was busy; the men, some in hunting and bringing in the meat when the weather permitted, some in sawing boards in the saw-pit, and building the boats, about thirty feet long and six feet beam, which go as far as York Factory, and are found more convenient for carrying goods on the Saskatchewan and Red River than canoes. They are mostly built at Edmonton, because there are more boats required to take the peltries to York Factory than is required to bring goods back; and more than one-half of the boats built here never return.   This system requires them to keep constantly building.

The women find ample employment in making mocassins and clothes for the men, putting up pemmican in ninety-pound bags, and doing all the household drudgery, in which the men never assist them.   The evenings are spent round their large fires in eternal gossiping and smoking.   The sole musician of the establishment, a fiddler, is now in great requisition amongst the French part of the inmates, who give full vent to their national vivacity, whilst the more sedate Indian looks on with solemn enjoyment.

No liquor is allowed to the men or Indians; but the want of it did not in the least seem to impair their cheerfulness.   True, the gentlemen of the fort had liquor brought out at their own expense; but the rules respecting its use were so strict and so well known, that none but those to whom it belonged either expected, or asked, to share it.

On Christmas day the flag was hoisted, and all appeared in their best and gaudiest style, to do honour to the holiday.   Towards noon every chimney gave evidence of being in full blast, whilst savoury steams of cooking pervaded the atmosphere in all directions. About two o'clock we sat down to dinner.   Our party consisted of Mr. Harriett, the chief, and three clerks, Mr. Thebo, the Roman Catholic missionary from Manitou Lake, about thirty miles off, Mr. Rundell,

the Wesleyan missionary, who resided within the
pickets, and myself, the wanderer, who, though returning from the shores of the Pacific, was still the latest
importation from civilized life.

The dining-hall in which we assembled was the largest room in the fort, probably about fifty by twenty-
five feet, well warmed by large fires, which are scarcely
ever allowed to go out.   The walls and ceilings are
boarded, as plastering is not used, there being no lime-
stone within reach; but these boards are painted in a
style of the most startling barbaric gaudiness, and the
ceiling filled with centre-pieces of fantastic gilt scrolls,
making altogether a saloon which no white man would
enter for the first time without a start, and which the
Indians always looked upon with awe and wonder.

The room was intended as a reception room for the
wild chiefs who visited the fort; and the artist who designed the decorations was no doubt directed to "aston-
ish the natives." If such were his instructions, he deserves the highest praise for having faithfully complied
with them, although, were he to attempt a repetition
of the same style in one of the rooms of the Vatican, it
might subject him to some severe criticisms from the
fastidious.   No tablecloth shed its snowy whiteness
over the board; no silver candelabra or gaudy china in-
terfered with its simple magnificence.   The bright tin
plates and dishes reflected jolly faces, and burnished
gold can give no truer zest to a feast.

Perhaps it might be interesting to some dyspeptic
idler, who painfully strolls through a city park, to coax
an appetite to a sufficient intensity to enable him to pick
an ortolan, if I were to describe to him the fare set before us, to appease appetites nourished by constant out-
door exercise in an atmosphere ranging at 40° to 50°

below zero. At the head, before Mr. Harriett, was a
large dish of boiled buffalo hump; at the foot smoked
a boiled buffalo calf. Start not, gentle reader, the calf
is very small, and is taken from the cow by the Cæsar-
ean operation long before it attains its full growth.
This, boiled whole, is one of the most esteemed dishes
amongst the epicures of the interior.   My pleasing
duty was to help a dish of mouffle, or dried moose nose;
the gentleman on my left distributed, with graceful impartiality, the white fish, delicately browned in buffalo
marrow. The worthy priest helped the buffalo tongue,
whilst Mr. Rundell cut up the beavers' tails. Nor was
the other gentleman left unemployed, as all his spare
time was occupied in dissecting a roast wild goose. The
centre of the table was graced with piles of potatoes,
turnips, and bread conveniently placed, so that each
could help himself without interrupting the labours of
his companions. Such was our jolly Christmas dinner
at Edmonton; and long will it remain in my memory,
although no pies, or puddings, or blanc manges, shed
their fragrance over the scene.

In the evening the hall was prepared for the dance
to which Mr. Harriett had invited all the inmates of
the fort, and was early filled by the gaily dressed guests.
Indians, whose chief ornament consisted in the paint on
their faces, voyageurs with bright sashes and neatly
ornamented mocassins, half-breeds glittering in every
ornament they could lay their hands on; whether civilized or savage, all were laughing, and jabbering in as
many different languages as there were styles of dress.
English, however, was little used, as none could speak
it but those who sat at the dinner-table. The dancing
was most picturesque, and almost all joined in it. Occasionally I, among the rest, led out a young Cree

squaw, who sported enough beads round her neck to have made a pedlar's fortune, and having led her into the centre of the room, I danced round her with all the agility I was capable of exhibiting, to some highland-reel tune which the fiddler played with great vigour, whilst my partner with grave face kept jumping up and

Cun-ne-wa-bum [Half-breed Cree, Fort Edmonton]
Courtesy of Royal Ontario Museum

down, both feet off the ground at once, as only an Indian can dance. I believe, however, that we elicited a great deal of applause from Indian squaws and children, who sat squatting round the room on the floor. Another lady with whom I sported the light fantastic toe, whose poetic name was Cun-ne-wa-bum, or "One that looks at the Stars," was a half-breed Cree girl; and I was so much struck by her beauty, that I prevailed upon her to promise to sit for her likeness, which she afterwards did with great patience, holding her fan, which was made of the tip end of swan's wing with an ornamental handle of porcupine's quills, in a most coquettish manner.

After enjoying ourselves with such boisterous vigor for several hours, we all gladly retired to rest about twelve o'clock, the guests separating in great good humour, not only with themselves but with their entertainers.

A few days afterwards, when we had recovered from the effects of our Christmas festivities, I went out with François Lucie, the half-breed voyageur, of whom Sir George Simpson, in his "Journey round the World," tells the following story:—

"A band of Assiniboines had carried off twenty-four horses from Edmonton, and, being pursued, they were overtaken at the small river Boutbière. One of the keepers of the animals, a very courageous man, of the name of François Lucie, plunged into the stream, grappling in the midst with a tall savage, and, in spite of his inferiority of strength, he kept so close that his enemy could not draw his bow; still, however, the Indian continued to strike his assailant on the head with the weapon in question, and thereby knocking him off his horse into the water. Springing immediately to his feet, Lucie was about to smite the Assiniboine with his dagger, when the savage arrested his arm by seizing a whip, which was hanging to his wrist by a loop, and then turning round the handle, with a scornful laugh, he drew the string so tight as to render the poor man's

hand nearly powerless. François continued nevertheless to saw away at the fellow's fingers with his dagger
till he had nearly cut them off, and when at length the
Assiniboine of necessity relaxed his grasp, François,
with the quickness of thought, sheathed the weapon in
his heart." François told me the story himself, much
as related above, except, he said, that the savage did
not die immediately, although he had ripped his breast
so open that he could see his heart throbbing, and that
he never let go the lasso of the stolen horses until it
ceased, which was for some minutes, though he tried
to pull it from his hand.

We had not left the fort more than five or six miles
behind us, when we fell in with an enormous grizzly bear,
but François would not fire at him, nor allow me to do
so, although I told him I had helped to kill one before.
A younger man than he, who had his character to make,
might have been foolish enough to have run the risk,
for the sake of the standing it would have given him
amongst his companions; but François had a character
established, and would not risk attacking so formidable
an animal with only two men. In fact, their enormous
strength, agility, and wonderful tenacity of life, make
them shunned even by large numbers, and few are killed,
except by young men, for the sake of proudly wearing
the claws—one of the most esteemed ornaments to an
Indian chief—round their necks.

The bear walked on, looking at us now and then,
but seeming to treat us with contempt. My fingers
were itching to let fly at him; it seemed so easy, and
his skin was in such fine condition. But though my gun
had two barrels, and François was by my side, with the
almost certainty of putting three balls well in; yet we
well knew that it was ten chances to one that three

balls would not kill him quick enough to prevent a hand-to-hand encounter, a sort of amusement that neither were Quixotic enough to desire.   After we had proceeded a few miles further, we fell in with a small band of buffaloes, and François initiated me into the mysteries of "making a calf."

This ruse is generally performed by two men, one covering himself with wolf skin, the other with buffalo skin.   They then crawl on all fours within sight of the buffaloes, and as soon as they have engaged their attention, the pretended wolf jumps on the pretended calf, which bellows in imitation of a real one.   The buffaloes seem to be easily deceived in this way.   As the bellowing is generally perfect, the herd rush on to the protection of their supposed young with such impetuosity that they do not perceive the cheat until they are quite close enough to be shot; indeed, François' bellowing was so perfect, that we were nearly run down. As soon, however, as we jumped up, they turned and fled, leaving two of their number behind, who paid the penalty of their want of discernment with their lives.

We shortly afterwards fell in with a solitary bull and cow, and again "made a calf."   The cow attempted to spring towards us, but the bull seeming to understand the trick, tried to stop her by running between us; the cow, however, dodged and got round him, and ran within ten or fifteen yards of us, with the bull close at her heels, when we both fired and brought her down. The bull instantly stopped short, and bending over her, tried to raise her up with his nose, evincing the most persevering affection for her in a rather ridiculous manner; nor could we get rid of him so as to cut up the cow, without shooting him also, although bull flesh is not desirable at this season of the year, when the female can be procured.

Having loaded our horses with the choice parts of the three cows we had killed, we proceeded home, François having taken particular care to secure the mesenteries or monyplies, as he called them, a part much esteemed in the interior, although I must confess I did not like it myself.

Another mode of hunting buffaloes, which we often practised with great success at Edmonton, was accompanied however with considerable fatigue: it consisted in crawling on our bellies and dragging ourselves along by our hands, being first fully certain that we were to the leeward of the herd, however light the wind, lest they should scent us until we came within a few yards of them, which they would almost invariably permit us to do.   Should there be twenty hunters engaged in the sport, each man follows exactly in the track of his leader, keeping his head close to the heels of his predecessor: the buffaloes seem not to take the slightest notice of the moving line, which the Indians account for by saying that the buffalo supposes it to be a big snake winding through the snow or grass.

Tired as I was at night after my day's hunt, I was kept long from my bed, fascinated by the appearance of the heavens, which presented to the view one of the most splendid meteoric phenomena I had ever witnessed.   Soon after dark a zone of light began to appear, increasing rapidly in brilliancy until nine or ten o'clock, when it attained its greatest intensity.   It was about four degrees in breadth, and extended from the east to the west across the zenith.   In its centre, immediately overhead, appeared a blood-red ball of fire, of greater diameter than the full moon rising in a misty horizon;

from the ball emanated rays of crimson light, merging into a brilliant yellow at the northern edges.   The belt also on the northern side presented the same dazzling brightness; while the snow and every object surrounding us was tinted by the same hues.   I continued lost in admiration of this splendid phenomenon until past one in the morning, when it still shone with undiminished, if not increasing, brilliancy.   Tired out at last, I was compelled to retire to bed, but those who still sat up told me that it faded away about three o'clock in the morning, without varying its position or form.   The Indians have a poetical superstition in regard to the Aurora Borealis, which is in this high latitude remarkably brilliant, shooting up coruscations of surprising splendour.   These, they think, are "the spirits of the dead dancing before the Manitou, or Great Spirit."

CHAPTER XXIII

On the 6th of January, 1848, we had a wedding at
Edmonton; the bride was the daughter of the gentleman in charge, the bridegroom Mr. Rowand, junior,
who resided at Fort Pitt, a distance of 200 miles from
the establishment. After the ceremony, which was
performed by the Rev. Mr. Rundell, the Methodist
missionary, we spent a pleasant evening, feasting and
dancing until midnight. Having received an invitation to accompany the happy pair on the journey home,
I gladly accepted it, as I began to find my amusements
rather monotonous. Next morning I was awoke by
the yelping of the dogs and the ringing of the bells on
the dog-collars, accompanied by the shouts of the men
thrashing the brutes into something like discipline, as
they harnessed them to the sledges and carioles. On
coming out into the yard, I found our party nearly
ready to start. It consisted of Mr. Rowand and his
bride with nine men. We had three carioles and six
sledges, with four dogs to each, forming when on route
a long and picturesque cavalcade: all the dogs gaudily
decorated with saddle-cloths of various colours, fringed
and embroidered in the most fantastic manner, with innumerable small bells and feathers, producing altogether a pleasing and enlivening effect (sketch No. 14).

Our carioles were also handsomely decorated, the bride's more particularly, which had been made expressly for the occasion, and was elaborately painted and ornamented, and was drawn by a set of dogs recently imported from Lower Canada by Mr. Rowand.

14. Winter Travelling in Dog Sleds
Courtesy of Royal Ontario Museum

The cariole is intended for carrying one person only; it is a thin flat board, about eighteen inches wide, bent up in front, with a straight back behind to lean against; the sides are made of green buffalo hide, with the hair scraped completely off and dried, resembling thick parchment; this entirely covers the front part, so that a person slips into it as into a tin bath.

We started as the day dawned, the dogs running at a furious rate, as they invariably do at first starting, and require all the strength and agility of the men to keep the sledges and carioles from upsetting, which they manage to do as well as they can by holding on to a

cord attached to each side from behind. Two men go
before on the run in snowshoes to beat a track, which
the dogs instinctively follow: these men are relieved
every two hours, as it is very laborious. The dogs
generally used are of a breed peculiar to the country,
and partake largely of the character and disposition of
the wolf, which they often so resemble in appearance
as sometimes to have been shot in mistake. Their
ferocity is so great that they are often dangerous. Some
of them this winter attacked a horse belonging to Mr.
Harriett, harnessed to a sledge. Mr. Harriett had
tied him to a stake and left him; on his return, in about
half an hour, he found the dogs tearing him to pieces;
nor would the dogs leave their prey until he had shot
five of them: the horse died almost immediately.

Mr. Rundell was himself attacked one evening,
while walking a short distance form the fort, by a band
of these brutes, belonging to the establishment; they got
him down, and, but for his cries bringing the assistance
of a squaw, they would have served him in a similar
manner.

Immediately on leaving the fort, we got on the ice
of the Saskatchewan River, and travelled down it all
day, having, in the true voyageur style, trusted to our
prowess as hunters for a supply of food on our journey,
although of 200 miles; and, having literally brought
nothing with us but the kettles, we were unable to break
our fast until we had killed a fat cow, which was soon
demolished by ourselves and the dogs. This apparent
absence of foresight is, in reality, aften affected by the
voyageurs out of bravado, for they are quite as much
disinclined to hunger and abstinence as other people.
In our case we might certainly have brought plenty of
food if we liked, but, on the other hand, buffaloes were

plentiful, and there was almost a certainty of obtaining them.

January 9th—Left our encampment three hours before day, and about daylight we killed two buffaloes and stopped to breakfast. The wind blew very cold and strong all day, with continued snow. After breakfast we left the circuitous windings of the river, and the friendly shelter of its banks and woods, to cut across the bleak and open plains, where we were exposed to the full fury of the chill blast; but this shortened our journey by many miles. In the evening we killed two more buffaloes, and encamped in a clump of pines, the last sheltered spot we might expect on our journey.

January 10th—Our spirit thermometer stood this morning at 47° below zero, Fahrenheit. Finding it impossible to keep myself warm in my cariole, in spite of plenty of skins and blankets, I put on a pair of snowshoes and walked all day. The snow was three feet deep on an average, and was drifted by the wind with such violence in our faces as to nearly blind us; notwithstanding which our guides seemed to find no difficulty in pursuing their course—such is the instinctive faculty of these men in tracing their way over this trackless desert, where not a stick or a shrub is to be met with to guide them. Towards evening we arrived at a sort of enclosure, which had evidently been erected by the Blackfoot Indians for a protection from the Crees, whose country this is, but where the Blackfeet sometimes come to steal horses. In the evening we only got one cow, which seemed barely to satisfy our dogs.

January 11th—Started as usual this morning three hours before daylight, the days being short: this early start is necessary to allow the men to stop and make the encampment before dark. We met two of the Company's men on their way from Carlton to the place we had so recently left. We killed only one buffalo to-day, and were obliged to sleep on the snow, no pine branches being within reach to make our beds. These we missed much, as they add much to the comfort of an encampment.

January 12*th*—We again got on the river. Hav-brought a small quantity of meat from our last night's supper with us, but not sufficient for all, some of our party went on in advance to hunt, whilst we stopped to take a scanty breakfast. About two hours afterwards we came up to them, sitting round a good fire cooking a fine fat cow, the delicate pieces of which they were demolishing with considerable rapidity, owing to the lateness of their meal.

During the day a diverting occurrence took place, although it might have turned out very serious. A herd of buffaloes had come down the bank on to the ice, and did not perceive our approach until the foremost sledge was so near them as to excite the dogs, who rushed furiously after them, notwithstanding all the efforts of the men to stop them. The spirit of the hunt was at once communicated through the whole line, and we were soon all, carioles and sledges, dashing along at a furious rate after the buffaloes. The frightened animals made a bold dash at last through a snow bank, and attempted to scramble up the steep bank of the river, the top of which the foremost one had nearly reached, when, slipping, he rolled over and knocked those behind, one on top of another, down into the snow-drift amongst the men and dogs, who were struggling in it. It would be impossible to describe the wild scene of uproar and confusion that followed.

Some of our sledges were smashed, and one of the men was nearly killed; but at last we succeeded in getting clear and repairing damages. We continued on our wedding tour.

January 13*th*—Started at half-past 1 A.M.. We followed a buffalo track along the river, in the deep ruts of which our carioles were frequently upset, rolling us into the snow. Having killed three buffaloes on the banks of the river, we stopped to breakfast: two calves, evidently belonging to the slaughtered animals, remained within a hundred yards of our fire the whole time.

Leaving the river, we passed over a succession of hills and valleys until dark, when we arrived at a camp of Cree Indians, consisting of about forty lodges. We went to the lodge of the chief named "Broken Arm", who received us very kindly, spreading buffalo robes in the best part of his tent for us to sit on and placing before us the best his stock afforded. After supper, the chief having cut some tobacco and filled a handsome stone pipe, took a few whiffs from it himself, and then presented it to me. On my doing the same, and offering it to him again, as is the custom, he told me that he wished me to accept it as a gift.

The lodge was soon filled with Indians, anxious to learn the news, which they are always eager to hear from strangers. Amongst our visitors was the son-in-law of the chief; and, according to the Indian custom, he took his seat with his back towards his father and mother-in-law, never addressing them but through the medium of a third party, and they preserving the same etiquette towards him. This rule is not broken through until the son-in-law proves himself worthy of personally speaking to him, by having killed an enemy with white hairs; they then become entitled to wear a dress trimmed with human hair, taken from the scalps of their foes.   I remarked that one of the leggings of the young man was spotted with some red earth, and the other not: on inquiring the reason, I was told that the spotted leg had been wounded, and the red earth was intended to indicate blood.

We sat up very late talking to the chief, who seemed to enjoy our society very much. Amongst other topics of discourse, he began talking about the efforts of the missionaries amongst his people, and seemed to think that they would not be very successful; for though he did not interfere with the religious belief of any of his tribe, yet many thought as he did; and his idea was, that as Mr. Rundell had told him that what he preached was the only true road to heaven, and Mr. Hunter told him the same thing, and so did Mr. Thebo, and as they all three said that the other two were wrong, and as he did not know which was right, he thought they ought to call a council among themselves, and that then he would go with them all three; but that until they agreed he would wait.   He then told us that there was a tradition in his tribe of one of them having become a Christian, and was very good, and did all that he ought; and that when he died he was taken up to the white man's heaven, where everything was very good and very beautiful, and all were happy amongst their friends and relatives who had gone before them, and where they had everything that the white man loves and longs for; but the Indian could not share their joy and pleasure, for all was strange to him, and he met none of the spirits of his ancestors, and there was none to welcome him, no hunting nor fishing, nor any of those joys in which he used to delight, and his spirit grew sad. Then the Great Manitou called him, and asked him, "Why art thou sad in this beautiful heaven which I have made for your joy and happiness?" and the Indian told him that he sighed for the company of the spirits of his relations, and that he felt lone and sorrowful. So the Great Manitou told him that he could not send him to the Indian heaven, as he had, whilst on earth, chosen this one, but that as he had been a very good man, he would send him back to earth again, and give him another chance.

January 14th—We travelled to-day through a hilly country until we arrived at another encampment of about thirty lodges. Our dogs rushed down amongst the lodges, dragging the sledges and carioles after them, and were immediately attacked by all the dogs in the Indian camp, barking, howling, and fighting, until all the sledges were upset, and some of them broken to pieces. It was half an hour before we could separate the enraged brutes.

These Indians had a buffalo pound within a short distance of their encampment, which was literally crammed with the dead frozen carcases they had slaughtered in it. On nearing Fort Pitt we fell in with two buffaloes, immediately in our track, and as we did not want the meat, they might have been allowed to escape, but for the large development of the bump of destructiveness in our men's heads.

We reached the fort soon after dark, having been seven days on our route from Edmonton. We had killed seventeen buffaloes in this journey, for feeding ourselves and dogs. The animals had, we were told, never appeared in such vast numbers, nor shown themselves so near the Company's establishments; some have even been shot within the gates of the fort. They killed with their horns twenty or thirty horses in their attempt to drive them off from the patches of grass which the horses had pawed the snow from with their hoofs for the purpose of getting at the grass, and severely gored many others, which eventually recovered.

These remarks convey but a faint idea of the astonishing numbers of these animals: within the whole distance we had travelled on this journey we were never out of sight of large herds of them, and we had not found it necessary to go a step out of our direct course to find more than we required for our use. They were probably migrating northwards, to escape from the human migrations which are so rapidly filling up the southern and western regions, which were formerly their pasture grounds.

I spent a very pleasant and interesting month at Fort Pitt, surrounded by Cree Indians, this being one of their principal places of resort, and had ample opportunity of studying their habits and manners. I took an elaborate sketch of a pipe-stem carrier with his medicine pipe-stem. The pipe-stem carrier is elected every four years by the band of the whole tribe to which he belongs, and is not allowed to retain the distinction beyond that period, all being eligible for the situation who have sufficient means to pay for it. But the expense is considerable, as the new officer elect has to pay his predecessor for the emblems of his dignity, which frequently are valued at from fifteen to twenty horses. Should he not possess sufficient means, his friends usually make up the deficiency, otherwise the office would in many cases be declined. It is, however, compulsory upon the person elected to serve if he can pay. The official insignia of the pipe-stem carrier are numerous, consisting of a highly ornamental skin tent, in which he is always expected to reside; a bear's skin upon which the pipe-stem is to be exposed to view when any circumstance requires it to be taken out from its mani-fold coverings in which it is usually wrapped up, such as a council of war, or a medicine pipe-stem dance, or on a quarrel taking place in the tribe, to settle which the medicine-man opens it for the adverse parties to smoke out of,—their superstitions leading them to fear a re-fusal of the reconciling ceremony, lest some calamity should be inflicted on them by the Great Spirit for their presumption;—a medicine rattle, which is employed in their medicine dances, and a wooden bowl, from which the dignitary always takes his food,—this he always carries about his person, sometimes in his hand, and often on his head;—besides numerous small articles.

It requires two horses to carry them when on the move. The pipe-stem itself is usally carried by the favourite wife of the official, and should it under any circumstances fall on the ground, it is regarded as a bad omen, and many ceremonies must be gone through to reinstate it. A young man, a half-breed, assured me that he had once a pipe-stem committed to his charge by an official who had gone out on a hunting excursion, and that being well aware of the sanctity at-tributed to it by the Crees, he was determined to try himself the effect of throwing it down and kicking it about, and that shortly after this act of desecration, as it would be considered, the pipe-stem carrier was killed by the Blackfeet. From that time he became a firm believer in the sanctity of the pipe-stem, and, as may be supposed, told me this story as a great secret.

A pipe-stem carrier always sits on the right side of his lodge as you enter, and it is considered a great mark of disrespect to him if you pass between him and the fire, which always occupies the centre of the lodge. He must not condescend to cut his own meat, but it is always cut for him by one of his wives, of whom he usually has five or six, and placed in his medicine bowl, which, as before said, he has always with him. One of the greatest inconveniences attached to the office, particularly to an Indian, who has always innumerable parasitical insects infesting his person, is, that the pipe-stem carrier dares not scratch his own head without compromising his dignity, without the intervention of a stick, which he always carries for that purpose. The pipe-stem, enclosed in its wrappers, always hangs in a large bag, when they can procure it, of parti-coloured woollen cloth, on the outside of the lodge, and is never taken inside either by night or by day, nor allowed to be uncovered when any woman is present.

About a fortnight after my arrival, Kee-a-kee-ka-sa-coo-way, "the Man who gives the War-whoop," whom I mentioned before as having met on the Saskatchewan on my journey out, arrived at Fort Pitt with his sub-chief, Muck-e-too, "Powder."

Kee-a-kee-ka-sa-coo-way is the head chief of all the Crees, and was now travelling through all their camps to induce them to take up the tomahawk and follow him on a war excursion in the following spring. He had eleven medicine pipe-stems with him, ten of which belonged to inferior chiefs, who had already consented to join in the expedition. Being curious to witness the opening of these pipe-stems and see the ceremonial accompanying it, I travelled with him to the camp, situated a few miles from Fort Pitt. On our arrival the wrappers of the stems were removed and carried in procession, headed by the chief in person, through the camp. The procession halted in front of nearly every lodge, where he delivered a continuous harangue, the burden of which was to rouse them to take up arms and revenge the death of the warriors who had been killed in former wars. During the whole of this address the tears continued to stream down his face as if at his entire command.   This the Indians call crying for war.

The weather was most intensely cold, notwithstanding which, and his being half naked, so strongly was every feeling concentrated on the subject, that he appeared altogether insensible to its severity, although the thermometer must have indicated at least thirty to forty degrees below zero. On the day following, I endeavoured to prevail on him to open the pipe-stems, in order that I might sketch some of them. This he at first declined, until he had been told that I was a great medicine-man, and that my sketching them would very much increase their efficiency when opened on the field of battle. He thereupon opened them with the following ceremonies. He first took a coal from the fire, and sprinkled upon it the dried leaves of a plant collected on the Rocky Mountains, the smoke of which filled the place with a fragrant odour resembling that of the incense burned in Catholic churches; while this was burning, he filled the bowls of these pipes with tobacco and some other weed, after which he took off all his clothes, with the exception of the breechcloth.

On my looking rather suspiciously at the clothes he had taken off, seeing they were rather old and filthy, he took notice of my doing so, and remarked, that although he possessed better, he was not allowed by the customs of his tribe to wear them, as he was then mourning the death of four of his relations who had been killed by the Blackfeet the year before. (He, however, put on his good clothes for me afterwards, when I took sketch

No. 15, as I told him that the picture would be shown
to the Queen.)   He then threw over his shoulders the
skin of a wolf highly ornamented after the Indian fashion, and immediately removed the wrappers of leather,
&c., that covered one of the stems, and inserting it into

15. Kee-a-kee-ka-sa-coo-way
[Head Chief of the Crees with his pipe-stem]
Courtesy of the Royal Ontario Museum

one of the bowls he had previously filled with tobacco,
commenced a song which I could not understand.

On finishing, he lighted the pipe, and inhaled a
mouthful of smoke; then turning his face upwards and
pointing in the same direction with the stem, he blew

upwards a long stream of smoke, and called on the Great Spirit to give them success in war, to enable them to take many scalps, and set their enemies asleep whilst they carried off their horses; that their own wives might continue virtuous and never grow old.   He then turned the stem to the earth, after blowing another puff of smoke, and called upon the earth to produce abundance of buffalo and roots for the coming season.   He then pointed the stem towards me, and requested that, if I possessed any influence with the Great Spirit, I would intercede with him for the supply of all their wants. A half-breed woman happening to look into the lodge at this moment, the ceremony was instantly suspended, and she as instantly shrunk back; a woman never being allowed to be present when the medicine pipe-stem is exposed to view.

After some little prolonged ceremony, consisting principally of all present smoking from each stem as it was opened, he permitted me to sketch them, but never left the lodge until I had finished and he had carefully recovered and removed them.   He told me he had been on this war mission to nearly every camp in his tribe, and intended to visit the whole of them; the distance he would have to travel in snowshoes to accomplish this would not be less than six or seven hundred miles.   It is the custom of the Indians after such a call to assemble at a place appointed on the Saskatchewan River, where they continue feasting and dancing three days previously to their starting for the enemy's country.   Here all their pipe-stems and medicine dresses are exhibited, and they decorate themselves with all the finery they can command, in which they continue their advance until they reach the enemy.   But no sooner are they in view, than their ornaments and their whole clothing are hastily thrown aside, and they fight naked.

A year before my arrival amongst them, a war party of 700 left for the Blackfeet country, which nation the Crees regard as their natural enemies, and are never at peace with them. After travelling for some fifteen or twenty days, a sickness broke out among them, affecting numbers and carrying off a few. This was considered by some of their great men a judgment upon them from the Great Spirit for some previous misconduct, and they, therefore, returned home without having accomplished anything. On another occasion a similar party fell in with a great warrior among the Blackfeet, named "Big Horn,"and six of his tribe, who were out on the legitimate calling of horse stealing,—for the greater the horse thief the greater the warrior. This small band, seeing their inferiority to their enemies, attempted flight; but finding escape impossible, they instantly dug holes sufficiently deep to intrench themselves, from which they kept up a constant fire with guns and arrows, and for nearly twelve hours held at bay this large war party, bringing down every man who ventured within shot, until their ammunition and arrows were entirely exhausted, when they of course fell an easy prey to their enemies, thirty of whom had fallen before their fire. This so enraged the Crees that they cut them in pieces, and mangled the dead bodies in a most brutal manner, and carried their scalps back as trophies.

It is said that Big Horn frequently sprang out from his intrenchment, and tried to irritate his foes by recounting the numbers of them he had destroyed, and boasting his many war exploits, and the Cree scalps that then hung in his lodge. So exasperated were they against him, that they tore out his heart from his quivering body, and savagely devoured it amongst them.

I returned to Edmonton by the same route, and in the same manner I had come from it, and as nothing material occurred in the route, I omit the details.

I remained at Emonton until the 12th of April,
when, having heard that a large band of Blackfeet were
shortly expected to visit Rocky Mountain House,
situated about 180 miles south-west of Edmonton, on
the Saskatchewan, for the purpose of trading, and being anxious to see them, I started with a small party of
six men and about twenty horses, ten of which were
loaded with goods. The snow had not left the ground,
and our horses were in a very bad condition, from living
out all the winter, except the one which I rode, which
had been kept in, and was the most vicious brute I ever
met. When I dismounted from him the first evening,
he tried to get away from me, and when he found that
I held on to the lasso, he attacked me with open mouth,
and had not one of the men knocked him down with a
stick, he might have seriously injured me. Our progress was, therefore, necessarily slow, as I would not
ride away from the party.

We found buffaloes in places where the Indians
said they had never been seen before, and remained two
days at a place called Battle River, to rest our horses,
as we had plenty of food for ourselves and grass for the
horses. I went out with an Indian and killed a cow,
which was followed by her calf. Wishing to take the
calf alive, so that it might carry itself to the camp, I

pursued and caught it, and, tying my sash round its neck, endeavoured to drag it along; but it plunged and tried so violently to escape that I was about to kill it, when the Indian took hold of its head, and turning up its muzzle, spat two or three times into it, when, much to my astonishment, the animal became perfectly docile, and followed us quietly to the camp, where it was immediately cooked for supper.

Finding three of the rivers in our route much flooded, we were obliged to make rafts to cross upon, so as to keep the goods dry. At the fourth river we were fortunate to find a raft formed by nature, in the shape of a large mass of floating ice, which one of the men swimming out dragged ashore. It was sufficiently buoyant to support two or three men, and by attaching our lassoes to it, and drawing it backwards and forwards, we soon got all our goods over dry. The horses we made swim.

Some of the men suffered severely from what is called "snow blind," which is a species of inflammation, brought on by the strong glare of the sun reflected from the snow. The pain in the eyeballs is excessive, and resembles the feeling produced by having sand in the eyes; the sufferers are sometimes blinded by it for weeks. This can be prevented by wearing a veil, which I did, and is generally adopted when they can be procured.

We arrived at Rocky Mountain Fort on the 21st of April. This fort is beautifully situated on the banks of the Saskatchewan, in a small prairie, backed by the Rock Mountains in the distance. In the vicinity was a camp of Assiniboine lodges, formed entirely of pine branches. It was built for the purpose of keeping a supply of goods to trade with the Blackfoot Indians, who come there every winter, and is abandoned and left empty every summer. It is built like most of the other forts, of wood, but with more than ordinary regard to strength, which is thought necessary on account of the vicious disposition of the Blackfoot tribe, who are, without exception, the most warlike on the northern continent. I may state that beds of coal are seen protruding here along the banks of the river, similar to those at Edmonton.

There is also a small band of Assiniboines in the neighbourhood of the fort. The Blackfeet attacked them last year, and carried off two girls, captives. One of them, after having been carried away a long distance, was stripped naked, and told to find her way back as best she could, and as she was never heard of afterwards, it was supposed that she perished from cold and hunger; the other girl was taken charge of by a chief, who sent her relations word that she should be returned safe, which promise he fulfilled.

We found a man at the establishment, called Jemmy Jock, a Cree half-breed, who had temporary charge of it; he had obtained much Blackfoot celebrity. He was sent out when a clerk of Hudson's Bay Company, by them, to the Blackfoot Indians, in order to learn their language, for the purpose of facilitating the trade with them. He then married a daughter of one of their chiefs, and taking a fancy to their mode of life, he left the Company's service, and stayed with them. He afterwards became one of their chiefs, and being a man of singular acuteness, soon acquired great influence. The missionaries entertained very little respect for him, and have spoken very badly of him throughout the whole country; but as far as my intercourse with him went, I always found him trustworthy and hospitable. I learned much from him relative to the customs of the Blackfoot tribe, of which, owing to his long residence amongst them, thirty or forty years, he possessed a greater knowledge probably than any other man with the same education.

Shortly after my arrival a report was brought in that the Blackfoot Indians had killed a party of Crees, and that amongst the slain was a pipe-stem carrier, whom they had skinned and stuffed with grass; the figure was then placed in a trail which the Crees were accustomed to pass in their hunting excursions. The Assiniboines, who reside in the vicinity of this fort, I found the most kind and honourable of any tribe that I met with. They constitute a very small part (say forty or fifty families) of a very large tribe who live in a more easterly direction. Mah-Min, "The Feather," their head chief, permitted me to take his likeness, and after I had finished it, and it was shown to the others, who all recognized and admired it, he said to me, "You are a greater chief than I am, and I present you with this collar of grizzly bear's claws, which I have worn for twenty-three summers, and which I hope you will wear as a token of my friendship." This collar I have, of course, brought home with me.

The second chief, Wah-he-joe-tasse-e-neen, "The half-white Man," seeing that I was so successful with his head chief's likeness, and probably feeling a little jealous, came and requested me to take his also, which I willingly did, as he had one of the most extraordinary countenances I had met with for some time. He was a man, however, noted as a great hunter, and as an evidence of his tremendous powers of endurance, it was related to me that one morning he had started on snowshoes in pursuit of two moose, and pursued them until they separated. He then followed one track until he

killed his prey, cut it up, and put it on scaffolding to
secure it from the wolves. He then returned to where
the tracks separated, and followed the other; this he
also killed, and placed, as he had done the former, returning to his lodge late in the evening. In the morning he sent off three men with dog sledges to bring in
the game, and they were three days following his tracks
before they got home.

Mah-Min gave one of the missionaries who was up
here last summer a very long and serious lecture upon
lying. It seems the missionary, who did not smoke
himself, had brought with him a carat of tobacco for
the purpose of purchasing horses and food from the
Indians, should he require them. Immediately on his
arrival, the Indians, who had exhausted their stock,
eagerly inquired if he had any tobacco, but he was afraid
that if he acknowledged he had any they would want it
all, and leave him without anything to barter with them,
and denied that he had any. Shortly afterwards, when
he was about to return, he went to Mah-Min, and
told him that he wanted horses and some provisions to
return, and that he would pay him for them in tobacco,
when Mah-Min said to him, "You preach to the Indians
many things, and tell them not to steal or lie; how can
they believe or listen to you? You are the father of
lies. You said you had no tobacco, and now you say
you have plenty."

We had nothing to eat at Rocky Mountain House
but rabbits, and even of those we could not get as much
as we wanted; this was in consequence of the *cache,* in
which the dried meat was placed, having been robbed by
the Assiniboines, who, if they could not be honest
against the temptations of hunger, at least tried to be
as much so as they could, for they placed furs of con-

siderable value in the place of the meat they had stolen. This was the second year they had played the same game; but however satisfactory the arrangement might be to the Hudson's Bay Company, it certainly was anything but pleasant either to their servants or myself; so that after being half starved for ten days, and seeing no signs of the Blackfoot Indians coming in, I persuaded Jemmy Jock to come back with me to Edmonton. This he agreed to do, and he said he had a *cache* of dried meat on the road which would supply us with plenty, so that all we had to do was to ride fast until we came to it.

Early in the morning, we started, taking four extra horses with us as relays. This is done by one man riding in front, then the loose horses, and the other man follows and drives them on; the horses seldom stray or give trouble in this way, and, as they carry no weight, are comparatively fresh when the horse you ride has broken down. We rode the whole day at a tremendous pace, stimulated by hunger, and arrived at the *cache* towards dusk. Having tied our horses, Jemmy went to the *cache,* which was made of logs built together, something like a log house, but not very closely fitted together, and began throwing off the heavy logs which covered the top and concealed it. He heard a regular rumpus within, so he called to me to fetch the guns; when I got up, he removed part of the top, and a fine fat wolverine jumped out, which I immediately shot down. The brute must have been starved and desperately thin to have squeezed himself through the openings between the logs, and no doubt impelled by hunger, and the smell of the meat inside, had not thought much of a slight squeeze. However, when he was once in, and had had a good meal, he could not get out again, and the idea of starving himself as long as the meat lasted, did not seem to have occurred to him. This was a great disappointment to us, as there was very little left, and that mangled, torn, and tossed about in the dirt by the animal. We, however, contrived to make a supper, and saved some for the future; but it was so little, that instead of taking our time on the road as we had intended, we had nothing for it but to ride as fast as we could.

The next day was most uncomfortable, as we had a heavy snowstorm blowing in our faces the whole day; but we pushed on gallantly, and finished our provisions between supper and breakfast next morning, and on the afternoon of the third day we got into Edmonton, but only with two horses, the others having been fagged out and left behind.

May 22nd—Mr. Low arrived from the east side of the Rocky Mountains, in company with Mr. de Merse, the Roman Catholic Bishop of Vancouver, and Mr. Paul Frazer. The boats and their cargoes had been long prepared, and we only waited for a favourable break in the weather to commence our journey home.

May 25th—The weather having cleared up, we embarked with the before-mentioned gentlemen for Norway House. We had twenty-three boats, and 130 men, with Mr. Harriett as our chief. We saw great numbers of dead buffaloes along the shore of the river, which, from the long continuance of the snow covering the herbage, had become so exhausted, that they were drowned in attempting to swim across the river, in their accustomed migration to the south every spring, and now lay in thousands along the banks. At night we drifted down with the current, the men tying several boats together, so as to be under the guidance of one man, whilst the rest lay down and slept.

May 26*th*—We saw several large herds of buffaloes swimming across the river, all going south.

May 27*th*—What with the strong current, the men pulling all day, and our drifting all night, we again arrived at Fort Pitt, where we got an addition to our party of two more boats. These boats are all loaded with the furs and pemmican of the Saskatchewan district. The furs are taken down to York Factory, in the Hudson's Bay, where they are shipped to Europe; the pemmican is intended for those posts where provisions are difficult to be procured. We remained at Fort Pitt for two days whilst the other boats were getting ready, and I took advantage of the delay to sketch a Cree chief. He was dressed in full costume, with a pipe-stem in his hand.

May 29*th*—We left Fort Pitt, quite filling the river with our fleet of boats, presenting a most imposing and animated appearance, considering that we were navigating inland waters so far from the boundaries of civilization. We saw great numbers of wolves busily employed in devouring the carcases of the drowned buffaloes, and had some amusing hunts with our boats after them, our men greatly enjoying the sport. We continued our course in great humour and comfort, without meeting with anything which I considered particularly worthy of recording at the time, until

June 1*st*—When we saw a large party of mounted Indians, riding furiously towards us. On their nearer approach they proved to be a large war party, consisting of Blackfoot Indians, Blood Indians, Sar-cees, Gros Ventres, and Pay-gans. We had a Cree Indian in one of our boats, whom we had to stow away under the skins which covered the goods, lest he should be discovered by the party, who were expressly bound on an

expedition against his tribe, and whom our dispropor-
tionate number could not have opposed had they sought
to take him from us.   We instantly put ashore to meet
them, and Mr. Harriett and myself met them on the
banks of the river, leaving strict orders with the men to
keep the boats afloat sufficiently near the shore for us
to re-embark promptly in case of danger.   They received Mr. Harriett, however, in a most friendly manner, he being personally known to numbers of them. They
immediately spread a buffalo skin for us to sit down
upon, depositing all their arms, consisting of knives,
guns, and bows and arrows, on the ground in front of us,
in token of amity.

There was, however, one exception to this pacific
demonstration, in the case of an Indian I had frequently heard spoken of before, named Omoxesisixany, "Big
Snake".   This chief walked round the party, cracking
and flourishing a whip, and singing a war song, evidently desirous of getting up a fight, and refusing to lay
down his arms with the rest, although frequently requested to do so.   At length, however, he put them
down, and sat with the rest, and taking (though with
evident reluctance) a few puffs from the pipe which was
going the round of the party, in token of peace, he
turned to Mr. Harriett and said, that as he had smoked
with the white man, he would present him with his horse,
at the same time leading up a beautiful brown animal
which I had seen him alight from on our arrival, he
handed Mr. Harriett, the lasso.   Mr. Harriett declined
his gift, explaining that it was impossible for him to
take it with him in the boats.

They told us they were a party of 1,500 warriors,
from 1,200 lodges, who were then "pitching on" towards
Fort Edmonton; that is, they were making short

journeys, and pitching their tents on towards Edmonton, leaving few behind capable of bearing arms.   They were in pursuit of the Crees and Assiniboines, whom they threatened totally to annihilate, boasting that they themselves were as numerous as the grass on the plains. They were the best mounted, the best looking, the most

16. Indian Horse Race
Courtesy of the Royal Ontario Museum

warlike in appearance, and the best accoutred of any tribe I had ever seen on the continent during my route. As Mr. Harriett was very anxious to cultivate the acquaintance and friendship of such questionable characters, he accepted of their invitation to "camp" with them until the following morning, which was exceedingly acceptable to me, as it enabled me to make several sketches, and to hear something about them.   After our smoke several of the young Braves engaged in a horse race, to which sport they are very partial, and at which they bet heavily; they generally ride on those occasions stark naked, without a saddle, and with only a lasso fastened to the lower jaw of the horse as represented in Sketch No. 16. I had some difficulty at first in getting their chiefs to let me take their likenesses, but after they comprehended what I wanted, they made no objections.

Big Snake's brother was the first who sat to me, and while I was sketching, he told me the following anecdote of his brother, of whom he seemed to be very proud. Mr. Harriett understood the language and acted as interpreter. Some time back, Big Snake had the free admission to one of the American forts near the Rocky Mountains. Coming up one day with two other Indians, to enter the gate, it was shut rudely in his face by the orders of the commander, who had only lately arrived in the country. This his pride led him to regard as a direct insult; he rode away, and falling in with some cattle that he knew belonged to the fort, he commenced firing on them, and killed thirteen. As soon as the sentinel, who had given offence, heard the shots, he suspected the reason, and informed the superintendent, who immediately collected his men, and sallied out with them well armed, in the direction of the firing. Big Snake being on the watch, hid himself with his two companions behind a small hill.

The party from the fort apprehending there might be a large number of Indians hid, hesitated to advance within gun-shot; but a negro of the party offered to proceed and reconnoitre. Approaching the hill with great caution, and seeing no one, he began to think they had escaped; but, when within about twenty yards of the top, Big Snake sprang up from his lair and fired, bringing him down, and the next moment bore off his scalp, and waved it in derision towards the Americans.

A short time afterwards, Big Snake met a large party of Blackfeet, "pitching" towards the fort on a trade. On his arrival amongst them, he stated what he had done, and dared any one to censure his conduct on peril of making him his enemy. Although the band well knew that what he had done amounted to an open declaration of war, and would of course cut off any communication or trade with the establishment, unless they actually gave up Big Snake as a prisoner, yet they suffered their disappointment in silence rather than incur the anger of one whom they so much feared. Another band of the same tribe, ignorant of the circumstance, arrived at the fort a few days afterwards. The Americans, thinking this a good opportunity of chastising the aggressors, loaded one of their cannons with musket-balls, and while the unsuspecting Indians were standing huddled together at the gate, waiting for admittance, applied the fusee. Fortunately it did not explode, and the Indians, seeing the unusual stir and the flash, became alarmed, and fled. On a second application of the fusee, it discharged its murderous projectiles amongst the fugitives, and killed ten persons, principally women and children.

Some time after, Big Snake heard that one of the most influential Indians of the tribe had blamed him, in a speech, for involving the tribe in much inconvenience and destroying their trade. On hearing these remarks, he directly went in search of the censurer, armed with a scalping-knife, and, on coming up with him, attempted to stab him; his foot, however, slipped in the attempt, which saved the other's life, although he received a severe wound in the side. These two continued for some time after in a state of deadly hostility, until Big Snake was persuaded by many of his friends to make peace, to which he at length consented, and proceeded towards his lodge for that purpose. In the meantime he had told his wife, if she saw any disturbance, to move her lodge instantly to the top of a small hill, a few hundred yards distant, which might be more easily defended. On his arrival at the man's lodge, he found him seated with his wife and children around him, and, taking up one of the children, he began to caress it, and asked it to intercede with its father for the injury he had done him. The man, however, moodily held down his head without any reply, whilst Big Snake again asked the child to take pity on him still. The father remained silent. On which Big Snake, getting enraged at the rejection of the friendly overtures he had condescended to make to one whom he regarded so much as an inferior, and feeling himself humiliated by the refusal, rushed from the tent, seized his gun, which he had taken the precaution of placing within reach in case of emergency, and commenced firing through the skin covering of the tent, killing two of its inmates, and wounding a third; after which he returned to the hill, where his wife was pitching a tent, according to his orders, where he remained and defied the whole camp to molest him.

After I had finished this picture, and the others had examined it with great attention, a general impression seemed to prevail amongst them all that I must be a great medicine-man. And as we encouraged the idea, which afforded us no inconsiderable protection from any treachery on their part, I had no trouble in getting as many sitters as I could possibly manage. Amongst others, I sketched group, No. 17, consisting of Big Snake, the centre figure; Mis-ke-me-kin, "The Iron Collar," a Blood Indian chief, with his face painted red; to the extreme left of the picture, is a chief called "Little

17. Six Indian Chiefs [in full war costume]
Courtesy of Royal Ontario Museum

Horn," with a buffalo robe draped round him, and between him and Big Snake is Wah-nis-stow, "The White
Buffalo," principal chief of the Sar-cee tribe.   In the
background stand two chiefs of inferior quality, one of
them has his face painted half black, being in half-
mourning for some friend.   As they were expecting to
have a fight with the Crees next day, they got up a
medicine dance in the afternoon, and I was solemnly
invited to attend, that I might add my magical powers
in increasing its efficacy.   Amongst all the tribes here
assembled, the sacredness of the medicine pipe-stem is
held in very high estimation, and it was with much
solemnity that I was placed in the best position, to work
my incantations; that is to say, to make the sketch
No. 18.

Next morning we embarked, after having presented
the chiefs with eight or ten pounds of tobacco to be
distributed amongst the rest, and had not proceeded
many miles, when we had to put ashore again to gratify
an old Blood Indian chief, who had arrived at the camp
shortly after our departure, and had galloped immediately after us, for the purpose of having a talk with
Mr. Harriett, whom he had known many years before,
and for whom he entertained the warmest friendship.
After the talk, he stripped himself naked, excepting his
breech-cloth.   Mr. Harriett, not to be behindhand with
him, gave him everything but his shirt and pantaloons:
it was rather a losing operation for him; although the
chief's leather shirt and leggings were quite new and
highly ornamented, yet they were not exactly what Mr.
Harriett would like to wear, so he gave them to me to
add to my stock of Indian costumes.   One of the
Indians who had accompanied the old chief, noticing
I had a new capote on, thought he would try what could

18. Medicine Pipe-stem Dance
Courtesy of Royal Ontario Museum

be done by an interchange of civilities with me. He accordingly took off a dirty old greasy shirt he had on, and laid it down before me; but as I had no other clothes with me but what I had on, I was forced to decline this most endearing mark of friendship, much to his disappointment, although the scamp could not help grinning as I shook my head in token of refusal.

June 3rd—We were obliged to lie by the whole of this day, on account of the violence of the wind and snow, which rendered any attempt at proceeding very uncomfortable, and almost useless.

June 14th—Early in the forenoon, we arrived at Carlton, and Bishop De Merse immediately took horses to cross by land to Red River Settlement, a distance of sixteen days' journey.

Chapter XXV

The Crees around this post all took to the woods on hearing of the large party of Blackfeet in their vicinity, and, as we heard, were collecting in large numbers in a camp, about fourteen miles off, for the purpose of opposing the invasion of the hostile tribes.

June 5th—We remained at Carlton during the day, as Mr. Harriett was anxious to hear of the proceedings of the hostile tribes; indeed, he felt rather apprehensive of the treachery of the Blackfeet, and knew that the large numbers of our party would check them from attempting anything which might hereafter call for redress.

June 6th—In the morning a fugitive arrived, bringing news of a battle between the hostile Indians. It appears that the Crees had a medicine dance, and had, according to their custom, erected an ornamental pole, around which they hung their medicine bags, &c., whilst dancing. After the conclusion of their dance, they returned to their camp, a distance of about three miles, which consisted of ninety lodges, leaving the medicine pole standing; shortly after, the invading war party we had met discovered the pole, and on one of their number climbing to the top, to tear off the ornaments, he from the height perceived the Cree camp in the distance, upon which the party prepared themselves for battle.

One of the Cree scouts had also perceived them, but had formed a very erroneous idea of their numbers, and had mentioned them only as a small party. Upon this the Crees immediately proceeded to the attack, thinking to overwhelm them by their superior numbers, and did not discover their error until they were actually engaged. When they perceived that they were so much outnumbered, they retreated to their camp; all but one chief, Pe-ho-this, who, disdaining to fly, dashed madly into the midst of his enemies, dealing death around him with his poke-a-mau-gun or war club. On every side, bullet and arrow pierced his body; but he continued the unequal conflict, until his bridle arm was shattered by a ball, when his wounded and frightened horse, no longer under control, dashed with him from the tumult, and carried him still living to his lodge, but with only just sufficient strength to enable him to beg his tribe to take care of his wives and children for his sake, when he fell dead from his charger.

The whole camp now fled with their women and children, leaving their lodges standing; except two old and enfeebled chiefs, who, as is not unusual amongst Indians under such circumstances, remained in the best lodge, and having dressed themselves in their gayest clothes and ornaments, painted their faces, lit their pipes, and sat singing their war songs, until the Blackfeet came up and soon despatched them.

The Crees had nineteen killed and forty wounded, besides losing their lodges and a good deal of property, which they could not carry with them. The Sar-cees lost Wah-nis-stow, before mentioned, and having taken six scalps, thought they had done enough, and returned from the battle to have a dance with the scalps. The Blood Indians, after losing three of their party, also retired after taking a few scalps, leaving the Blackfeet, who had lost six, to bear the brunt of the battle; the Pay-gans and Gros Ventres not having arrived until the fight was over, of course suffered no loss.

Immediately after hearing this, Mr. Harriett ordered us to embark, as he knew that the Blackfeet and their allies would immediately return to their own country after meeting with any success, and having a few scalps to take home, according to the invariable custom of the Indians. We embarked early in the forenoon, and glided quickly down the rapid stream, aided by our oars. We now were out of the buffalo country altogether, and had no fresh meat but some little that we had brought with us for the use of the gentlemen of the party; the men, however, were plentifully supplied with pemmican.

June 10th—We arrived at Cumberland House, which we left next morning, having received an addition to our party of three more boats and their crews.

June 12th—We arrived at the Paw, where my old friend Mr. Hunter gave me a most hearty welcome. Mrs. Hunter had died during my absence, and he had been waiting for us for the purpose of going down to Norway House. We met here Sir John Richardson and Dr. Rae, *en route* to Mackenzie River, with two canoes in search of Sir John Franklin. From them we first heard of the events that had recently occurred in Europe, the flight of Louis Philippe from Paris, and the revolutionary movements then agitating the Continent.

Whilst walking past the small trading post established here, Mr. Hunter asked me to go in, and we were received very kindly by a little shrivelled up French Canadian, married to a Cree squaw, one of the most extraordinary looking women I have ever seen. She was so fat that she was obliged to sit on a small waggon, in which they drew her about, and her mode of going to bed was by rolling off this on to a buffalo skin. She had not been able to use her legs for many years. I have generally noticed that all Indian women, when brought into the forts, and when relieved from the toils and exposures of their native life, become fat, lazy and unwieldy.

We left the same evening, bringing Mr. Hunter with us. Few incidents worth noticing occurred on our route. Mr. Harriett's boat, in which I sat, was generally a-head of the party, being lighter and rather better built than the rest. One evening we got to the place Mr. Harriett selected for encampment considerably before any of the others, and I got out my drawing materials and took a sketch of the brigade, as it was coming up with a fair breeze, crowding on all sail to escape a thunder storm rolling fast after them.

June 17th—We arrived at the Grand Rapids, and the whole brigade shot down them, a distance of three and a half miles; this is the same rapid where Paulet Paul achieved his herculean feat before mentioned. No rapid in the whole course of the navigation on the eastern side of the mountains is at all to be compared to this in point of velocity, grandeur, or danger to the navigator. The brigade flies down as if impelled by a hurricane, many shipping a good deal of water in the perpendicular leaps which they often have to take in the descent. The whole course is one white sheet of foam, from one end to the other.

We passed here the brigade of boats bound upwards for Mackenzie River; they were laboriously making the portage up, whilst we were shooting down with lightning speed. The heavily laden men, as they toiled along the banks, cast many an envious look at our flying company, who yelled and shouted with excitement whilst plunging down the foaming cataract. Having run the rapids in safety, we arrived in a few minutes more at Lake Winnipeg, and encamped on the shore, where we cooked and ate our supper. From this point we had to make a traverse of seventy miles as the crow flies to Mossy Point, the entrance to Jack Fish River; but as the wind was against us, we lay down to sleep.

About 1 o'clock in the morning we were all aroused, and found the wind blowing fresh and fair, so that we put off immediately to take advantage of the fortunate occurrence. I was soon asleep again in the boat, and did not awake till after sunrise, when I found we were far out of sight of land and the wind blowing a heavy gale. About 2 o'clock P.M. we rounded Mossy Point, and at 5 o'clock arrived at Norway House, where the brigade left me, they going on to York Factory, and I remaining to meet Major McKenzie, who was expected soon to pass on his way to Fort Frances.

The annual council of chief factors, which is usually held at Red River, was this year held at Norway House, and I had the pleasure of again meeting with Sir George Simpson, and several gentlemen to whose kindness I had before been deeply indebted. I was detained here for more than a month, and though the weather was clear and fine, yet we could not sit in the house in comfort without having the stove lighted. I amused myself in fishing and shooting. I speared a good many sturgeon, which are here very fine and numerous, and also great lots of gold eyes, which are a peculiar species of fish, like the herring, though larger and thicker, but not worth catching. Mr. Rowand said that they eat like mud. I certainly never tasted them but once, and I was not tempted to repeat the experiment.

I was often accompanied in the canoe by Ogemawwah
Chack, "The Spirit Chief" (Sketch No. 19), an Esqui-
mau from the Hudson's Bay who had attained to an
extreme old age. According to received opinion, he was
110 years old, and the events which he related as having

19. The Esquimalt [Fort Victoria, Vancouver's Island]
Courtesy of Royal Ontario Museum

witnessed seemed to warrant the belief. He had an only
son, whom I often met, quite elderly in appearance.
The mother of this boy had died very shortly after his
birth, and there being no woman giving suck near at the
time, the father, to soothe the cries of the starving infant,
placed the child's mouth to his own breast, and finding

that the child derived some benefit from it, he continued the practice for some days, and, strange to say, milk flowed from his nipple, and he brought up the child without the assistance of any woman.

Before leaving Norway House, some Cree Indians arrived, and boasted that one of their war chiefs had vanquished the great Blackfoot chief, Big Snake, in single combat. Big Snake had ridden away from the main body of his tribe, in hopes of stealing some horses, as he thought that the Crees in their precipitate flight were likely to have left them behind; and, hoping to have all he got for himself, he took no comrades with him. The Cree chief discovered him from behind a hill, riding alone on the plain beneath, and, burning with vengeance, rushed at him, without waiting for his other warriors, who were not, however, far off. Big Snake did not see the others, and disdaining to fly from a single foe, he boldly galloped to meet his enemy; but the fight was short, as the Cree succeeded in piercing him with his spear at the first meeting, and he was scalped and dead before the others came up.

July 24*th*—Major McKenzie at last arrived with five boats, manned principally with Indians; he only remained a few hours, when I embarked with him; but we only proceeded about six miles when it became dark, and we encamped for the night.

July 25*th*—We stopped to breakfast ot a picturesque little island near the outlet of Lake Winnipeg, after which we passed the Spider Islands, so called from the countless myriads of these insects which infest them. In the evening we encamped at Point de Tremble, on Poplar Point.

July 26*th*—We left in the morning with a strong breeze, which changed into a perfect gale, making many of our Indians sea-sick. The swells of Lake Winnipeg, from the shallowness of this wide expanse of water when set in motion by a heavy wind, are far more abrupt and dangerous for boats than those of the Atlantic; and I could not but feel very apprehensive for our safety,— a feeling which was evidently shared by Major McKenzie, for he kept a signal flying from his mast-head, which the guide well knew meant for him to put ashore, but which he would not obey, as he considered it a most dangerous alternative to change his course; and the shore, from its rocky character, being very difficult of approach in stormy weather. We, however, by dint of constant baling continued our course in safety until we arrived at the mouth of Behring's River, which we entered in safety, much to the relief of the Major's anxiety for both cargoes and crews. Here we remained windbound for the rest of the day and part of the following.

By way of passing the time, I took my gun and strolled up the river, accompanied by the guide, and fell in with a solitary Sotto woman and child sitting under a tree. She was quite alone, as her husband had gone up the river fishing in the morning. She did not appear to be at all alarmed or confused at our approach, and freely entered into conversation with the guide, to whom she told her name, Caw-kee-ka-keesh-e-ko, "The Constant Sky." Tempted by the beauty of the scene, and she seeming to be in no wise unwilling, I sketched her likeness and the surrounding landscape with considerable care.

July 27th—We started rather late, and being only able to make Rabbit Point, we encamped. We here found immense flocks of wild pigeons, and killed a good supply. Our Indians killed several skunks, which they prize very much as delicate eating, preferring them to the pigeons, although the bare smell of them in our vicinity almost took away my appetite for the former.

July 28*th*—About 2 o'clock P.M., we endeavoured to proceed, but only got as far as the Dog's Head, the wind being so strong and unfavourable, that it was thought useless to run any risk for the short distance that we would be able to make against it. In the evening our Indians constructed a jonglerie, or medicine lodge, the main object of which was to procure a fair wind for next day. For this purpose they first drive ten or twelve poles, nine or ten feet long, into the ground, enclosing a circular area of about three feet in diameter, with a boat sail open at the top. The medicine-man, one of whom is generally found in every brigade, gets inside and commences shaking the poles violently, rattling his medicinal rattle, and singing hoarse incantations to the Great Spirit for a fair wind. Being unable to sleep on account of the discordant noises, I wrapped a blanket round me, and went out into the woods, where they were holding their midnight orgies, and lay down amongst those on the outside of the medicine lodge, to witness the proceedings. I had no sooner done so than the incantations at once ceased, and the performer exclaimed that a white man was present. How he ascertained this fact I am at a loss to surmise, as it was pitch dark at the time, and he was enclosed in the narrow tent, without any apparent opening through which he could espy me, even had it been light enough to distinguish one person from another.

The Major, who, with many other intelligent persons, is a firm believer in their medicine, told me that a Canadian once had the temerity to peep under the covering which enclosed the jonglerie, but that he got such a fright that he never fairly recovered from it, nor could he ever be prevailed upon to tell what it was that had so appalled him. After about two hours' shaking and singing, the medicine-man cried out that he saw five boats with the sails set running before the wind, which communication was greeted by the whole party with their usual grunt of satisfaction and assent.

After this, many questions were asked him by the Indians, some inquiring after the health of their families at home, whom they had not seen for many months. Upon putting the question, the inquirer threw a small piece of tobacco over the covering of the tent, upon which the medicine-man agitated the tent, and shook his rattle violently, and then replied that he saw one family enjoying themselves over a fat sturgeon, another engaged in some pleasing employment, &c., &c.   I then put a question to him myself, accompanying it with a double portion of tobacco, for which I got a double portion of noise. I asked about my curiosities which I had left at Norway House (for want of room in our boats), to be brought on by the canoes which had taken up Sir John Richardson on their return, they not being engaged to carry him further than Prairie River. The medicine-man told me that he saw the party with my baggage encamped on a sandy point, which we had ourselves passed two days before.

However singular the coincidence may appear, it is a fact, that on the next day we had a fair wind, for which the medicine-man of course took all the credit; and it is no less true, that the canoes with my baggage were on the sandy point on the day stated, for I inquired particularly of them when they came up to us.

July 29*th*—We started very early in the morning, with a fair wind, and stopped to breakfast at the Loon

Narrows.   We reached Otter Head in the evening, and then encamped.

July 30*th*—We breakfasted at Point Mille-Lacs, and arrived at 10 o'clock A.M. at Fort Alexander, where we found a great number of Saulteaux Indians, who come in large numbers about this season of the year, and disperse themselves among the small lakes, where they gather great quantities of wild rice, resembling our own in taste, but much larger and black.   The scarcity of other provisions in these parts renders the rice very valuable, but the Indians are so lazy, that they will not collect much more than they want for themselves without being bribed to do so, and the clerk in charge of the establishment is obliged to give them, for that purpose, a certain quantity of rum to induce them to go to collect rice for the establishment, and also to give them some on their return, besides paying them in goods for the quantity they bring in.   Major McKenzie here met his wife and two daughters, who had been on a visit to Red River. We remained at Fort Alexander four days, changing our crews, the Indians who had been with us belonging here.

Before leaving Lake Winnipeg, I would remark that the whole of its eastern shore, which I had just coasted, presented a most wild, rocky, rough, hilly, and almost impassable country, and several of the Indians, who had been through, described it as being of the same character far back from the lake, and interspersed with innumerable lakes and swamps.

August 3*rd*—We left with four boats, manned with thirty men, twenty-seven of whom were Indians, two French Canadians, and one Orkney man, and commenced the ascent of the Winnipeg River.   Mrs. McKenzie and her two daughters were to follow us in a light canoe, with a crew of Indians. We had to make several portages during the day, and in the evening got over the portage of the Prancing Horses, a cascade about twenty feet high. We had a whole fleet of light canoes following us, containing the Indian wives and children. Two of them contained brides, who had been married in the morning without any ceremony that I heard of.

August 4th—In the morning, we made the White Mud Portage, which was very picturesque, and of which I took a sketch, No. 20, with the Indians and squaws who were following us, carrying their canoes across; and in the course of the day made another called Little Rock, about seven feet high, and camped at the upper end of it.

August 5th—Left at 4 o'clock A.M., and arrived at the Grand Bonnet, a portage of a mile in length, which it took us the whole day to drag the boats across; the weather was burning hot, and the mosquitoes in legions. The canoes, containing the women and children, kept close at our heels, and always came up to our encampment for provisions; this so reduced our stock, that out of regard to our own safety, we were obliged to put them upon short allowance.

August 6th—We crossed the Second Bonnet, and met some Indians, who sold us a few sturgeon, and crossing Lac de Bonnet, where several of our Indian followers left us for the rice-grounds, we encamped for the night on the banks of the river Malaine. Owing to the low marshy state of the country hereabouts, we were dreadfully tormented with mosquitoes. The poor Orkney man, in particular, seemed to be an especial favourite, and there had been evidently an attempt made to eat him up altogether. In the morning, his face presented the appearance of a person in the smallpox.

20. White Mud Portage [Winnipeg River]
Courtesy of Royal Ontario Museum

August 7th—Passed six portages to-day, one of which is called the Wooden Horse, and encamped at the Grande Gullete. The chief's son, of Rat Portage, who was one of our engaged men, here deserted us, and stole off in a canoe with his two wives.

August 8th—To-day we had to make several portages, and in the evening encamped three miles above the Grand Rapid of this river, having still thirteen canoes of Indians paddling in our wake. This evening we found some smooth flat rocks, which the voyageurs always prefer to grass or earth to make their bed on, and I can say, from experience, that they have formed a judicious estimate of the superior comfort they afford after a hard day's travel; for grass or sand is certainly the worst surface to sleep upon, however soft it may feel at first.

August 9th—We breakfasted at the Barrière Portage, and arrived about noon at the Slave Falls, of which I made a sketch. Three military officers, Captain Moody, Mr. Brown, and Mr. Constable, caught up to us in their light canoes; they were on their way from Red River to Canada, and pushed on after a very short stay. We had hardly bid them good-bye, when Mrs. McKenzie and her two lovely daughters came up, and stayed with us until next morning. Our Indians now refused to proceed further, unless they received an allowance of rum; and the Major was obliged to promise them a supply as soon as he arrived at Rat Portage.

August 10th—Our starting was delayed this morning in consequence of a dense fog, and we only got as far as the Rochers Boules before breakfast; after which, the ladies left us for their residence at Rat Portage. During the day we passed the Aux Chênes, and encamped about four miles below the Point of Woods.

August 11*th*—Our provisions were now getting very low, and we had still further to restrict our distributions to the women and children.   On each side of the river for a long distance are innumerable small shallow lakes, bearing usually large quantities of rice; but the water in them had sunk so low this season, that the Indians were apprehensive of a failure in the crop, which would be attended with the most serious consequences, as upon it was placed their whole dependence for food.   When we arrived at the Grand Equerre we stopped for the night.

August 12*th*—We passed to-day the deserted Catholic mission called Wabe-samung, "White Dog," from the name of the portage next above it.   This was established by Rev. Belcour, a Catholic priest, but he had left it the year before, as he found there was not enough of land near it that would pay for cultivation. The whole country between this and Fort Alexander was rocky and barren, so that no mission could hope to get any Indians to settle permanently near it.   In the evening we encamped at the White Dog Portage.

August 13*th*—We got to the Yellow Mud Portage by breakfast-time, and afterwards crossed the "Grande Décharge," so called from its being the place where the boats are hauled up after the goods are discharged from them, in distinction from a portage, at which latter place, as I have already observed, it is necessary to carry the boats as well as the cargoes.   In the evening we encamped at what is called the Fishery, or the place where the people from Rat Portage come to fish.   It was with great difficulty we could find a place to sleep on free from ants, whose hillocks we disturbed at every step.   I made several attempts to lie down, but they annoyed me so much, that at last I got into one of the boats.

August 14*th*—Left our encampment at 3 A.M., and arrived at Rat Portage at 10, where we were received by Mrs. McKenzie with the greatest hospitality and kindness. The Indians here subsist on sturgeon and white fish in the summer, and rice and rabbits in the winter. We rested ourselves here two days, and employed themselves principally in feasting on white fish, to make up for the short allowance of food under which we had lately been suffering.

August 16*th*—It was with great regret that I parted with the kind major and his family. The men having made the portage from which this post is named, we left about 2 in the afternoon, and soon entered the Lake of the Woods, where we chose a comfortable little island, and encamped for the night.

August 17*th*—We threaded our way among innumerable islands, many of them thickly covered with woods, from which circumstance the lake takes it name. We saw on one of them about five acres of cultivated corn, the only instance of the kind I had seen since I left Norway House. There is another island called Garden Island, which lay to the west of our route, about six miles long and about three wide, on which I was told some Indians raised yearly a few bushels of corn and potatoes. At night we again chose an island for our resting place.

August 18*th*—We were wind-bound until 5 P.M., during which time we were visited by a large party of Saulteaux Indians; we embarked in the evening, but only succeeded in getting on about six miles before we were again obliged to stop and remained all the next day.

August 20*th*—Made an early start with a fair wind, which carried us into the mouth of the River La Pluie. Here we found some Indians who were gathering snow-berries and sand-berries; the latter are the size of large grapes, of a reddish blue colour. They grow on long vines trailing upon the sand, and are very good eating when washed free of the particles which adhere to them. We encamped about four miles up the river, and were again tortured by our old enemies the mosquitoes, aided by detachments of black flies.

August 21*st*—Roused by the flies, we started early. Our route up the river was much enlivened by the antics of the Indians when tracking, that is, hauling the boats up the current, which they do for days together when-ever the banks, or indeed the bed of the river, will admit of it; for they seemed to be perfectly amphibious, wading about in the water, and swimming from side to side as a matter of course, without thinking of getting into the boat, and making great fun of one of our Can-adians who had got into a canoe with two squaws, to cross.

August 22*nd*—The men woke me up at 2 o'clock in the morning from my warm blankets, for the purpose of getting under way; but when just ready to start, we were prevented by a violent storm of rain, which continued until about 6 o'clock, when we immediately set off. The country about here is very swampy, but, from its height, I think much of it might be drained, and adapted for cultivation. I noticed all along the banks of this river, that wherever pine trees had been burned down, poplars invariably sprung up in their places, although no other poplars could be seen in the vicinity.

August 23rd—We left our encampment at 1 A.M., so as to make sure of arriving at Fort Frances before night. The Indians tracked with the line the whole day, frequently up to their middles in the water, and often swimming; this wearisome toil they kept up for sixteen hours, with the exception of one hour, during which we stopped for breakfast, never for one moment losing their cheerfulness and good humour. I scarcely think that any other race of people could go through such fatigue with the same alacrity and energy.

At 5 o'clock P.M., we reached Fort Frances, so named after the sister of Lady Simpson. Here the annual three months' voyage terminates, that being the time it takes to convey furs to York Factory, in Hudson's Bay, and bring back the outfit of goods. The fort is situated near where Rainy Lake disembogues into a river of the same name, forming a beautiful cascade. The Indians catch great quantities of sturgeon at the foot of these falls in the month of June. The sturgeon here are very small—seldom weighing more than 40 or 50 lbs—at least in comparison with those taken at the mouth of Frazer's River on the west side of the mountains, which often weigh from 5 to 7 cwt.

Fort Frances has usually about 250 Indians in its neighbourhood, who have a half-breed missionary of the Methodist church resident amongst them; but I understood he was about to leave them disheartened by the small success attendant upon his exertions. The Indians live here as at Rat Portage, on rice, fish, and rabbits. The last are so numerous in the winter, that one man caught eighty-six in one night, being only unsuccessful with fourteen snares out of the hundred he had set in the evening.

The skins, like the Canadian, are far inferior to the European rabbits': the only use to which I have seen them applied has been in the manufacture of rabbit-skin robes, which are made by cutting the skin with the hair on into strips, which are twisted and netted together in such a manner as to keep the hair outward on both sides of the robe. The people of the fort grow some wheat and potatoes, but though there is some very good land about, they find it impossible to induce the Indians to cultivate it. The crop of wheat which they got in while I was there, was almost entirely spoiled by smut, and they were obliged to wash it before they could turn it to any account. I remained here eighteen days waiting for the passing of the express canoe which annually carries the letters from the interior posts to Lachine.

September 10*th*—The express canoe arrived in the evening with Mr. M'Tavish. He was come direct from York Factory, where he had been stationed for fourteen years, and gave a most dismal account of the climate and country; he was now going to the Sault Ste. Marie, to the charge of which post he had been recently appointed by way of giving him a little taste of civilization, of which he rather stood in need.

September 11*th*—We started at 6 o'clock in the morning, and got through Lac la Pluie by 5 in the afternoon; after this we had to make two portages, and encamped just before dark at the second.

September 12*th*—Started at 3 o'clock A.M. The morning was very cold and foggy; and we had a severe frost during the night. We breakfasted at the Grand Chute, and had a very severe day's work afterwards, as we had to make four bad portages, and did not encamp until 9 o'clock at night, the men having worked eighteen hours steadily. We were lucky enough to meet some Indians after dark, from whom we obtained a good supply of delicious white fish. We now exerted all our energies to hasten our journey as the danger of ice setting in was becoming imminent, and with great labour we arrived at the Mountain Portage on the evening of the 18th.

September 19*th*—I got up at the first appearance of day, that I might have the opportunity whilst the men were making the portage, of again visiting the Kakabakka falls. As the day dawned the magnificent spectacle gradually cleared to my view in all its mighty grandeur and magnificence, and I felt more impressed than ever with the opinion that these falls far surpass the Niagara in beauty and picturesque effect, and would have much liked to have taken another sketch of them; but my admiring contemplations were hastily cut short by a peremptory summons from the canoes, which were waiting for me. I hastily rejoined them, and we dashed down the uninterrupted current forty miles to Fort William, where we arrived early in the afternoon. On leaving Fort William, we suffered a great deal the next five days from the high cold wind, which frequently stopped our progress.

September 24*th*—We were wind-bound at the mouth of a small river, and as there seemed no prospect of a change, I followed the stream up about ten miles until I came to a cascade. The interior of the country as far as I went seemed to be of the same character as the coast, high mountain rocks, interspersed with a few trees of stunted growth and scanty herbage. I was lucky enough to shoot four ducks, which proved a most acceptable addition to the pemmican and fish which we had brought with us. We got off next day, although the weather was still bad, but we were anxious to get to Michipicoton, as there is a post there, and we might obtain some little comfort at least, if we were detained.

September 27*th*—We arrived at the post about 9 o'clock in the evening, and remained there the whole of next day. The post is situated in a deep bay at the mouth of the river, and is surrounded by some of the best land to be found on the British shores of Lake Superior. The head chief of the Ojibbeways, who resides near the post, sat for me in his red coat trimmed with gold lace. These coats are given by the Company to such Indian chiefs as have been friendly and service-able to them, and are very highly prized by their possessors. His name was Maydoc-game-kinungee, "I hear the Noise of the Deer."

September 29*th*—We started very early in the morning, and encamped that evening opposite to Montreal Island.

September 30*th*—We got to Montreal River, where we stopped for two hours for breakfast, passed Micah Bay at 1 o'clock, and encamped at night at the Isle aux Sables.

October 1*st*—We stopped to breakfast at 4 o'clock near Gros-cap, a porphyry rock rising 1,500 feet above the level of the lake, and got to the post at Sault Ste. Marie by 2 o'clock P.M. Here I consider that my Indian travels finish, as the rest of my journey home to Toronto was performed on board steamboats; and the greatest hardship I had to endure, was the difficulty in trying to sleep in a civilized bed.

NOTES

1—(p. 18) 'Mackinaw,'—an important point in the western fur trade from the earliest times. Known to the French as Michilimackinac, a corruption of the Chippewa *mitchi makinak*, signifying 'big turtle'. An alternative derivation is from *Mishinimakinunk*, 'place of the big wounded person', or *Mishinimakinagog*, the name of an extinct Algonquin tribe.

2—(p. 33) 'El Royal'. Isle Royale, which enjoyed a certain notoriety in connection with the international boundary controversies. Among other eccentricities, it had masqueraded for a time as two distinct islands, Isle Royale and Isle Phillipeaux, the error apparently arising from conflicting reports of the island as seen by different observers from opposite sides of the lake.

3—(p. 33) 'a gentleman named Lane'. Afterward Chief Trader W. D. Lane.

4—(p. 34) 'The Mountain Portage'. This is the beautiful Kakabeka Falls. They are about 150 feet in height.

5—(p. 43) 'sturgeon'. For many years large quantities of this fish were obtained from the Lake of the Woods. Indeed at one time much of the caviare consumed in America came not from Russia but from the Lake of the Woods. The sturgeon fishery is now, however, pretty well exhausted.

6—(p. 51) 'a chief named Grant'. Cuthbert Grant, son of one of the leading traders of the North-West Company, of the same name, and an Indian mother. He was educated at Montreal, entered the service of the North-West Company, led the Half-breeds in the Seven Oaks affair. He afterwards settled near White Horse Plains, on the Assiniboine; was appointed Warden of the Plains by the Council of Assiniboia, and became a member of that body.

7—(p. 55) 'Saulteaux'. This name was applied by the French to the Ojibway, or Chippewa. Ojibway means 'to roast till puckered up', referring to the puckered seam on their moccasins, according to White's *Handbook of Indians of Canada*.

8—(p. 57) 'an immense herd'. Evidence as to the extraordinary numbers of the buffalo might be multiplied
almost indefinitely, as it is found in all narratives of the
western plains, from the days of La Vérendrye down to
the middle of the last century. Indeed the incredible
thing is that at one time they were seen in millions, and
only a few short years afterward nothing remained but
piles of bleached bones. Fortunately the rapidly increasing herd in Wainwright Park dispels the fear that this
interesting animal will become extinct.

9—(p. 65) 'The gentleman in charge was Mr Christie'.
Several generations of Christies were prominent in the
history of the Hudson's Bay Company. Alexander
Christie, mentioned here, rose to the rank of Chief Factor,
and was twice Governor of Assiniboia. His son, of the
same Christian name, became Chief Trader, and another
son, Wm Christie, Chief Factor.

10—(p. 67) 'Mr Le Fleck and Mr Taché'. Père Laflèche
(afterward Bishop of Three Rivers) and Père Taché
(afterward Archbishop of St Boniface). See Morice,
Dictionnaire historique des Canadiens de l'Ouest.

11—(p. 71) Donald Ross, who became Chief Factor. Was
for many years in charge of Norway House.

12—(p. 71) 'Reverend Mr Mason'. He was sent out by the
Church Missionary Society.

13—(p. 71) 'Mr Rowand'. John Rowand, who had been
made Chief Factor in 1826. Of the many stories that are
told of him, none is perhaps more singular than that which
relates the fate of his ashes. He had, it appears, expressed
a strong wish that he might be buried in the old cemetery
at Montreal. As he died at Edmonton, how to carry
out his request proved a difficult problem. Finally a
huge pot was brought into requisition, the body boiled
down, and the bones packed in a small keg for the long
journey. All went well until the brigade reached Fort
Frances, when for some reason the superstitious voyageurs
refused to take that particular keg any farther. It was
shipped back to Fort Garry, and eventually reached its
resting place by way of York Factory, London, and
Montreal.

14—(p. 74) 'the Pau'. Le Pas, on the lower Saskatchewan,
still known by that name. The name is probably a
corruption of the old Indian name of Pasquia. Fort
Pasquia, built in La Vérendrye's day, stood near this spot.

15—(p. 76) 'the Blackfeet being the most hostile tribe'. It is an interesting fact that while, in Paul Kane's day and for many years before, the Blackfeet had a most unenviable reputation among the whites, the first white trader, in fact the first white man, who is known to have visited them, Anthony Hendry of the Hudson's Bay Company, has left it on record that he spent the winter with them and was treated with the utmost friendliness. One wonders if the fault lay with the Indian or with his civilized brother.

16—(p. 80) 'endeavour to cross in front of his horse'. This curious propensity has been noted also among some of the deer family in Mongolia.

17—(p. 106) 'His proper location is a long distance to the north-east'. Kane must have misunderstood the direction, as the home of the Shuswap was south-west, rather than north-east, west of the mountains, between the Columbia and the Fraser rivers.

18—(p. 107) 'La Row's Prairie'. Probably Larue's Prairie.

19—(p. 116) 'Mr Douglas and Mr Ogden'. James (afterward Sir) Douglas (1803-1877) and Peter Skene Ogden (1794-1854), were two of the most remarkable men contributed by the North-West Company to the service of the Hudson's Bay Company. A third, and even greater, was Dr John McLoughlin (1784-1857), mentioned on page 117. Townsend, in his *Narrative* of 1834, describes him as "a large, dignified and very noble looking man, with a fine expressive countenance, and remarkably bland and pleasing manners." He had resigned from the service of the Hudson's Bay Company shortly before Kane's visit, his friendliness and humanity to the Oregon settlers having been more than the Company thought necessary, and having led to a reprimand.

20—(p. 121) Duncan McDougall, who left the North-West Company to take charge of the new venture at Astoria.

21—(p. 122) Samuel Black. Bryce tells the story of the murder in his *Hudson's Bay Company*. Black had originally been in the service of the North-West Company. Had charge of Dunvegan, for the H.B.C., in 1823, and Walla-Walla, 1828. He was in charge of Kamloops at the time of his murder, 1841.

22—(p. 125)   John Clarke (1781-1852), a native of Montreal, and associated with Astor in his Pacific coast ventures. An account of his life is given in *Old Montreal*, written by his daughter, and published in 1906.

23—(p. 131)   'the Walhamette'. Settlement in the valley of the Willamette, according to De Smet, dates from 1829. McLoughlin, after leaving the Hudson's Bay Company, settled at Oregon City, where he spent the remainder of his life.

24—(p. 140)   'We landed at the Cowlitz farm'. Thwaites says that in 1837 Simon Plomondeau was advised by McLoughlin to settle on Cowlitz Prairie. Others followed, and in 1839 a large farm was surveyed by Charles Ross, John Work and James Douglas as a company settlement. It grew but little until the advent of the Americans in 1853-54.

25—(p. 144)   Nichol Finlayson, Chief Factor. Like the Christies, the Finlaysons gave several generations to the service of the Hudson's Bay Company.

26—(p. 144)   'Its Indian name is the Esquimalt'. Scholefield, in *British Columbia*, notes that Kane "confuses the old name of Fort Victoria, Camosun, with that of Esquimalt."

27—(p. 144)   'Clover grows plentifully'. This was wild clover, native to the place. Scholefield says, "His account of the origin of the clover which grew so luxuriantly at Victoria is obviously at fault; for Douglas in his Report of 1842 remarks upon the rank growth of the plant in the vicinity of Camosun."

28—(p. 178)   Probably John L. Lewes, who became Chief Factor in 1828.

29—(p. 202)   'Nezperees'. A corruption, doubtless, of Nez Perces, a name given to this Indian tribe by the Franco-Canadian fur-traders. They inhabited the regions about the Columbia River until 1877, when they made a sanguinary outbreak. They murdered settlers and fought United States soldiers, and then fled eastward for hundreds of miles; but they were overtaken and their hostile spirit crushed. Some of their descendants may be found in Washington and Idaho, under the name of Sahaptins or Shahapkins.

30—(p. 225)   Mr T. C. Elliott, of Walla-Walla, draws my
    attention to a curious error in Kane's narrative.   The
    Whitman Massacre took place on November 27th-29th,
    1847, about six miles from Walla-Walla.   Kane says,
    under date of September 21st., (p. 222)   "This evening
    two men arrive from Walla-Walla," and goes on to
    describe the massacre.   He was then at Fort Colville,
    two hundred miles north of Walla-Walla.   On the actual
    date of the massacre, he was at or near Fort Assiniboine
    on the Athabaska.   Either his dates are all wrong, or he
    must have heard the story east of the mountains some
    time afterward, and got his facts mixed when he came
    to write the book.

31—(p. 233)   'botanical research'.   The gentleman engaged
    in botanical research seems to point to David Douglas,
    after whom the Douglas fir was named, but Douglas's
    visit to the coast was in 1825.

32—(p. 255)   John E. Harriott, who became a Chief Factor
    in 1846.   De Smet, who visited him at Rocky Mountain
    House in 1845, describes him as an Englishman by birth,
    and "among the most amiable gentlemen I have ever had
    the pleasure of meeting."   He had been working for
    many years among the Blackfeet.

33—(p. 261)   'Mr Thebo'.   Rev. Jean Baptiste Thibault
    (1810-1879).

34—(p. 302)   Mgr. Louis-Benjamin Demers (1809-1871).

35—(p. 317)   Rev. Georges Antoine Belcourt (1803-1874).

36—(p. 321)   William McTavish, afterward Governor of
    Assiniboia.

A CATALOG OF SELECTED DOVER
BOOKS IN ALL FIELDS OF INTEREST

CONCERNING THE SPIRITUAL IN ART, Wassily Kandinsky. Pioneering work by father of abstract art. Thoughts on color theory, nature of art. Analysis of earlier masters. 12 illustrations. 80pp. of text. 5⅜ × 8½.   23411-8 Pa. $3.95

ANIMALS: 1,419 Copyright-Free Illustrations of Mammals, Birds, Fish, Insects, etc., Jim Harter (ed.). Clear wood engravings present, in extremely lifelike poses, over 1,000 species of animals. One of the most extensive pictorial sourcebooks of its kind. Captions. Index. 284pp. 9 × 12.   23766-4 Pa. $12.95

CELTIC ART: The Methods of Construction, George Bain. Simple geometric techniques for making Celtic interlacements, spirals, Kells-type initials, animals, humans, etc. Over 500 illustrations. 160pp. 9 × 12. (USO)   22923-8 Pa. $9.95

AN ATLAS OF ANATOMY FOR ARTISTS, Fritz Schider. Most thorough reference work on art anatomy in the world. Hundreds of illustrations, including selections from works by Vesalius, Leonardo, Goya, Ingres, Michelangelo, others. 593 illustrations. 192pp. 7⅛ × 10¼.   20241-0 Pa. $9.95

CELTIC HAND STROKE-BY-STROKE (Irish Half-Uncial from "The Book of Kells"): An Arthur Baker Calligraphy Manual, Arthur Baker. Complete guide to creating each letter of the alphabet in distinctive Celtic manner. Covers hand position, strokes, pens, inks, paper, more. Illustrated. 48pp. 8¼ × 11.

24336-2 Pa. $3.95

EASY ORIGAMI, John Montroll. Charming collection of 32 projects (hat, cup, pelican, piano, swan, many more) specially designed for the novice origami hobbyist. Clearly illustrated easy-to-follow instructions insure that even beginning papercrafters will achieve successful results. 48pp. 8¼ × 11.   27298-2 Pa. $2.95

THE COMPLETE BOOK OF BIRDHOUSE CONSTRUCTION FOR WOOD-WORKERS, Scott D. Campbell. Detailed instructions, illustrations, tables. Also data on bird habitat and instinct patterns. Bibliography. 3 tables. 63 illustrations in 15 figures. 48pp. 5¼ × 8½.   24407-5 Pa. $1.95

BLOOMINGDALE'S ILLUSTRATED 1886 CATALOG: Fashions, Dry Goods and Housewares, Bloomingdale Brothers. Famed merchants' extremely rare catalog depicting about 1,700 products: clothing, housewares, firearms, dry goods, jewelry, more. Invaluable for dating, identifying vintage items. Also, copyright-free graphics for artists, designers. Co-published with Henry Ford Museum & Green-field Village. 160pp. 8¼ × 11.   25780-0 Pa. $9.95

HISTORIC COSTUME IN PICTURES, Braun & Schneider. Over 1,450 costumed figures in clearly detailed engravings—from dawn of civilization to end of 19th century. Captions. Many folk costumes. 256pp. 8⅜ × 11¾.   23150-X Pa. $11.95

CATALOG OF DOVER BOOKS

STICKLEY CRAFTSMAN FURNITURE CATALOGS, Gustav Stickley and L. & J. G. Stickley. Beautiful, functional furniture in two authentic catalogs from 1910. 594 illustrations, including 277 photos, show settles, rockers, armchairs, reclining chairs, bookcases, desks, tables. 183pp. 6½ × 9¼.   23838-5 Pa. $9.95

AMERICAN LOCOMOTIVES IN HISTORIC PHOTOGRAPHS: 1858 to 1949, Ron Ziel (ed.). A rare collection of 126 meticulously detailed official photographs, called "builder portraits," of American locomotives that majestically chronicle the rise of steam locomotive power in America. Introduction. Detailed captions. xi + 129pp. 9 × 12.   27393-8 Pa. $12.95

AMERICA'S LIGHTHOUSES: An Illustrated History, Francis Ross Holland, Jr. Delightfully written, profusely illustrated fact-filled survey of over 200 American lighthouses since 1716. History, anecdotes, technological advances, more. 240pp. 8 × 10¾.   25576-X Pa. $11.95

TOWARDS A NEW ARCHITECTURE, Le Corbusier. Pioneering manifesto by founder of "International School." Technical and aesthetic theories, views of industry, economics, relation of form to function, "mass-production split" and much more. Profusely illustrated. 320pp. 6⅛ × 9¼. (USO)   25023-7 Pa. $9.95

HOW THE OTHER HALF LIVES, Jacob Riis. Famous journalistic record, exposing poverty and degradation of New York slums around 1900, by major social reformer. 100 striking and influential photographs. 233pp. 10 × 7⅞.
22012-5 Pa $10.95

FRUIT KEY AND TWIG KEY TO TREES AND SHRUBS, William M. Harlow. One of the handiest and most widely used identification aids. Fruit key covers 120 deciduous and evergreen species; twig key 160 deciduous species. Easily used. Over 300 photographs. 126pp. 5⅜ × 8½.   20511-8 Pa. $3.95

COMMON BIRD SONGS, Dr. Donald J. Borror. Songs of 60 most common U.S. birds: robins, sparrows, cardinals, bluejays, finches, more—arranged in order of increasing complexity. Up to 9 variations of songs of each species.
Cassette and manual 99911-4 $8.95

ORCHIDS AS HOUSE PLANTS, Rebecca Tyson Northen. Grow cattleyas and many other kinds of orchids—in a window, in a case, or under artificial light. 63 illustrations. 148pp. 5⅜ × 8½.   23261-1 Pa. $4.95

MONSTER MAZES, Dave Phillips. Masterful mazes at four levels of difficulty. Avoid deadly perils and evil creatures to find magical treasures. Solutions for all 32 exciting illustrated puzzles. 48pp. 8¼ × 11.   26005-4 Pa. $2.95

MOZART'S DON GIOVANNI (DOVER OPERA LIBRETTO SERIES), Wolfgang Amadeus Mozart. Introduced and translated by Ellen H. Bleiler. Standard Italian libretto, with complete English translation. Convenient and thoroughly portable—an ideal companion for reading along with a recording or the performance itself. Introduction. List of characters. Plot summary. 121pp. 5¼ × 8½.
24944-1 Pa. $2.95

TECHNICAL MANUAL AND DICTIONARY OF CLASSICAL BALLET, Gail Grant. Defines, explains, comments on steps, movements, poses and concepts. 15-page pictorial section. Basic book for student, viewer. 127pp. 5⅜ × 8½.
21843-0 Pa. $4.95

BRASS INSTRUMENTS: Their History and Development, Anthony Baines. Authoritative, updated survey of the evolution of trumpets, trombones, bugles, cornets, French horns, tubas and other brass wind instruments. Over 140 illustrations and 48 music examples. Corrected and updated by author. New preface. Bibliography. 320pp. 5⅜ × 8½. 27574-4 Pa. $9.95

HOLLYWOOD GLAMOR PORTRAITS, John Kobal (ed.). 145 photos from 1926–49. Harlow, Gable, Bogart, Bacall; 94 stars in all. Full background on photographers, technical aspects. 160pp. 8⅜ × 11¼. 23352-9 Pa. $11.95

MAX AND MORITZ, Wilhelm Busch. Great humor classic in both German and English. Also 10 other works: "Cat and Mouse," "Plisch and Plumm," etc. 216pp. 5⅜ × 8½. 20181-3 Pa. $5.95

THE RAVEN AND OTHER FAVORITE POEMS, Edgar Allan Poe. Over 40 of the author's most memorable poems: "The Bells," "Ulalume," "Israfel," "To Helen," "The Conqueror Worm," "Eldorado," "Annabel Lee," many more. Alphabetic lists of titles and first lines. 64pp. 5³⁄₁₆ × 8¼. 26685-0 Pa. $1.00

SEVEN SCIENCE FICTION NOVELS, H. G. Wells. The standard collection of the great novels. Complete, unabridged. First Men in the Moon, Island of Dr. Moreau, War of the Worlds, Food of the Gods, Invisible Man, Time Machine, In the Days of the Comet. Total of 1,015pp. 5⅜ × 8½. (USO) 20264-X Clothbd. $29.95

AMULETS AND SUPERSTITIONS, E. A. Wallis Budge. Comprehensive discourse on origin, powers of amulets in many ancient cultures: Arab, Persian, Babylonian, Assyrian, Egyptian, Gnostic, Hebrew, Phoenician, Syriac, etc. Covers cross, swastika, crucifix, seals, rings, stones, etc. 584pp. 5⅜ × 8½. 23573-4 Pa. $12.95

RUSSIAN STORIES/PYCCKNE PACCKA3bl: A Dual-Language Book, edited by Gleb Struve. Twelve tales by such masters as Chekhov, Tolstoy, Dostoevsky, Pushkin, others. Excellent word-for-word English translations on facing pages, plus teaching and study aids, Russian/English vocabulary, biographical/critical introductions, more. 416pp. 5⅜ × 8½. 26244-8 Pa. $8.95

PHILADELPHIA THEN AND NOW: 60 Sites Photographed in the Past and Present, Kenneth Finkel and Susan Oyama. Rare photographs of City Hall, Logan Square, Independence Hall, Betsy Ross House, other landmarks juxtaposed with contemporary views. Captures changing face of historic city. Introduction. Captions. 128pp. 8¼ × 11. 25790-8 Pa. $9.95

AIA ARCHITECTURAL GUIDE TO NASSAU AND SUFFOLK COUNTIES, LONG ISLAND, The American Institute of Architects, Long Island Chapter, and the Society for the Preservation of Long Island Antiquities. Comprehensive, well-researched and generously illustrated volume brings to life over three centuries of Long Island's great architectural heritage. More than 240 photographs with authoritative, extensively detailed captions. 176pp. 8¼ × 11. 26946-9 Pa. $14.95

NORTH AMERICAN INDIAN LIFE: Customs and Traditions of 23 Tribes, Elsie Clews Parsons (ed.). 27 fictionalized essays by noted anthropologists examine religion, customs, government, additional facets of life among the Winnebago, Crow, Zuni, Eskimo, other tribes. 480pp. 6⅛ × 9¼. 27377-6 Pa. $10.95

FRANK LLOYD WRIGHT'S HOLLYHOCK HOUSE, Donald Hoffmann. Lavishly illustrated, carefully documented study of one of Wright's most controversial residential designs. Over 120 photographs, floor plans, elevations, etc. Detailed perceptive text by noted Wright scholar. Index. 128pp. 9¼ × 10¾.
27133-1 Pa. $11.95

THE MALE AND FEMALE FIGURE IN MOTION: 60 Classic Photographic Sequences, Eadweard Muybridge. 60 true-action photographs of men and women walking, running, climbing, bending, turning, etc., reproduced from rare 19th-century masterpiece. vi + 121pp. 9 × 12.
24745-7 Pa. $10.95

1001 QUESTIONS ANSWERED ABOUT THE SEASHORE, N. J. Berrill and Jacquelyn Berrill. Queries answered about dolphins, sea snails, sponges, starfish, fishes, shore birds, many others. Covers appearance, breeding, growth, feeding, much more. 305pp. 5¼ × 8¼.
23366-9 Pa. $7.95

GUIDE TO OWL WATCHING IN NORTH AMERICA, Donald S. Heintzelman. Superb guide offers complete data and descriptions of 19 species: barn owl, screech owl, snowy owl, many more. Expert coverage of owl-watching equipment, conservation, migrations and invasions, etc. Guide to observing sites. 84 illustrations. xiii + 193pp. 5⅜ × 8½.
27344-X Pa. $8.95

MEDICINAL AND OTHER USES OF NORTH AMERICAN PLANTS: A Historical Survey with Special Reference to the Eastern Indian Tribes, Charlotte Erichsen-Brown. Chronological historical citations document 500 years of usage of plants, trees, shrubs native to eastern Canada, northeastern U.S. Also complete identifying information. 343 illustrations. 544pp. 6½ × 9¼.
25951-X Pa. $12.95

STORYBOOK MAZES, Dave Phillips. 23 stories and mazes on two-page spreads: Wizard of Oz, Treasure Island, Robin Hood, etc. Solutions. 64pp. 8¼ × 11.
23628-5 Pa. $2.95

NEGRO FOLK MUSIC, U.S.A., Harold Courlander. Noted folklorist's scholarly yet readable analysis of rich and varied musical tradition. Includes authentic versions of over 40 folk songs. Valuable bibliography and discography. xi + 324pp. 5⅜ × 8½.
27350-4 Pa. $7.95

MOVIE-STAR PORTRAITS OF THE FORTIES, John Kobal (ed.). 163 glamor, studio photos of 106 stars of the 1940s: Rita Hayworth, Ava Gardner, Marlon Brando, Clark Gable, many more. 176pp. 8⅜ × 11¼.
23546-7 Pa. $11.95

BENCHLEY LOST AND FOUND, Robert Benchley. Finest humor from early 30s, about pet peeves, child psychologists, post office and others. Mostly unavailable elsewhere. 73 illustrations by Peter Arno and others. 183pp. 5⅜ × 8½.
22410-4 Pa. $5.95

YEKL and THE IMPORTED BRIDEGROOM AND OTHER STORIES OF YIDDISH NEW YORK, Abraham Cahan. Film Hester Street based on Yekl (1896). Novel, other stories among first about Jewish immigrants on N.Y.'s East Side. 240pp. 5⅜ × 8½.
22427-9 Pa. $6.95

SELECTED POEMS, Walt Whitman. Generous sampling from *Leaves of Grass.* Twenty-four poems include "I Hear America Singing," "Song of the Open Road," "I Sing the Body Electric," "When Lilacs Last in the Dooryard Bloom'd," "O Captain! My Captain!"—all reprinted from an authoritative edition. Lists of titles and first lines. 128pp. 5³⁄₁₆ × 8¼.
26878-0 Pa. $1.00

THE BEST TALES OF HOFFMANN, E. T. A. Hoffmann. 10 of Hoffmann's most important stories: "Nutcracker and the King of Mice," "The Golden Flowerpot," etc. 458pp. 5⅜ × 8½. 21793-0 Pa. $8.95

FROM FETISH TO GOD IN ANCIENT EGYPT, E. A. Wallis Budge. Rich detailed survey of Egyptian conception of "God" and gods, magic, cult of animals, Osiris, more. Also, superb English translations of hymns and legends. 240 illustrations. 545pp. 5⅜ × 8½. 25803-3 Pa. $11.95

FRENCH STORIES/CONTES FRANÇAIS: A Dual-Language Book, Wallace Fowlie. Ten stories by French masters, Voltaire to Camus: "Micromegas" by Voltaire; "The Atheist's Mass" by Balzac; "Minuet" by de Maupassant; "The Guest" by Camus, six more. Excellent English translations on facing pages. Also French-English vocabulary list, exercises, more. 352pp. 5⅜ × 8½. 26443-2 Pa. $8.95

CHICAGO AT THE TURN OF THE CENTURY IN PHOTOGRAPHS: 122 Historic Views from the Collections of the Chicago Historical Society, Larry A. Viskochil. Rare large-format prints offer detailed views of City Hall, State Street, the Loop, Hull House, Union Station, many other landmarks, circa 1904–1913. Introduction. Captions. Maps. 144pp. 9⅜ × 12¼. 24656-6 Pa. $12.95

OLD BROOKLYN IN EARLY PHOTOGRAPHS, 1865–1929, William Lee Younger. Luna Park, Gravesend race track, construction of Grand Army Plaza, moving of Hotel Brighton, etc. 157 previously unpublished photographs. 165pp. 8⅞ × 11¾. 23587-4 Pa. $13.95

THE MYTHS OF THE NORTH AMERICAN INDIANS, Lewis Spence. Rich anthology of the myths and legends of the Algonquins, Iroquois, Pawnees and Sioux, prefaced by an extensive historical and ethnological commentary. 36 illustrations. 480pp. 5⅜ × 8½. 25967-6 Pa. $8.95

AN ENCYCLOPEDIA OF BATTLES: Accounts of Over 1,560 Battles from 1479 B.C. to the Present, David Eggenberger. Essential details of every major battle in recorded history from the first battle of Megiddo in 1479 B.C. to Grenada in 1984. List of Battle Maps. New Appendix covering the years 1967–1984. Index. 99 illustrations. 544pp. 6½ × 9¼. 24913-1 Pa. $14.95

SAILING ALONE AROUND THE WORLD, Captain Joshua Slocum. First man to sail around the world, alone, in small boat. One of great feats of seamanship told in delightful manner. 67 illustrations. 294pp. 5⅜ × 8½. 20326-3 Pa. $5.95

ANARCHISM AND OTHER ESSAYS, Emma Goldman. Powerful, penetrating, prophetic essays on direct action, role of minorities, prison reform, puritan hypocrisy, violence, etc. 271pp. 5⅜ × 8½. 22484-8 Pa. $5.95

MYTHS OF THE HINDUS AND BUDDHISTS, Ananda K. Coomaraswamy and Sister Nivedita. Great stories of the epics; deeds of Krishna, Shiva, taken from puranas, Vedas, folk tales; etc. 32 illustrations. 400pp. 5⅜ × 8½. 21759-0 Pa. $9.95

BEYOND PSYCHOLOGY, Otto Rank. Fear of death, desire of immortality, nature of sexuality, social organization, creativity, according to Rankian system. 291pp. 5⅜ × 8½. 20485-5 Pa. $8.95

A THEOLOGICO-POLITICAL TREATISE, Benedict Spinoza. Also contains unfinished Political Treatise. Great classic on religious liberty, theory of government on common consent. R. Elwes translation. Total of 421pp. 5⅜ × 8½. 20249-6 Pa. $8.95

MY BONDAGE AND MY FREEDOM, Frederick Douglass. Born a slave, Douglass became outspoken force in antislavery movement. The best of Douglass' auto-biographies. Graphic description of slave life. 464pp. 5⅜ × 8½.   22457-0 Pa. $8.95

FOLLOWING THE EQUATOR: A Journey Around the World, Mark Twain. Fascinating humorous account of 1897 voyage to Hawaii, Australia, India, New Zealand, etc. Ironic, bemused reports on peoples, customs, climate, flora and fauna, politics, much more. 197 illustrations. 720pp. 5⅜ × 8½.   26113-1 Pa. $15.95

THE PEOPLE CALLED SHAKERS, Edward D. Andrews. Definitive study of Shakers: origins, beliefs, practices, dances, social organization, furniture and crafts, etc. 33 illustrations. 351pp. 5⅜ × 8½.   21081-2 Pa. $8.95

THE MYTHS OF GREECE AND ROME, H. A. Guerber. A classic of mythology, generously illustrated, long prized for its simple, graphic, accurate retelling of the principal myths of Greece and Rome, and for its commentary on their origins and significance. With 64 illustrations by Michelangelo, Raphael, Titian, Rubens, Canova, Bernini and others. 480pp. 5⅜ × 8½.   27584-1 Pa. $9.95

PSYCHOLOGY OF MUSIC, Carl E. Seashore. Classic work discusses music as a medium from psychological viewpoint. Clear treatment of physical acoustics, auditory apparatus, sound perception, development of musical skills, nature of musical feeling, host of other topics. 88 figures. 408pp. 5⅜ × 8½.   21851-1 Pa. $9.95

THE PHILOSOPHY OF HISTORY, Georg W. Hegel. Great classic of Western thought develops concept that history is not chance but rational process, the evolution of freedom. 457pp. 5⅜ × 8½.   20112-0 Pa. $9.95

THE BOOK OF TEA, Kakuzo Okakura. Minor classic of the Orient: entertaining, charming explanation, interpretation of traditional Japanese culture in terms of tea ceremony. 94pp. 5⅜ × 8½.   20070-1 Pa. $3.95

LIFE IN ANCIENT EGYPT, Adolf Erman. Fullest, most thorough, detailed older account with much not in more recent books, domestic life, religion, magic, medicine, commerce, much more. Many illustrations reproduce tomb paintings, carvings, hieroglyphs, etc. 597pp. 5⅜ × 8½.   22632-8 Pa. $10.95

SUNDIALS, Their Theory and Construction, Albert Waugh. Far and away the best, most thorough coverage of ideas, mathematics concerned, types, construction, adjusting anywhere. Simple, nontechnical treatment allows even children to build several of these dials. Over 100 illustrations. 230pp. 5⅜ × 8½.   22947-5 Pa. $7.95

DYNAMICS OF FLUIDS IN POROUS MEDIA, Jacob Bear. For advanced students of ground water hydrology, soil mechanics and physics, drainage and irrigation engineering, and more. 335 illustrations. Exercises, with answers. 784pp. 6⅛ × 9¼.   65675-6 Pa. $19.95

SONGS OF EXPERIENCE: Facsimile Reproduction with 26 Plates in Full Color, William Blake. 26 full-color plates from a rare 1826 edition. Includes "The Tyger," "London," "Holy Thursday," and other poems. Printed text of poems. 48pp. 5¼ × 7.   24636-1 Pa. $4.95

OLD-TIME VIGNETTES IN FULL COLOR, Carol Belanger Grafton (ed.). Over 390 charming, often sentimental illustrations, selected from archives of Victorian graphics—pretty women posing, children playing, food, flowers, kittens and puppies, smiling cherubs, birds and butterflies, much more. All copyright-free. 48pp. 9¼ × 12¼.   27269-9 Pa. $5.95

PERSPECTIVE FOR ARTISTS, Rex Vicat Cole. Depth, perspective of sky and sea, shadows, much more, not usually covered. 391 diagrams, 81 reproductions of drawings and paintings. 279pp. 5⅜ × 8½. 22487-2 Pa. $6.95

DRAWING THE LIVING FIGURE, Joseph Sheppard. Innovative approach to artistic anatomy focuses on specifics of surface anatomy, rather than muscles and bones. Over 170 drawings of live models in front, back and side views, and in widely varying poses. Accompanying diagrams. 177 illustrations. Introduction. Index. 144pp. 8⅜ × 11¼. 26723-7 Pa. $8.95

GOTHIC AND OLD ENGLISH ALPHABETS: 100 Complete Fonts, Dan X. Solo. Add power, elegance to posters, signs, other graphics with 100 stunning copyright-free alphabets: Blackstone, Dolbey, Germania, 97 more—including many lower-case, numerals, punctuation marks. 104pp. 8⅛ × 11. 24695-7 Pa. $8.95

HOW TO DO BEADWORK, Mary White. Fundamental book on craft from simple projects to five-bead chains and woven works. 106 illustrations. 142pp. 5⅜ × 8. 20697-1 Pa. $4.95

THE BOOK OF WOOD CARVING, Charles Marshall Sayers. Finest book for beginners discusses fundamentals and offers 34 designs. "Absolutely first rate . . . well thought out and well executed."—E. J. Tangerman. 118pp. 7¾ × 10⅝. 23654-4 Pa. $5.95

ILLUSTRATED CATALOG OF CIVIL WAR MILITARY GOODS: Union Army Weapons, Insignia, Uniform Accessories, and Other Equipment, Schuyler, Hartley, and Graham. Rare, profusely illustrated 1846 catalog includes Union Army uniform and dress regulations, arms and ammunition, coats, insignia, flags, swords, rifles, etc. 226 illustrations. 160pp. 9 × 12. 24939-5 Pa. $10.95

WOMEN'S FASHIONS OF THE EARLY 1900s: An Unabridged Republication of "New York Fashions, 1909," National Cloak & Suit Co. Rare catalog of mail-order fashions documents women's and children's clothing styles shortly after the turn of the century. Captions offer full descriptions, prices. Invaluable resource for fashion, costume historians. Approximately 725 illustrations. 128pp. 8⅜ × 11¼. 27276-1 Pa. $11.95

THE 1912 AND 1915 GUSTAV STICKLEY FURNITURE CATALOGS, Gustav Stickley. With over 200 detailed illustrations and descriptions, these two catalogs are essential reading and reference materials and identification guides for Stickley furniture. Captions cite materials, dimensions and prices. 112pp. 6½ × 9¼. 26676-1 Pa. $9.95

EARLY AMERICAN LOCOMOTIVES, John H. White, Jr. Finest locomotive engravings from early 19th century: historical (1804–74), main-line (after 1870), special, foreign, etc. 147 plates. 142pp. 11⅜ × 8¼. 22772-3 Pa. $10.95

THE TALL SHIPS OF TODAY IN PHOTOGRAPHS, Frank O. Braynard. Lavishly illustrated tribute to nearly 100 majestic contemporary sailing vessels: Amerigo Vespucci, Clearwater, Constitution, Eagle, Mayflower, Sea Cloud, Victory, many more. Authoritative captions provide statistics, background on each ship. 190 black-and-white photographs and illustrations. Introduction. 128pp. 8⅞ × 11¾. 27163-3 Pa. $13.95

EARLY NINETEENTH-CENTURY CRAFTS AND TRADES, Peter Stockham (ed.). Extremely rare 1807 volume describes to youngsters the crafts and trades of the day: brickmaker, weaver, dressmaker, bookbinder, ropemaker, saddler, many more. Quaint prose, charming illustrations for each craft. 20 black-and-white line illustrations. 192pp. 4⅜ × 6. 27293-1 Pa. $4.95

VICTORIAN FASHIONS AND COSTUMES FROM HARPER'S BAZAR, 1867–1898, Stella Blum (ed.). Day costumes, evening wear, sports clothes, shoes, hats, other accessories in over 1,000 detailed engravings. 320pp. 9⅜ × 12¼. 22990-4 Pa. $13.95

GUSTAV STICKLEY, THE CRAFTSMAN, Mary Ann Smith. Superb study surveys broad scope of Stickley's achievement, especially in architecture. Design philosophy, rise and fall of the Craftsman empire, descriptions and floor plans for many Craftsman houses, more. 86 black-and-white halftones. 31 line illustrations. Introduction. 208pp. 6½ × 9¼. 27210-9 Pa. $9.95

THE LONG ISLAND RAIL ROAD IN EARLY PHOTOGRAPHS, Ron Ziel. Over 220 rare photos, informative text document origin (1844) and development of rail service on Long Island. Vintage views of early trains, locomotives, stations, passengers, crews, much more. Captions. 8⅞ × 11¾. 26301-0 Pa. $13.95

THE BOOK OF OLD SHIPS: From Egyptian Galleys to Clipper Ships, Henry B. Culver. Superb, authoritative history of sailing vessels, with 80 magnificent line illustrations. Galley, bark, caravel, longship, whaler, many more. Detailed, informative text on each vessel by noted naval historian. Introduction. 256pp. 5⅜ × 8½. 27332-6 Pa. $6.95

TEN BOOKS ON ARCHITECTURE, Vitruvius. The most important book ever written on architecture. Early Roman aesthetics, technology, classical orders, site selection, all other aspects. Morgan translation. 331pp. 5⅜ × 8½. 20645-9 Pa. $8.95

THE HUMAN FIGURE IN MOTION, Eadweard Muybridge. More than 4,500 stopped-action photos, in action series, showing undraped men, women, children jumping, lying down, throwing, sitting, wrestling, carrying, etc. 390pp. 7⅞ × 10⅝. 20204-6 Clothbd. $24.95

TREES OF THE EASTERN AND CENTRAL UNITED STATES AND CANADA, William M. Harlow. Best one-volume guide to 140 trees. Full descriptions, woodlore, range, etc. Over 600 illustrations. Handy size. 288pp. 4½ × 6⅜. 20395-6 Pa. $5.95

SONGS OF WESTERN BIRDS, Dr. Donald J. Borror. Complete song and call repertoire of 60 western species, including flycatchers, juncoes, cactus wrens, many more—includes fully illustrated booklet. Cassette and manual 99913-0 $8.95

GROWING AND USING HERBS AND SPICES, Milo Miloradovich. Versatile handbook provides all the information needed for cultivation and use of all the herbs and spices available in North America. 4 illustrations. Index. Glossary. 236pp. 5⅜ × 8½. 25058-X Pa. $6.95

BIG BOOK OF MAZES AND LABYRINTHS, Walter Shepherd. 50 mazes and labyrinths in all—classical, solid, ripple, and more—in one great volume. Perfect inexpensive puzzler for clever youngsters. Full solutions. 112pp. 8⅛ × 11. 22951-3 Pa. $4.95

PIANO TUNING, J. Cree Fischer. Clearest, best book for beginner, amateur. Simple repairs, raising dropped notes, tuning by easy method of flattened fifths. No previous skills needed. 4 illustrations. 201pp. 5⅜ × 8½.   23267-0 Pa. $5.95

A SOURCE BOOK IN THEATRICAL HISTORY, A. M. Nagler. Contemporary observers on acting, directing, make-up, costuming, stage props, machinery, scene design, from Ancient Greece to Chekhov. 611pp. 5⅜ × 8½.   20515-0 Pa. $11.95

THE COMPLETE NONSENSE OF EDWARD LEAR, Edward Lear. All nonsense limericks, zany alphabets, Owl and Pussycat, songs, nonsense botany, etc., illustrated by Lear. Total of 320pp. 5⅜ × 8½. (USO)   20167-8 Pa. $6.95

VICTORIAN PARLOUR POETRY: An Annotated Anthology, Michael R. Turner. 117 gems by Longfellow, Tennyson, Browning, many lesser-known poets. "The Village Blacksmith," "Curfew Must Not Ring Tonight," "Only a Baby Small," dozens more, often difficult to find elsewhere. Index of poets, titles, first lines. xxiii + 325pp. 5⅜ × 8¼.   27044-0 Pa. $8.95

DUBLINERS, James Joyce. Fifteen stories offer vivid, tightly focused observations of the lives of Dublin's poorer classes. At least one, "The Dead," is considered a masterpiece. Reprinted complete and unabridged from standard edition. 160pp. 5³⁄₁₆ × 8¼.   26870-5 Pa. $1.00

THE HAUNTED MONASTERY and THE CHINESE MAZE MURDERS, Robert van Gulik. Two full novels by van Gulik, set in 7th-century China, continue adventures of Judge Dee and his companions. An evil Taoist monastery, seemingly supernatural events; overgrown topiary maze hides strange crimes. 27 illustrations. 328pp. 5⅜ × 8½.   23502-5 Pa. $7.95

THE BOOK OF THE SACRED MAGIC OF ABRAMELIN THE MAGE, translated by S. MacGregor Mathers. Medieval manuscript of ceremonial magic. Basic document in Aleister Crowley, Golden Dawn groups. 268pp. 5⅜ × 8½.   23211-5 Pa. $8.95

NEW RUSSIAN-ENGLISH AND ENGLISH-RUSSIAN DICTIONARY, M. A. O'Brien. This is a remarkably handy Russian dictionary, containing a surprising amount of information, including over 70,000 entries. 366pp. 4½ × 6⅛.   20208-9 Pa. $9.95

HISTORIC HOMES OF THE AMERICAN PRESIDENTS, Second, Revised Edition, Irvin Haas. A traveler's guide to American Presidential homes, most open to the public, depicting and describing homes occupied by every American President from George Washington to George Bush. With visiting hours, admission charges, travel routes. 175 photographs. Index. 160pp. 8¼ × 11. 26751-2 Pa. $10.95

NEW YORK IN THE FORTIES, Andreas Feininger. 162 brilliant photographs by the well-known photographer, formerly with *Life* magazine. Commuters, shoppers, Times Square at night, much else from city at its peak. Captions by John von Hartz. 181pp. 9¼ × 10¾.   23585-8 Pa. $12.95

INDIAN SIGN LANGUAGE, William Tomkins. Over 525 signs developed by Sioux and other tribes. Written instructions and diagrams. Also 290 pictographs. 111pp. 6⅛ × 9¼.   22029-X Pa. $3.50

ANATOMY: A Complete Guide for Artists, Joseph Sheppard. A master of figure drawing shows artists how to render human anatomy convincingly. Over 460 illustrations. 224pp. 8⅜ × 11¼. 27279-6 Pa. $10.95

MEDIEVAL CALLIGRAPHY: Its History and Technique, Marc Drogin. Spirited history, comprehensive instruction manual covers 13 styles (ca. 4th century thru 15th). Excellent photographs; directions for duplicating medieval techniques with modern tools. 224pp. 8⅜ × 11¼. 26142-5 Pa. $11.95

DRIED FLOWERS: How to Prepare Them, Sarah Whitlock and Martha Rankin. Complete instructions on how to use silica gel, meal and borax, perlite aggregate, sand and borax, glycerine and water to create attractive permanent flower arrangements. 12 illustrations. 32pp. 5⅜ × 8½. 21802-3 Pa. $1.00

EASY-TO-MAKE BIRD FEEDERS FOR WOODWORKERS, Scott D. Campbell. Detailed, simple-to-use guide for designing, constructing, caring for and using feeders. Text, illustrations for 12 classic and contemporary designs. 96pp. 5⅜ × 8½.
25847-5 Pa. $2.95

OLD-TIME CRAFTS AND TRADES, Peter Stockham. An 1807 book created to teach children about crafts and trades open to them as future careers. It describes in detailed, nontechnical terms 24 different occupations, among them coachmaker, gardener, hairdresser, lacemaker, shoemaker, wheelwright, copper-plate printer, milliner, trunkmaker, merchant and brewer. Finely detailed engravings illustrate each occupation. 192pp. 4⅝ × 6. 27398-9 Pa. $4.95

THE HISTORY OF UNDERCLOTHES, C. Willett Cunnington and Phyllis Cunnington. Fascinating, well-documented survey covering six centuries of English undergarments, enhanced with over 100 illustrations: 12th-century laced-up bodice, footed long drawers (1795), 19th-century bustles, 19th-century corsets for men, Victorian "bust improvers," much more. 272pp. 5⅜ × 8¼. 27124-2 Pa. $9.95

ARTS AND CRAFTS FURNITURE: The Complete Brooks Catalog of 1912, Brooks Manufacturing Co. Photos and detailed descriptions of more than 150 now very collectible furniture designs from the Arts and Crafts movement depict davenports, settees, buffets, desks, tables, chairs, bedsteads, dressers and more, all built of solid, quarter-sawed oak. Invaluable for students and enthusiasts of antiques, Americana and the decorative arts. 80pp. 6½ × 9¼. 27471-3 Pa. $7.95

HOW WE INVENTED THE AIRPLANE: An Illustrated History, Orville Wright. Fascinating firsthand account covers early experiments, construction of planes and motors, first flights, much more. Introduction and commentary by Fred C. Kelly. 76 photographs. 96pp. 8¼ × 11. 25662-6 Pa. $8.95

THE ARTS OF THE SAILOR: Knotting, Splicing and Ropework, Hervey Garrett Smith. Indispensable shipboard reference covers tools, basic knots and useful hitches; handsewing and canvas work, more. Over 100 illustrations. Delightful reading for sea lovers. 256pp. 5⅜ × 8½. 26440-8 Pa. $7.95

FRANK LLOYD WRIGHT'S FALLINGWATER: The House and Its History, Second, Revised Edition, Donald Hoffmann. A total revision—both in text and illustrations—of the standard document on Fallingwater, the boldest, most personal architectural statement of Wright's mature years, updated with valuable new material from the recently opened Frank Lloyd Wright Archives. "Fascinating"—*The New York Times*. 116 illustrations. 128pp. 9¼ × 10¾.
27430-6 Pa. $10.95

PHOTOGRAPHIC SKETCHBOOK OF THE CIVIL WAR, Alexander Gardner. 100 photos taken on field during the Civil War. Famous shots of Manassas, Harper's Ferry, Lincoln, Richmond, slave pens, etc. 244pp. 10⅝ × 8¼.
22731-6 Pa. $9.95

FIVE ACRES AND INDEPENDENCE, Maurice G. Kains. Great back-to-the-land classic explains basics of self-sufficient farming. The one book to get. 95 illustrations. 397pp. 5⅜ × 8½.
20974-1 Pa. $7.95

SONGS OF EASTERN BIRDS, Dr. Donald J. Borror. Songs and calls of 60 species most common to eastern U.S.: warblers, woodpeckers, flycatchers, thrushes, larks, many more in high-quality recording.
Cassette and manual 99912-2 $8.95

A MODERN HERBAL, Margaret Grieve. Much the fullest, most exact, most useful compilation of herbal material. Gigantic alphabetical encyclopedia, from aconite to zedoary, gives botanical information, medical properties, folklore, economic uses, much else. Indispensable to serious reader. 161 illustrations. 888pp. 6½ × 9¼. 2-vol. set. (USO)
Vol. I: 22798-7 Pa. $9.95
Vol. II: 22799-5 Pa. $9.95

HIDDEN TREASURE MAZE BOOK, Dave Phillips. Solve 34 challenging mazes accompanied by heroic tales of adventure. Evil dragons, people-eating plants, bloodthirsty giants, many more dangerous adversaries lurk at every twist and turn. 34 mazes, stories, solutions. 48pp. 8¼ × 11.
24566-7 Pa. $2.95

LETTERS OF W. A. MOZART, Wolfgang A. Mozart. Remarkable letters show bawdy wit, humor, imagination, musical insights, contemporary musical world; includes some letters from Leopold Mozart. 276pp. 5⅜ × 8½.
22859-2 Pa. $7.95

BASIC PRINCIPLES OF CLASSICAL BALLET, Agrippina Vaganova. Great Russian theoretician, teacher explains methods for teaching classical ballet. 118 illustrations. 175pp. 5⅜ × 8½.
22036-2 Pa. $4.95

THE JUMPING FROG, Mark Twain. Revenge edition. The original story of The Celebrated Jumping Frog of Calaveras County, a hapless French translation, and Twain's hilarious "retranslation" from the French. 12 illustrations. 66pp. 5⅜ × 8½.
22686-7 Pa. $3.95

BEST REMEMBERED POEMS, Martin Gardner (ed.). The 126 poems in this superb collection of 19th- and 20th-century British and American verse range from Shelley's "To a Skylark" to the impassioned "Renascence" of Edna St. Vincent Millay and to Edward Lear's whimsical "The Owl and the Pussycat." 224pp. 5⅜ × 8½.
27165-X Pa. $4.95

COMPLETE SONNETS, William Shakespeare. Over 150 exquisite poems deal with love, friendship, the tyranny of time, beauty's evanescence, death and other themes in language of remarkable power, precision and beauty. Glossary of archaic terms. 80pp. 5³⁄₁₆ × 8¼.
26686-9 Pa. $1.00

BODIES IN A BOOKSHOP, R. T. Campbell. Challenging mystery of blackmail and murder with ingenious plot and superbly drawn characters. In the best tradition of British suspense fiction. 192pp. 5⅜ × 8½.
24720-1 Pa. $5.95

THE WIT AND HUMOR OF OSCAR WILDE, Alvin Redman (ed.). More than 1,000 ripostes, paradoxes, wisecracks: Work is the curse of the drinking classes; I can resist everything except temptation; etc. 258pp. 5⅜ × 8½. 20602-5 Pa. $5.95

SHAKESPEARE LEXICON AND QUOTATION DICTIONARY, Alexander Schmidt. Full definitions, locations, shades of meaning in every word in plays and poems. More than 50,000 exact quotations. 1,485pp. 6½ × 9¼. 2-vol. set.
Vol. I: 22726-X Pa. $16.95
Vol. 2: 22727-8 Pa. $15.95

SELECTED POEMS, Emily Dickinson. Over 100 best-known, best-loved poems by one of America's foremost poets, reprinted from authoritative early editions. No comparable edition at this price. Index of first lines. 64pp. 5³⁄₁₆ × 8¼.
26466-1 Pa. $1.00

CELEBRATED CASES OF JUDGE DEE (DEE GOONG AN), translated by Robert van Gulik. Authentic 18th-century Chinese detective novel; Dee and associates solve three interlocked cases. Led to van Gulik's own stories with same characters. Extensive introduction. 9 illustrations. 237pp. 5⅜ × 8½.
23337-5 Pa. $6.95

THE MALLEUS MALEFICARUM OF KRAMER AND SPRENGER, translated by Montague Summers. Full text of most important witchhunter's "bible," used by both Catholics and Protestants. 278pp. 6⅝ × 10. 22802-9 Pa. $11.95

SPANISH STORIES/CUENTOS ESPAÑOLES: A Dual-Language Book, Angel Flores (ed.). Unique format offers 13 great stories in Spanish by Cervantes, Borges, others. Faithful English translations on facing pages. 352pp. 5⅜ × 8½.
25399-6 Pa. $8.95

THE CHICAGO WORLD'S FAIR OF 1893: A Photographic Record, Stanley Appelbaum (ed.). 128 rare photos show 200 buildings, Beaux-Arts architecture, Midway, original Ferris Wheel, Edison's kinetoscope, more. Architectural emphasis; full text. 116pp. 8¼ × 11. 23990-X Pa. $9.95

OLD QUEENS, N.Y., IN EARLY PHOTOGRAPHS, Vincent F. Seyfried and William Asadorian. Over 160 rare photographs of Maspeth, Jamaica, Jackson Heights, and other areas. Vintage views of DeWitt Clinton mansion, 1939 World's Fair and more. Captions. 192pp. 8⅞ × 11. 26358-4 Pa. $12.95

CAPTURED BY THE INDIANS: 15 Firsthand Accounts, 1750–1870, Frederick Drimmer. Astounding true historical accounts of grisly torture, bloody conflicts, relentless pursuits, miraculous escapes and more, by people who lived to tell the tale. 384pp. 5⅜ × 8½. 24901-8 Pa. $8.95

THE WORLD'S GREAT SPEECHES, Lewis Copeland and Lawrence W. Lamm (eds.). Vast collection of 278 speeches of Greeks to 1970. Powerful and effective models; unique look at history. 842pp. 5⅜ × 8½. 20468-5 Pa. $14.95

THE BOOK OF THE SWORD, Sir Richard F. Burton. Great Victorian scholar/adventurer's eloquent, erudite history of the "queen of weapons"—from prehistory to early Roman Empire. Evolution and development of early swords, variations (sabre, broadsword, cutlass, scimitar, etc.), much more. 336pp. 6⅛ × 9¼. 25434-8 Pa. $8.95

AUTOBIOGRAPHY: The Story of My Experiments with Truth, Mohandas K. Gandhi. Boyhood, legal studies, purification, the growth of the Satyagraha (nonviolent protest) movement. Critical, inspiring work of the man responsible for the freedom of India. 480pp. 5⅜ × 8½. (USO) 24593-4 Pa. $8.95

CELTIC MYTHS AND LEGENDS, T. W. Rolleston. Masterful retelling of Irish and Welsh stories and tales. Cuchulain, King Arthur, Deirdre, the Grail, many more. First paperback edition. 58 full-page illustrations. 512pp. 5⅜ × 8½.
26507-2 Pa. $9.95

THE PRINCIPLES OF PSYCHOLOGY, William James. Famous long course complete, unabridged. Stream of thought, time perception, memory, experimental methods; great work decades ahead of its time. 94 figures. 1,391pp. 5⅜ × 8½. 2-vol. set.
Vol. I: 20381-6 Pa. $12.95
Vol. II: 20382-4 Pa. $12.95

THE WORLD AS WILL AND REPRESENTATION, Arthur Schopenhauer. Definitive English translation of Schopenhauer's life work, correcting more than 1,000 errors, omissions in earlier translations. Translated by E. F. J. Payne. Total of 1,269pp. 5⅜ × 8½. 2-vol. set. Vol. 1: 21761-2 Pa. $11.95
Vol. 2: 21762-0 Pa. $11.95

MAGIC AND MYSTERY IN TIBET, Madame Alexandra David-Neel. Experiences among lamas, magicians, sages, sorcerers, Bonpa wizards. A true psychic discovery. 32 illustrations. 321pp. 5⅜ × 8½. (USO) 22682-4 Pa. $8.95

THE EGYPTIAN BOOK OF THE DEAD, E. A. Wallis Budge. Complete reproduction of Ani's papyrus, finest ever found. Full hieroglyphic text, interlinear transliteration, word-for-word translation, smooth translation. 533pp. 6½ × 9¼.
21866-X Pa. $9.95

MATHEMATICS FOR THE NONMATHEMATICIAN, Morris Kline. Detailed, college-level treatment of mathematics in cultural and historical context, with numerous exercises. Recommended Reading Lists. Tables. Numerous figures. 641pp. 5⅜ × 8½. 24823-2 Pa. $11.95

THEORY OF WING SECTIONS: Including a Summary of Airfoil Data, Ira H. Abbott and A. E. von Doenhoff. Concise compilation of subsonic aerodynamic characteristics of NACA wing sections, plus description of theory. 350pp. of tables. 693pp. 5⅜ × 8½. 60586-8 Pa. $14.95

THE RIME OF THE ANCIENT MARINER, Gustave Doré, S. T. Coleridge. Doré's finest work; 34 plates capture moods, subtleties of poem. Flawless full-size reproductions printed on facing pages with authoritative text of poem. "Beautiful. Simply beautiful."—*Publisher's Weekly*. 77pp. 9¼ × 12. 22305-1 Pa. $6.95

NORTH AMERICAN INDIAN DESIGNS FOR ARTISTS AND CRAFTSPEOPLE, Eva Wilson. Over 360 authentic copyright-free designs adapted from Navajo blankets, Hopi pottery, Sioux buffalo hides, more. Geometrics, symbolic figures, plant and animal motifs, etc. 128pp. 8⅜ × 11. (EUK) 25341-4 Pa. $7.95

SCULPTURE: Principles and Practice, Louis Slobodkin. Step-by-step approach to clay, plaster, metals, stone; classical and modern. 253 drawings, photos. 255pp. 8⅛ × 11. 22960-2 Pa. $10.95

THE INFLUENCE OF SEA POWER UPON HISTORY, 1660-1783, A. T. Mahan. Influential classic of naval history and tactics still used as text in war colleges. First paperback edition. 4 maps. 24 battle plans. 640pp. 5⅜ × 8½.
25509-3 Pa. $12.95

THE STORY OF THE TITANIC AS TOLD BY ITS SURVIVORS, Jack Winocour (ed.). What it was really like. Panic, despair, shocking inefficiency, and a little heroism. More thrilling than any fictional account. 26 illustrations. 320pp. 5⅜ × 8½. **20610-6 Pa. $8.95**

FAIRY AND FOLK TALES OF THE IRISH PEASANTRY, William Butler Yeats (ed.). Treasury of 64 tales from the twilight world of Celtic myth and legend: "The Soul Cages," "The Kildare Pooka," "King O'Toole and his Goose," many more. Introduction and Notes by W. B. Yeats. 352pp. 5⅜ × 8½. **26941-8 Pa. $8.95**

BUDDHIST MAHAYANA TEXTS, E. B. Cowell and Others (eds.). Superb, accurate translations of basic documents in Mahayana Buddhism, highly important in history of religions. The Buddha-karita of Asvaghosha, Larger Sukhavativyuha, more. 448pp. 5⅜ × 8½. 25552-2 Pa. $9.95

ONE TWO THREE . . . INFINITY: Facts and Speculations of Science, George Gamow. Great physicist's fascinating, readable overview of contemporary science: number theory, relativity, fourth dimension, entropy, genes, atomic structure, much more. 128 illustrations. Index. 352pp. 5⅜ × 8½. **25664-2 Pa. $8.95**

ENGINEERING IN HISTORY, Richard Shelton Kirby, et al. Broad, nontechnical survey of history's major technological advances: birth of Greek science, industrial revolution, electricity and applied science, 20th-century automation, much more. 181 illustrations. ". . . excellent . . ."—Isis. Bibliography. vii + 530pp. 5⅜ × 8¼.
26412-2 Pa. $14.95

Prices subject to change without notice.

Available at your book dealer or write for free catalog to Dept. GI, Dover Publications, Inc., 31 East 2nd St., Mineola, N.Y. 11501. Dover publishes more than 500 books each year on science, elementary and advanced mathematics, biology, music, art, literary history, social sciences and other areas.